PEACE

MEDJUGORJE MIRACLE AND MESSAGE

A PILGRIM'S REFLECTION

Jeffrey Maria D. Arnold

McLennan Publishing
Laguna Hills, California

The author is available for missions and other speaking engagements on the contents of this book. He employs a PowerPoint® presentation with pictures of Medjugorje in a mini-retreat format. Please schedule your parish or group by calling the publisher toll free at 866 585-1555 or 949 463-1730 or e-mail jmdarnold@hotmail.com .

Library of Congress Control Number: 2003112618

Published by McLennan Publishing
Laguna Hills, California
USA

ISBN 0-9745156-0-4

Cover by FR Graphics

Printed in USA

F G R

Central Plains
BOOK MANUFACTURING

This book is dedicated to all priests everywhere who are servants of the Holy Eucharist; also to the visionaries and locutionists of Medugorje who have done our Mother's bidding by patiently bringing her messages to their brothers and sisters for all these years; and to the Medugorje parishioners who all so graciously provide for us pilgrims.

Contents

Acknowledgements

Unless otherwise noted all Biblical quotations in this book are from The New American Bible extracted from a few different sources with Imprimatur.

Likewise, unless otherwise noted all of the messages of the Blessed Virgin Mary quoted in this book are with permission copied directly from MIR, Official Information Center for the Shrine of Peace in Medjugorje Website. See www.medjugorje.hr

All quotes from the *Catechism* are taken from the *Catechism of the Catholic Church* SECOND EDITION *revised in accordance with the official Latin text promulgated by Pope John Paul II.*

Special thanks to Patrick Newman and Jebb Johnson, my fellow Medjugorje pilgrims, for their helpful review of the draft manuscripts. And I am especially grateful for Monsignor Paul Martin who graciously took the time to read the manuscript and give his appraisal in the Forward to this book.

Thanks to Paul Millard for all his help and to Paul and Pat for their poignant testimonies.

Also, I very much appreciate the labor of Janice T. Connell who wrote *The Visions Of The Children, Revised Edition.*

And finally to Reverend Father Juan Caboboy who so graciously received me into the Church on December 30, 2001, which allowed me to receive our Lord in the Holy Eucharist 3 ½ months earlier than the normal time at Easter Vigil, 2002.

Forward

Peace is an elusive treasure in the Third Millennium, whether world, national or personal. In *Peace – Medjugorje Miracle and Message, A Pilgrim's Reflection*, one can find a blueprint for peace.

For myself, I found a rare treasure as I met in this book the author, the people and the life of Medjugorje and the application of our Blessed Mother's message to daily life. The 'five little stones' of prayer, mass, reading the Bible daily, confession monthly and fasting can lead a person willing to surrender to the will of God to find true peace.

Our Blessed Mother has changed the heart of the author, Jeffrey Maria D. Arnold, and can change the heart of all who read his reflections if one truly seeks a peace this world cannot give. May all who read this work find peace and lead others to the Prince of Peace.

Msgr. Paul Martin
Pastor Emeritus, Mission Basilica
San Juan Capistrano, California
September 2003

Prologue

Allow me to introduce myself to you the reader. I came into this world in January, 1947. I was baptized on March 30, 1958. I married Diane in September, 1967. We are still so joined and have been ever since without interruption. We are blessed with four grown children and four grandchildren. We hope for more grandchildren.

I was first spiritually awakened on Easter Day, 1977. After not setting foot in a church except to get married and baptize the children, for some reason just before Easter in 1977, I mentioned to Diane that we probably ought to start the children in Sunday School. She agreed and so on the appointed day we got all dressed up, Easter dresses and bonnets for the girls, coats and ties for the boys, and headed out for church. What little church background we had was Methodist so that seemed the logical choice. We attended the 11 AM service at First United Methodist Church in Medford, Oregon. Reverend Ross Knotts was the preacher for the service.

From the moment we walked into the narthex of the church something emotional came over me. I cannot explain it. I remember hardly anything of the service, except that at least three times I broke down in heart wrenching sobs. I could not control myself. Something like this had never happened to me before. I was the strong one. That was my nature. It proved out in various occupations: helicopter pilot, Army officer, Vietnam veteran, police officer, death investigator. But there I was, sitting in that pew crying like a baby in a church full of people. Finally the service was over and as we left I said to Diane, "I think we will be back." She had been similarly moved and said she thought the same thing.

The next Sunday we were back. There was no emotional charge. But, I felt somehow compelled to explore this Christian thing. So as we left I borrowed a Bible from the pew. We had no Bible at our house. Anyway, I began reading at the Gospel According To Matthew. When I came to the Sermon On The Mount and the Beatitudes at Chapter Five I knew I was reading the truth. I became like the Old Testament prophet, Jeremiah, who, when he found the words of God, devoured them as they became the joy and happiness of his heart (Jer 15:16). I too proceeded to devour the entire New Testament and continued on to the Old Testament. In about three months I read the whole Bible (Protestant). I then sat down and had a serious talk with myself. Did I want to give up the life I had been living and become a Christian? My decision was yes. After that, for several years, I concentrated my personal study on the Bible and Bible commentaries.

After my decision to become a Christian (even though I already was one through baptism, but didn't realize it) we joined the church and within about two years I began to feel the call to ministry. I enrolled as a candidate for ministry in the United Methodist Church. But that didn't work out. Reverend Knotts went into semi retirement and was pastor at a little rural church close by. I helped him for a while. I joined a charismatic men's breakfast fellowship. We explored Calvary Chapel in Applegate. But I was sort of frustrated. It did not seem to me that I could see in all these groups the deep spirituality the Gospel calls for. I went off on my own and started a little neighborhood fellowship. That lasted for about three years. Then we sort of drifted. Dark years of sin set in. I was barely hanging on – more back to the old ways than the way of Jesus.

We moved back to California in 1985, still drifting. We made occasional Sunday visits to the local Presbyterian

Church and that was about it. My prayer life and Bible reading were seriously depleted. Then long about 1993 our daughter became involved with a para-church organization of young adults that were attempting to follow the tenets of what is commonly known as Calvinism. This interested me and I too became involved. We were starting a church! I thought maybe this one would be like the early church of the New Testament. It didn't work out. The group has long since disbanded. But, it did rekindle the fire in me.

I began a personal study of Protestant reformed theology and Church history. I did some graduate theological work. Gradually, I built a personal reference library of some 1,000 volumes of reference works including a 38 volume set of the writings of the early fathers and 18 volumes on Church history. I became an amateur scholar and theologian.

In 1996 we began regular attendance locally at Geneva Presbyterian Church USA. We joined in 1997 and in 1999 I was ordained an elder in the church and appointed chairman of the adult education commission. Diane was elected a Deaconess in 2000. We were very active in the church. Personally, I enjoyed the fellowship and the physical work we were doing in Mexico and in building a new chapel. I especially favored our Sunday School class that I was honored to teach every Sunday. Our daughter attended on Sundays and our granddaughter was involved in the children's programs and choir. I sang in the adult choir. All was going well. We were happy.

Late in the year 2000 my office at work was moved. I noticed the fellow in the office next to me usually had his door closed when I arrived in the mornings. I wondered if he was reading his Bible during this time. So I kept an eye out and sure enough one morning he stepped out of his office, left the door open and there was an open Bible on his desk. That was all I needed. I engaged him in conversation and found out he was Catholic. Well, for about five months the debate was on – friendly of course. We discussed the Bible, Mary, the Pope and all the usual Catholic-Protestant differences. He would relate his understanding and feelings on the subjects. I would respond and help him with Bible interpretation. He told me he even told his friends that he met this Protestant who knew more about his Church than he did.

One day he brought a book in and wanted me to read it and let him know what I thought about it. He had been looking into alleged appearances of the Blessed Virgin Mary and this was a book on that subject. I began reading on Friday evening, March 23, 2001. I finished it on Sunday, March 25 – the Feast of the Annunciation – and I was converted that day. I had my second spiritual awakening. In my heart I was a Catholic Christian. The book was *The Visions Of The Children – The Apparitions of the Blessed Mother at Medjugorje* by Janice T. Connell. My office neighbor and friend is Jebb Johnson. He was pretty shocked Monday morning when I asked him to take me to Mass.

In reading Ms. Connell's book I experienced the same sort of conviction I had when I first read the Bible. I just knew it was true. There is no way to explain it except to say that the evidence she presented in the book was apparently sufficient for me to believe that indeed the Blessed Virgin Mary is appearing in Medjugorje. What converted me is what Mary is reported to say in messages she delivers through visionaries in Medjugorje. Rather quickly I realized that if I believed the Mother of the Son of God was appearing today and delivering messages for our salvation I better pay heed. That left no option. I had to come full circle and convert to Catholicism which is really a homecoming to the fullness of Christ. And that is because of Holy Eucharist – the real, physical and spiritual presence of Jesus in the consecrated bread and wine of Holy Communion. I was suddenly acutely aware of what I was missing all those past 24 years. Now, not only did I want to receive Jesus, I had a deep seated need.

I tried to get into the Church on Easter Vigil. It didn't work out. After Easter I went to the Pastor of the local Catholic Church and pleaded with him to examine me and receive me into the Church as soon as possible. Fr. Juan met with me on a regular basis and being the patient, thorough sort of guy he is, we started out slowly. I was anxious. He was calm and patient. A priest for over 25 years, I presumed he knew what he was doing. I had a lot to learn about humility and obedience. But he was most concerned about my marital relationship. Diane did not share my conviction. She chose to stay where she was. Fr. Juan met with Diane and was satisfied that we were not going to separate over this sudden and dramatic change in our relationship. So, on December 30, 2001, I was confirmed and received my first Holy Communion in a beautiful Mass celebrated by Reverend Father Juan Caboboy, Pastor of St. Nicholas Catholic Church, Diocese of Orange County, California, USA.

It was a tearful departure from Geneva for me and for many of my friends there. Sara Arndt was mad at me and says she still is but still wants me to come over to their house and enjoy their patio with them as usual. My building buddy, Dave Lammert, said it was like I was leaving the family. But we still get together now and then on projects and I see many of all who are too many to mention here (forgive me, all you wonderful people) when there is a dinner or what have you there at Geneva. In fact, Don Larsen, bless his soul, insisted that I help in the kitchen this year at the all church, annual, men's pancake breakfast. So, although I miss you all at Geneva, I hope you understand I could not ignore the tremendous spiritual conviction I received. God bless you all.

Looking back I can now see the signs I did not see then - mainly underscores in my reference books related to the Mass, Eucharist and Popes. The Holy Spirit was drawing me to the Eucharist. All that was left was a push from Mary. I remember many years ago, my friend Bill Cronin in Medford who is a Catholic Christian said in conversation one evening that I would someday be a Catholic. I have a special admiration for Bill and Marge Cronin, their seven children and I don't know how many grandchildren. Her family is Slavic as are the Croatian people of Medjugorje. Maybe there is a connection and maybe there is not. I don't know. But what I do know is that as of March 25, 2001, I had a very strong urge to go on pilgrimage to Medjugorje.

I put off a trip to Medjugorje for many months. First, I wanted to be able to receive Holy Eucharist in Medjugorje. The urge to go remained throughout the period of my preparation for Confirmation. Then after I was received into the Church I was concerned about the expense of the trip. But, in a totally unexpected way, I got some extra money. I still procrastinated until one day in prayer I was propelled into resolution to go. And so, on November 18, 2002, Jebb Johnson and I departed Los Angeles for Medjugorje. This book is about our spiritual experience in the "Oasis of Peace" – Medjugorje.

I write this prologue so you may have some idea of my spiritual journey thus far and how I wound up going to Medjugorje – how I found peace. The last couple of years have been an extraordinary blessing for me. I have been changed by the miracles and messages from our Blessed Mother Mary occurring at her Oasis of Peace. I want to share with you my Medjugorje experience and thoughts gathered and firmly rooted in my heart. My hope and prayer is that you too will be blessed.

JMDA, October 2003

Peace

The one thing in all the world that every sane person wants is peace. Even the most deviant ones desire to be left alone to practice their particular deviancy. A power hungry dictator is only at peace when in power. Those who are driven to increase financial wealth seek the realization of peace in the attainment of wealth. A young woman whose highest hope is to have a baby believes she will be at peace in mothering. A good job, home, car and some extra money for play, the right man, the right woman, adventure, achievement, work, knowledge, wisdom, etc. are all examples of goals and conditions most people strive to attain because we believe that is how we can have peace. However, I am sure most of us do not look at it that way.

If we stop and think about it, we may realize that to be at peace is to be in a state of tranquility, free from disturbance, untroubled and secure, in harmony with others around us, and unbothered by disquieting or oppressive thoughts and emotions. Isn't that basically, in one way or another, what we are all after? We travel down many different roads in life in search of what? Well, I say, peace. The classic example of the pursuit of peace is the idea of retirement – when I retire I will be free to do whatever I want to do or to do those things I have so long wanted to do. Whether we realize it or not, even if we do not consciously think about it, I for one am convinced that the pursuit of personal peace is what really drives humanity. Yet, if that is true then one would think there would be peace in the valley, so to speak.

Is there peace in the world? In your country? In your region? In your town or village? In your neighborhood? In your house? In your family? In your heart? Are you at peace? Do you feel it? Is your peace secured by truth or false notion? Do you have peace or an illusion of peace?

Answers to the first five of the preceding questions can be readily found on any given day in most any newspaper. For example, the Nation and World section of our local newspaper on December 28, 2002, contained the following headlines:

SKEPTICS AWAIT PROOF OF CLONE
PEACEFUL VOTE RAISES HOPES FOR FRESH START [Kenya]
DAD ARRESTED IN SHOOTING DEATH OF [his] 8-MONTH-OLD
4 ISRAELIS KILLED AT SABBATH DINNER
TWO GOLFERS ARRESTED IN ATTACK ON BOY
FBI TO ANALYZE VIDEOS IN ABDUCTION
FRANCE BREAKS UP REPUTED TERROR CELL
JAPANESE ABDUCTEES SPEAK OUT
U.S. CONFIRMS RAPE OF MINORITIES BY MYANMAR MILITARY
VIETNAM SENTENCES CHRISTIAN TRIBESMEN
FOCUS ON PEACE URGED IN SRI LANKA
IVORY COAST REBEL FORCES CLASH AGAIN WITH FRENCH
VENEZUELANS PROTEST AS STRIKE DRAGS ON
NIGERIA MAKES ARREST IN OFFICIAL'S KILLING

CONGO REBELS URGED TO REIN IN TROOPS
RUSSIA SAYS NO MORE PEACE CORPS WORKERS

There were a total of 20 headlines in that particular section of the newspaper from which the 16 above were taken. The example of these headlines obviously supports the notion that there is no peace or at least only fragmented peace in the world, nation, region and local areas. Of them, the two most illustrative for use in this book are the Dad who killed his baby daughter and the golfers who beat up the 14 year old boy. We shall address them below. But first I have some thoughts on peace in general.

Although, for the most part, it is self-evident that the majority of people in the world live in relatively safe neighborhoods and most are rarely, if ever, touched by serious violence, it is also obvious that the world in general is not at peace. To me, it feels like we are sitting on a powder keg. Sooner or later it will blow. Not only that, but there is always the threat of lost freedom and looming injustice. Where it exists, brotherly love is sectarian. The goal of lasting world peace has been illusive. And now, in the 21st Century it seems the situation in many countries is destabilizing. Mutual concord among governments is oriented to self-interest rather than common good. But most of that is way beyond you and me, except, of course, if you are well informed on the matters.

Closer to home, I think most of us desire domestic tranquility: peace in our families, at work and peace in our own hearts. We probably seldom think about another person's peace – even those within our sphere of regular contact and society. Yet, we want peace while slow to realize that peace only comes from harmony in personal relations and freedom from disquieting or oppressive thoughts or emotions. All else, in my opinion, is simply some measure of tolerance or intolerance as the case may be. Above everything it is disharmony in personal relationships that disturbs our peace. Such disturbance causes bad or sad thoughts and emotions which ignite and sustain conflict.

Consider the two headlines I mentioned above. Now, of course, few by comparison would likely beat up a teenage boy because he picked up one's golf ball from the course of play or kill an eight-month-old baby girl in a fit of jealousy. But that is what happened in these two events respectively. And I would like to examine these events just a little bit.

According to the news story, a 14 year old boy happened across a golf ball in a sand trap that was apparently in play on a golf course in Florida. The ball belonged to one of two men in their forties; seemingly two mature men. The boy picked up the ball and took it. He was chased down by one of the men, tackled to the ground and punched and kicked by the two men. Presumably, the one man took back his ball. The newspaper does not give any more detail than that so we are not privy to the exact transaction of the exchange between the boy and the men.

What could have motivated two mature men to attack a young teenage boy? Were there words, gestures, threats? The rules of golf say that a ball in play cannot be moved, except under certain conditions, and if moved a penalty is assessed. Did the men have a bet between them and their game was ruined, thus abolishing the bet? Or were they just highly incensed because they were wronged? The two men were arrested, but what about the boy? Was he trespassing on the golf course? Did he take a golf ball that did not belong to him? Probably so. That means that not only was the boy wronged by the two men but the men were wronged by the boy and the golf club was wronged by the boy and the men. Regardless, there is no justification for their resultant act of violence. Yet, we must ask ourselves how many times have we felt wronged for even the slightest thing and responded angrily or vengefully or with hurt feelings resulting in arguments small or large. We all know the answer and it is: many times. The golfers are an extreme example to be sure but the principle is the same.

The story on the baby killer is that he, a 38 year old man, believed his wife was having an affair with his brother and so he tried to shoot her in the heart. His wife, the mother of their eight-month-old daughter, was allegedly attempting to shield their daughter from harm. The baby's father fired his pistol and missed the mother's heart but hit and killed the baby. This all took place on Christmas Day. Details here also are minimal. However, the outcome vividly illustrates the all too frequent tragic consequences of jealous rage. Yet, we must ask ourselves how many times have we felt the heat of jealousy rise up in us? How many times have we felt betrayed? Wronged? Again, the example is extreme but the principle is the same.

It seems to me the common thread to these two examples is the same thread that weaves its way throughout the whole of human society. Something one could even call the bane of humanity – our sense of justice and injustice. I am not referring to civil justice or natural law but to the actual common practice of people everywhere. We might even call it the basic human instinct of justice. It is the instinct that will cause us to feel violated like in certain situations such as residential burglary victims feel or victims of robbery, rape and sodomy, etc. which are all crimes against person and property. Crimes such as these are codified as violations of law in all civilized societies precisely because, I think, we all recognize this basic instinct in each other. We desire to protect against violation through mutually beneficial arrangements called law. When violations occur, the violator is prosecuted and punished. The wrong done has then been dealt with justly.

But, I think there is more to our sense of justice and injustice than just law. It is the instinctive catalyst to our emotional response to perceived insult, ridicule, criticism, betrayal, deceit, trespass, desecration, etc. In other words, our instinctive sense of justice is the base line determinate for *perceived violations* against us personally or against our property. If we think or feel that we have been wronged we respond accordingly. Our response to such perceived violations can be emotional, physical, rational, irrational, and individually or all together involved. We are upset because things have not gone the way we want them to go. And this, of course, disturbs our peace.

I submit, then, that the two biggest roadblocks to peace, personal or otherwise, are: 1) an inherent sense of justice and injustice defined and applied individually and 2) conflicting personal agendas. I say the two 'biggest roadblocks' because I think they are the most common, everyday problem causers. We may think we are at peace if most everything seems to be going well or as well as can be expected. Yet, I ask, just because everything feels okay do we really have true peace or some illusion of peace? It seems we should examine the source, stability and end of our impression of such feelings.

Of course, many other things disturb peace. Fear, hate, sadness, war, injury, illness, etc. can and do disturb peace. However, these and those like them are usually temporary and are either directly or indirectly influenced by a matrix of individual personalities subject to their own sense of justice and personal agendas. For example, when enough individual agendas meld into a conglomerate or a collective feeling of violation emerges we have the makings of war. In time the war ends and we say we have peace. Or when we have lost a loved one, we grieve. Peace is disturbed during our bereavement. But time passes and eventually we come back to normal, so to speak. On the other hand, every time we feel wronged for anything, our personal peace is disturbed and usually, through our consequent response, our harmony in personal relations deteriorates. Every time we perceive, right or wrong, that we are blocked from getting what we want we either fight all the more for our desires or succumb reluctantly to the blocking entity. Both responses disturb our peace. We see this aspect of human nature in infants clear through to old age although I doubt we recognize it as springing from a primordial sense of justice.

So it is with us humans for our whole existence here on earth. That is why I said it is the bane or woe of humanity. On the one hand, as stated in the first sentence, we all *want* peace. On the other hand we seem to be unable to achieve lasting peace because of our injured feelings when we think we have been wronged and our resultant response thereto. We perceive an injustice to our person or property and seek justice to make it right which we think should bring peace but does not. Many times we take no immediate action to right the wrong we think has been done to us but let it fester inside. Or we explode on the spot. Or we argue, snarl and snap. In a flash, things are said and done that are just as quickly regretted. And because we thought we were wronged someone else has now been wronged. Isn't this the cycle and doesn't it persist day in and day out in the smallest and the biggest of things and persons with whom we are involved. Think about it. We can recall our last week's activity. I venture to say that there was at least one instance sometime during the week where we all felt the need to defend ourselves or somehow respond to a perceived injustice done to us. Our feelings may not have been hurt but we felt wronged and it upset, annoyed or angered us. Our peace was disturbed. How do we escape this paradox?

More than anything I think there is a false sense of peace in the world today. It seems most people think that if they have a good job, can provide for their necessities, be in relatively good health, are able to have some recreation and not have any hassles they are at peace. There are surveys that indicate this, especially in the USA.[1] The complication here, of course, is that if any one of those aspects is taken away, peace is disturbed. So if not a false sense of peace it is at least a fragile one. Furthermore, to my mind it is a superficial sense of peace simply because it is dependent upon material things and on the self. Therefore, the source of peace becomes the question. And therein is the problem.

I think that most of humanity searches for peace in all the wrong places. I believe there is only one source of true and lasting peace: God in, through and by Jesus Christ. But there is substantial testimony, clear evidence, to show that to receive peace from God we must first be *at peace* with God. So how can we be at peace with God and how can we eliminate or at least minimize our mutual trespasses?

---

[1] See www.barna.org April 24, 2003: *Views On Quality of Life Are Most Influenced By Money and Faith*

Medjugorje Introduction

Down the dark future, through long generations,
The echoing sounds grow fainter and then cease;
And like a bell, with solemn, sweet vibrations,
I hear once more the voice of Christ say "Peace!"

Henry Wadsworth Longfellow

How can we have peace; true and lasting peace? How do we learn peace? Where can we find peace? Believe it or not, the answers to these questions have always been present in the Catholic Church. Mary, Mother of the Church, today is making known the need and the way of peace like never before in recorded history. She established and sustains to this very day an oasis of peace in a place called:

Medugorje[1] (pronounced Medj'-u-gor-ree) is a small village in the southwestern part of the country Bosnia and Herzegovina which is one of the former people's republics of the former Yugoslavia. It is the name of a Roman Catholic Parish in the Diocese of Mostar-Duvno for a group of five hamlets served by the Franciscan priests at Saint James Church of Medjugorje. It is a place where the people of the parish have seen and continue, to this day, to see a great light. That light is reflected in them and in the pilgrims who visit Medjugorje. The light they all reflect is the Light of the World, Jesus Christ. The Light of Jesus shines in Medjugorje where an oasis of peace has been established by his ever virgin mother, Mary, Mother of the Church.[2]

She says her son, Jesus Christ, sent her from Heaven[3] to teach and guide all of humanity in the way of peace. The center of her school is Medjugorje where she is known as Gospa (Our Lady) and where she has let it be well known that she is the Queen of Peace and the mother of all people. Her way of tending to her children is as one who stands before God as an advocate for her children. At his pleasure she brings the graces of God to her children. As one from heaven our spiritual mother brings behavioral instruction to her children so we, her children, may avoid offending her son, Jesus, our brother and Lord, and bring us to reconciliation with God. She teaches us truthfully and faithfully so we will be moved to love the Lord our God and

---

[1] Medugorje is the Croatian spelling. Medjugorje is the Anglicized.

[2] See *Catechism of the Catholic Church, Second Edition*, paragraph 963 ff.

[3] According to the visionary Ivan Dragicevic in a talk he gave at the Mission Basilica, San Juan Capistrano, California on February 20, 2003, Our Lady said she was sent by Jesus.

Creator with all our heart, mind, spirit and body. Our Blessed Mother Mary does this *now*, in the 21st Century, primarily through messages delivered in apparition to six visionaries and, from late 1982 through 1987, by speaking inwardly to two locutionists. These eight are all from the Medjugorje parish but now only three are permanent residents. Although they are the primary apostles of Our Lady's messages, they are not alone. Many, perhaps thousands, associated with Medjugorje through pilgrimage or in some other capacity have heard from or seen Mary. Her messages are authenticated by the finger of God through physical miracles, healings and millions upon millions of individual spiritual regenerations. Her overriding concern is for PEACE for all of humanity – peace with God and peace with each other.

Sound incredible? Unbelievable? Why do I believe it is true? Well, I have been to Medjugorje and I bring to you my eyewitness testimony – testimony probably in principle much like that of those disciples of Christ who were in Jerusalem on the day of Pentecost almost 2,000 years ago. And like them I am compelled to tell what I experienced. In her message of November 25, 2001, Our Lady said: *That is why you who live my messages be the light and extended hands to this faithless world that all may come to know the God of Love.*[4] And as recently as January 25, 2003, through her chosen child, Marija Pavlovic-Lunetti, she said in her monthly message for the world: *Dear children! With this message I call you anew to pray for peace. Particularly now when peace is in crisis, you be those who pray and bear witness to peace. Little children, be peace in this peaceless world. Thank you for having responded to my*

---

[4] MIR, Official Information Center for the Shrine of Peace in Medjugorje. See www.Medjugorje.hr

call.[5] Out of love for Our Blessed Mother I am simply making an effort to do what she asks.

It was my personal blessing, honour and great privilege to be, along with my fellow pilgrim, Jebb Johnson, in attendance at this heavenly school in November 2002. There we celebrated with the parishioners of Medjugorje the Memorial of the Presentation of Mary, the Solemnity of Christ the King, and the second anniversary of Fr. Slavko Barbaric's passing from this world. We experienced the faith and culture of the Croatian people living in that part of the world who are kept safe under the mantle of the Blessed Virgin Mary, the Queen of Peace, Mother of God and Mother of the Church. In this book I share with you my personal reflections and conclusions inspired by my pilgrimage to Medjugorje. It is my own testimony and a compilation of the testimony of others. But I must stress that all I write in this book is my own conviction and reflection, testimony from others likewise convinced of the truth of Medjugorje and/or citation from other published documents.

The Magisterium of the Church is not opposed to the sharing of private revelation provided it does not attempt to "improve or complete Christ's definitive Revelation, but to help live more fully by it in a certain period of history."[6] I am confident that whoever reads this material will not find any hint of suggestion for improvement or completion of Our Lord's definitive Revelation which has been transmitted down through the centuries from the Apostles through the bishops and the whole Catholic Church. Rather, I think most readers, God willing, are more likely to find agreement with the writing of His Excellency, Dr. Frane Franic, who at the time was Archbishop of the Diocese of Split-Makarska, (Croatia): "Following my personal experience at Medjugorje

---

[5] Ibid.

[6] See *Catechism of the Catholic Church, Second Edition*, paragraph 67.

I have become convinced that the Holy Spirit is present there and that through His most innocent and most Holy Lady – the Virgin, the Mother Mary, the Queen of Peace, - He gives His grace, faith and love, thereby working for the restoration of the World and the Church."[7] And too, Cardinal Schönborn, Archbishop of Vienna (Austria) says "I would not like to pronounce myself about Medjugorje from the point of view of a Church judgment. However, I can establish only one thing, again and again and always again, that this is a place, where obviously there is an intensive mission station of Heaven, where thousands find prayer, confession, conversion, reconciliation, healing, and a deeper faith."[8]

Medjugorje is not just a phenomenon of the Catholic Church. It is indeed ecumenical in the sense that people of all different faiths come to Medjugorje. Mary invites the whole of humanity to hear and apply her messages of peace, love and holy living. She is showing the way to emerge from a daily existence that strives for peace without God and fails, to a successful life filled with the peace that only God provides. Medjugorje is about life. It is about personal revelation that convicts and liberates. It is about change that comes from a desire for the holy. It is about a serious and extensive revision of one's view on life. In short, Medjugorje is about Jesus Christ.

To begin to speak about Medjugorje, however, we must begin with the apparitions of the Blessed Virgin Mary that occur there. Following is a short history of the modern apparitional events written by Fr. Ljudevit Rupcic, O.F.M. copied by permission from MIR, Official Information Center

---

[7] *Medjugorje Today*, ©1990 by Sonnenhaus Verlag Jelenko Rastic, Medjugorje Publishing Group, ISBN 3-924902-03-8, page 63

[8] ©*Information Center "Mir" Medjugorje* www.medjugorje.hr , Archives, January 2003

for the Shrine of Peace in Medjugorje; see www.Medjugorje.hr

A SHORT HISTORY OF OUR LADY'S APPARITIONS IN MEDJUGORJE

For quite a while now, in Medjugorje (Citluk, Bosnia-Herzegovina) six trustworthy witnesses, testify firmly under oath, that since the 24th of June 1981, the Blessed Virgin Mary, or the "Gospa", as she is affectionately known as here, appears to them every day up to the present.

The first day

On the said date at approximately six o' clock in the evening, on the area of Crnica hill known as Podbrdo, the children, Ivanka [pronounced Evanka] Ivankovic, Mirjana [pronounced Miryana] Dragicevic, Vicka [pronounced Veatska] Ivankovic, Ivan [pronounced Evan] Dragicevic, Ivan Ivankovic and Milka [pronounced Mealka] Pavlovic saw an incredibly beautiful young woman with a little child in her arms. She didn't say anything to them but indicated with gestures that they should come closer. Surprised and frightened they were afraid to come near, even though they immediately thought her to be Our Lady.

The Second day

On the second day, the 25th of June 1981, the children agreed to meet once again at the same place that Our Lady had previously appeared, in the hope of seeing her again. All of a sudden there was a flash of light. The children looked up and saw Our Lady, this time without the child. She was smiling and joyful and was indescribably beautiful. With her hands she gestured to them to come closer. The children braced themselves and went up to her. They immediately fell to their knees and began to pray the "Our Father, Hail Mary and Glory Be". Our Lady prayed together with them except for when they prayed the "Hail Mary".

After the prayer she began to speak with the children. Ivanka, first of all, asked her about her mother who had died two months previously. And Mirjana asked Our Lady for some sign to be given to show to the people that they were neither lying nor crazy, as some people had said.

Our Lady finally left the children with the words," God be with you my angels!" Before that, when the children asked her if they would see her the following day, she replied by nodding her head.

According to the visionaries the whole encounter was indescribable. On that day two of the children, which made up the previous group were missing: Ivan Ivankovic and Milka Pavlovic. They were replaced by two others: Marija [pronounced Mariya] Pavlovic and Jakov [pronounced Yakov] Colo. And from that day onwards according to these six children, Our Lady regularly appears to them. Milka Pavlovic and Ivan Ivankovic, who were present on the first day of apparitions, did not see Our Lady again, even though they returned to the apparition site, in the hope of seeing her.

The third day

On the 26th of June 1981, the children full of anticipation waited at around six o' clock, which was when she previously appeared. They were going towards the same place, to meet her there. They were very happy, although their joy was mixed with fear wondering what would be the outcome of all this. Despite all this, the children could feel some sort of inner strength attracting them to meet with Our Lady.

Suddenly, while the children were still on their way a light flashed three times. To them and to those following them, it was a sign indicating Our Lady's whereabouts. On that third day Our Lady appeared even higher up than on the previous days. All at once Our Lady disappeared. But when the children began to pray, she reappeared. She was cheerful and smiling serenely and once again her beauty was overwhelming.

As they left their houses some older women advised them to carry holy water with them to make sure that it was not of Satan. When they were with Our Lady Vicka took the water and splashed it in the direction of the vision saying, “If you are Our Blessed Mother, please stay, and if you are not, go away from us". Our Lady smiled at this and remained with the children. Then Mirjana asked her name and she replied, “I am the Blessed Virgin Mary".

On the same day, coming down Podbrdo, Our Lady appeared one more time, this time however only to Maria saying, “Peace, peace, peace and only peace”. Behind her, Maria could see a cross. After which Our Lady repeated, in tears, the following words, “Peace must reign between man and God, and between all people!” The area where this took place is about half way up to the Apparition Site.

The fourth day

On the 27th of June 1981, Our Lady appeared three times to the children. On that occasion the children asked all kinds of questions and Our Lady responded. For priests, she gave this message. “May the priests firmly believe and may they take care of the faith of the people!" Once again, Jakov and Mirjana asked for a sign, because the people had begun to accuse them of lying and of taking drugs. "Do not be afraid of anything", Our Lady replied.

Before parting, when asked if she would come again, she indicated that she would. On the way down Podbrdo, Our Lady appeared one more time to say goodbye with the words, “May God be with you my angels, go in peace!"

The fifth day

On the 28th of June 1981, big crowds were gathering from all parts even from the early hours of the morning. By noon there were about fifteen thousand people. On the same day, the Parish Priest, Fr. Jozo Zovko,

examined the children on what they had seen and heard in the previous days.
At the usual time Our Lady appeared again. The children prayed with her, and afterwards they questioned her. Vicka, for example, asked "My dear Lady, what do you want from us and what do you want from our priests?" Our Lady replied, "The people should pray and firmly believe". Regarding priests, she replied that they should believe firmly and help others to do the same.
On that day Our Lady came and went many times. During one of these times the children asked her why she doesn't appear in the Parish Church for every-one to see. She replied," Blessed are those who have not seen and yet believe".
Even though the crowds were pushing them with their questions and curiosities and the day was heavy and sultry, the children felt as though they were in heaven.

The sixth day

On the 29th of June 1981, the children were taken to Mostar for a medical examination after which they were proclaimed "healthy". The statement of the head doctor was: "The children aren't crazy, the person who brought them here must be though"....
The crowds on Apparition Hill that day were greater than ever. As soon as the children arrived at the usual place and began to pray, Our Lady appeared. On that occasion the Blessed Mother exhorted them to have faith saying," The people should believe firmly and have no fear."

On that day, a doctoress who was following and observing them, during the apparition desired to touch Our Lady. The children guided her hand to the place where Our Lady's shoulder was, and she felt a tingling sensation. The doctor, even though an atheist had to admit that, "Here, something strange is happening!"
On that same day a child was miraculously healed by the name of Daniel Setka. Her parents had brought her to Medjugorje, praying specifically for a healing. Our Lady had promised that this would come about if the parents prayed and fasted and strongly believed. The child thereupon was healed.

The seventh day
On the 30th of June 1981 two young girls suggested to the children to go by car further away to be able to stroll in peace. Really their intention was to bring them away from the area and keep them until after the normal apparition time had passed. However, even though the children were far away from Podbrdo, at the usual time of the apparition, it was as if an interior call prompted them to ask to be let out of the car. As soon as they did, and said a prayer, Our Lady drew near to them, from the direction of Podbrdo, which was now over a kilometre away. She prayed seven "Our Fathers" etc. And so the girl's trick had no effect. Soon after this the police began to hinder the children and the pilgrims going on Podbrdo, the site of apparitions. The children, and soon afterwards even the crowds were forbidden to go there. But Our Lady

continued to appear to them in secret places, in their homes and in the fields. The children had already gained confidence, and openly spoke with Our Lady, eagerly seeking her advice, listening to her warnings and messages. The events of Medjugorje continued in this fashion up until the 15th of January 1982.

In the meantime, the Parish Priest began to host the pilgrims in the Church, enabling them to participate in the rosary and to celebrate the Eucharist. The children also gave out the rosary. Our Lady sometimes appeared to them in the church at that time. Even the Parish Priest himself once while praying the rosary, saw Our Lady. Immediately he broke off praying and spontaneously started to sing a popular hymn: "Lijepa si, lijepa, Djevo Marijo" - "O how beautiful you are, Most Blessed Virgin Mary". The whole church could see that something unusual was happening to him. Afterwards he stated that he had seen her. And so, he who up until then had not only been doubtful, but openly against even rumours of the apparitions, became their defender. He testified his support of the apparitions even to the point of serving a prison sentence.

From the 15th of January 1982 onwards the children saw Our Lady in a closed off area of the Parish Church. The Parish Priest arranged this because of the newly arisen difficulties and sometimes even dangers, which provided themselves for the visionaries. Previously the children had ensured that this was in accord with Our Lady's wishes. Because of the prohibitions of the Diocesan Bishop however, from April 1985 onwards the children ceased to use the area of the church as an apparition site. Instead, they went to a room in the Parish house.

All this time, from the beginning of the apparitions up until today, there have only been five days when none of the children saw Our Lady.

Our Lady didn't always appear in the same place either, nor to the same group, nor individuals, nor did her apparitions always last a specified period. Sometimes the apparitions lasted two minutes, sometimes an hour. Neither did Our Lady appear at the children's will. Sometimes they prayed and waited but Our Lady didn't appear until a little while afterwards, unexpectedly and unforewarned. And sometimes she appeared to one and not to the others. If she hadn't promised an appointed time, nobody knew when she would appear, or if she would appear. Neither did she appear always to just the aforesaid visionaries, but to others also of different age, stature, race, education and walks of life. All this suggests that the apparitions are not a product of the imagination. It depends neither on time nor place, nor desire nor the prayer of pilgrim or visionary, but moreover on the will of He who permits it.

MESSAGES

According to the united testimony of the visionaries, Our Lady on the occasion of her apparition gave a series of messages, to be transmitted to the people. Even though there are many messages, they can however be summarized in five themes, because all the messages basically underline or lead up to these five.

GENERAL OVERVIEW OF THE MESSAGES

PEACE

Already on the third day, Our Lady stressed peace as the first of her messages: "Peace, peace, peace and only peace!" after which she said twice, "Peace must reign between God and man and between people". Considering that Maria could see a cross, when Our Lady gave this message, the obvious conclusion is that this peace comes from God. God, who through Our Lady in Christ became our peace, (Ephesians 2:14) "For He is the peace between us"...This peace, "the world cannot give" (John 14:27) and that's why Christ commanded His apostles to bring it to the world (Matthew 10:11) so that all men could become "sons of peace"(Luke 10:6). That's why Our Lady as "Queen of Apostles" in Medjugorje specifically refers to herself as "Queen of Peace". Who better than she can more successfully convince today's world, which is faced with the threat of destruction, how great and how necessary peace is.

FAITH

The second of Our Lady's messages is faith. Already on the fourth, fifth and sixth day of apparitions, Our Lady exhorted those present to have strong faith. Understandably, she repeated this message many times. Without faith we cannot arrive at peace! Not only this but faith is itself an answer to God's Word, which he not only proclaims but actually gives to us. When we believe, we accept God's Word, which in Christ became "our peace" (Ephesians 2:14). Accepting it, the individual becomes a new creature, with a new life of Christ within, and a share in God's nature (1 Peter 1:4, Ephesians 2:18). In this way the individual ensures peace with God and with others.

Once again there is no one who can better understand the necessity and efficaciousness of faith than Our Lady. That's why she stressed it on every occasion and charged the visionaries to bring the light of faith to others. Our Lady presented faith as an answer to everything, no matter whatever people were looking for. She presented it as the prerequisite of all prayer, desires and demands, relating it to health, wholeness and to all other human necessities.

CONVERSION

Conversion was another one of Our Lady's frequent messages. This presupposes that she noticed either a weakness or a complete lack of faith in humanity today. And without conversion it is impossible to achieve peace. True conversion means, the purifying or cleansing of the heart, (Jeremiah 4:14), because a corrupt or 'deteriorated' heart is the basis of bad relations, which in turn brings social disorder, unjust laws, base constitutions etc. Without a radical change of heart, without the conversion of the heart, there is no peace. For this reason, Our Lady continually suggests frequent confession. The request is directed to all without differentiation because, “not one of us is just"...."all have wandered, not one does right"(Romans 3:11-12).

PRAYER

Almost daily, from the fifth day of apparitions onwards Our Lady recommends prayer. She requests everyone to "pray without ceasing" just as Christ himself taught (Mark 9:29; Matthew 9:38; Luke 11:5-13) Prayer, therefore stimulates and strengthens our faith, without which our relationship with God is disordered;-as is our relationship with each other. Prayer also reminds us of how close God is to us even in our daily lives: In prayer we acknowledge Him, we give Him thanks for His gifts to us, and we are filled with a hopeful expectancy of that which we need, but particularly our redemption. Prayer solidifies the equilibrium of the individual, and aids us in our 'ordered relationship with God', without which it is impossible to maintain peace either with God or with our neighbour. [sic]

The Word of the Lord acquainted itself with all humanity and awaits humanity's response. It is precisely this which gives prayer it's "justification". Our response should be "spoken faith", or "prayer". In prayer, faith animates, renews, strengthens and sustains itself. In addition to this, man's prayer really bears witness to the Gospel, and to the existence of God, thus provoking a response of faith in others.

FASTING

Already on the sixth day of the apparitions, Our Lady often recommended fasting because it aids faith. That is, the practice of fasting aids and ensures control over oneself. Only the person who can dominate himself is truly free, and is capable of abandoning himself to God and to his neighbour, [sic] as faith demands. Fasting guarantees him that his abandonment to faith is secure and sincere. It helps him to free himself from every slavery, but especially to the slavery to sin. Whoever is not in the possession of oneself is in some way enslaved. Therefore fasting helps the individual to restrain himself from disordered pleasure seeking which in turn leads him to a futile and useless existence often wasteful of the very goods which are necessary to others just for basic survival.

With fasting we also retrieve the gift, which creates within us a realistic love for the poor and the destitute, which up to a certain point eases the difference between rich and poor. It therefore heals the wants of the poor and also heals the excesses and over-indulgence of others. And in it's [sic] own way, it gives a dimension of peace which today in a special way, is threatened by the difference in the lifestyles of the rich and the poor. (e.g. North and South).

To sum up, we can say that Our Lady's messages underline that v [sic] peace is the greatest good, and that faith, conversion, prayer and fasting are the means by which we can attain it.

SPECIAL MESSAGES

Outside of the five messages which, as we have said are the important messages which Our Lady immediately gave to the whole world, she started from the 1st of March 1984, every Thursday, mainly through the visionary Marija Pavlovic to give special messages to the Parish of Medjugorje and to the pilgrims who come. Our Lady therefore, outside of the six visionaries chose the Parish of Medjugorje together with the pilgrims who come here to be her collaborators and witnesses. This is clear from the first of the Thursday messages, where she says: “I am choosing this Parish in a special way and I want to guide it." She emphasized this once again when she said, "I am choosing this Parish in a special way, which is dearer to me than others, where I joyfully went when the Almighty sent me."(25th March 1985). Our Lady gave a reason too for her choice saying: “Convert, you in the Parish, this is my second wish. In that way, all those who come here will convert."(8th March 1984)." I am asking you, especially the members of this Parish, to live my messages"(16th August 1984). First of all the parishioners and the pilgrims should become witnesses of her apparitions, and her messages, so that we can then unite with her and the visionaries in the realization of her plan for conversion of the world and reconciliation with God.

Our Lady well knows the weaknesses and the nature of the parishioners and pilgrims with whom she wishes to collaborate in the salvation of the world. She is aware of the need for supernatural strength. That's why she leads them to the fount of that strength. This primarily is prayer. She ardently and continuously exhorts us to pray. Of all prayer, she especially stresses the Holy Mass, (7th March 1985, 16th May 1985) and recommends continuous devotion to the Blessed Sacrament (15th March 1984). She also encourages devotion to the Holy Spirit (2nd June 1984; 9th June 1984; 11th April 1985; 23rd May 1988, etc.) and the reading of Sacred Scripture (8th Sept. 1984; 14th Feb. 1985).

With these special messages to the Parish and it's [sic] pilgrims, Our Lady wishes that the first messages, which in the beginning were intended for the whole world, are deepened, made more acceptable and understandable to others.

From the 25th of January 1987 Our Lady began to give the message on the 25th of every month instead of every Thursday, through the visionary Marija Pavlovic. This still continues today.

By Fr. Ljudevit Rupcic, Professor of Theology and translator of Sacred Scripture into the Croatian language[9]

Fr. Rupcic died June 25, 2003, at the age of 85. All Herzegovina mourned his loss.[10]

That is the short history of the apparitions of Our Blessed Mother at Medjugorje. Next I would like to share with you some of my cultural experiences and what I learned about the place between the mountains located in the Brotnjo region of western Herzegovina.

[9] ©*Information Center "Mir" Medjugorje* www.medjugorje.hr , Our Lady's Messages, Introduction
[10] Ibid. June, 2003, Archives

Medjugorje[1]
(between the mountains)
The Place

Location:

The parish of Medjugorje is located in the far southwestern extreme of Bosnia and Herzegovina, in the south of a region known as western Herzegovina (pronounced Her-ze-gov-ea-na). Western Herzegovina is bounded on the north by the Duvno Plains and several ranges of mountains, to the east by the Neretva River, to the south and west by the Dalmatian Mountains. More specifically, the area in which Medjugorje sits is known as Brotnjo (pronounced Brot-n-ya). Geographically, Medjugorje is approximately 43° 12' N by 17° 34' E in terrestrial latitude and longitude. The metropolitan center of western Herzegovina is Mostar located approximately 20 miles north of Medjugorje and about 60 miles southwest of Sarajevo.

---

[1] Most of the information presented in this section is derived from either my personal observation and conversation with the local people or from *Medugorje Today* © 1990 by Sonnehaus Verlag Jelenko Rastic, Medugorje Publishing Group, ISBN 3-924902-03-8.

Most visitors (pilgrims) from outside western Herzegovina fly into Split or Dubrovnik, Croatia and then take a three hour car or bus ride to Medjugorje.

The Land:

For the most part western Herzegovina is comprised of terrain that is barren brush, filled with limestone creating a geological region known as karst, and low mountains. But there are fertile areas with arable soil of red, sandy loam and of them all Brotnjo is reputed to be the best. Tobacco and grapes have been traditionally grown in the area, including Medjugorje, although tobacco is not evident in Medjugorje today. The grapes, however, bear a laudatory reputation for producing very good wines. There is some shepherding in and around Medjugorje and chickens in almost every backyard. Fruits and grains also are produced in Brotnjo.

Ancient Roman archeological finds in Brotnjo reveal that the area was originally heavily wooded. The timber was harvested and exported by the Romans and the forests never regenerated. There were also olive groves but none today.

Generally, the land is a gently rolling countryside. Where there is no cultivation or other human development the lay of the land would have to be called brushy and rocky, especially on the surrounding hills and mountains. Not surprising, all the houses and buildings are built of stone and/or concrete. There are, however, abundant patches of deciduous and conifer trees, most noticeable along the banks of the Neretva and Trebižat rivers. The Trebižat, near Medjugorje, generates the picturesque and pretty little waterfalls of Kravica. The falls are approximately 400 feet wide in a horseshoe formation and about 83 feet high. They are like a sort of mini Niagara Falls.

The climate is Mediterranean. Hot in the summer and cold in the winter. The local folks say it snows on the valley floor about four inches every other year. Most every day in summer is filled with clear skies and warm sun that provide a long growing season.

Travel is relatively easy in Herzegovina. Most all roads and streets are paved and they are in good condition. There are sufficient roads to get one to where one needs to go. The nearest commercial airport is in Mostar and then more distant are Split and Dubrovnik in bordering Croatia. Bus transportation is available and there are taxis everywhere.

Very Brief History of The People:

Brotnjo was originally settled by tribe people around 1300 B.C. and is included in what is known in historical and archeological terms as the ancient region of Illyria. Thus, the first known peoples of Brotnjo are called Illyrians. Illyria generally consisted of the modern day area of Albania and the former Yugoslavia of which both Croatia and Bosnia-Herzegovina were parts. There is some evidence of a Celtic presence in Brotnjo beginning around 400 B.C. It is, however, the Roman presence in the area that yields the greatest abundance of archeological treasures. Their arrival is confidently dated 229 B.C. Carved stone slabs, called stelae, used as commemorative markers for graves and other important sites and other Roman artifacts are housed at the Franciscan Monastery Museum in Humac which by car is located about 20 minutes away from Medjugorje. The museum collection also contains ancient Byzantine coinage found in Medjugorje and other parts of Brotnjo.

For nearly seven hundred years Brotnjo was ruled by Rome and populated by the indigenous people, Romans,

Greeks and maybe some leftover Celts. By the first half of the sixth century A.D., however, with the fall of the Western Roman Empire, Byzantium[2] came to rule in all of Herzegovina (then called Hum) and the entire Balkans. And at the invitation of the Emperor, the Croats came to western Herzegovina in the third decade of the seventh century. They have been there ever since. Croatia became a nation-state in the year 879 and according to tradition the first King of Croatia was crowned in the Duvno plains 25 miles to the north of Medjugorje. Brotnjo was assigned to the district of Hum within the national borders of Croatia. From that time forward Hum would alternately fall outside and inside the borders of Croatia depending on the political situation of the day. In 1322 Hum became part of Bosnia and in 1448 became known as Herzegovina. As it was, the Turks of the Ottoman Empire conquered the region in the same century and ruled for four centuries thereafter.

Only in the 1800's was the area released from Turkish tyranny as the Ottomans finally vanished. After the Russo-Turkish War, pursuant to the Treaty of San Stefano in 1878, Herzegovina was occupied and ruled by the Austria-Hungary Empire. Following the First World War in 1918 the Kingdom of Serbs, Croats and Slovenes came to be of which western Herzegovina was part. However, in 1929 King Alexander I changed the name of the kingdom to Yugoslavia. With the end of World War II, Communism came to power and under Tito the party ruled all of Yugoslavia with an iron hand. In June of 1981 the Blessed Virgin Mary first appeared in Bijakovici (pronounced Bee-

---

[2] Byzantium, modern day Istanbul, Turkey, was chosen for the imperial capital and renamed Constantinople by the Roman Emperor, Constantine the Great in the 4th century. In 364 the Roman Empire divided with Valentinian I ruling the West from Rome and Valens ruling the East from Constantinople. The East became known as the Byzantine Empire and survived until 1453 when the dreaded Ottoman Turks finally conquered Constantinople.

ya-kah-vea-chea), a hamlet of the Medjugorje parish. In 1988/89 Communism fell in Eastern Europe and Bosnia and Herzegovina sought independence from Yugoslavia. In 1992 civil war came to the region but Medjugorje was untouched. Mostar, on the other hand, was heavily damaged. The war ended in 1995 and there has been relative peace ever since.[3] Today, except for Mostar, the population of western Herzegovina and, therefore Brotnjo, is 99% Croatian.

In the last one hundred years there has been ebb and flow in the demographics of Medjugorje. By 1900 the parish had 266 families and 2,121 faithful. From 1916 to 1918 301 people died of Spanish Flu, yet the population grew. By 1932/33, the period in which the concrete cross was built on Šipovac, now called Križevac (Cross Mountain), there were 418 families and 4,504 inhabitants in Medjugorje which is the highest in its history. During the Communist regime, killings and emigration prevailed. The partisans killed 69 Herzegovian Franciscan Priests, one in the parish office of Medjugorje, and the people started searching for a safer place to live. Of those who stayed there was a "miraculously high birth rate"[4] that sustained the population level. However, by the 1960's emigration was in full swing and the number of inhabitants dropped dramatically. Then, in 1981... Our Lady, the Blessed Virgin Mary, appeared.

---

[3] Certain key dates are taken from Mark Mazower, professor of history at Birkbeck College, London, and a former professor of history at Princeton University, in his book *The Balkans – A Short History*, 2000, Random House, Inc., ISBN 0-8129-6621-X.

[4] Fr. Svetozar Kraljevic, O.F.M., Fr. Ivan Sesar, et al., *Medjugorje*, pg. 108, Informativni centar "Mir" Medjugorje, 2002, ISBN 9958-775-14-X. Demographic information is also from Father Svet's article.

The People Today:

To talk about people and their culture as "a people" one should really do a full anthropologic/sociological study. I have not done that. I am not qualified. However, I can give you my observations and impressions and information I gained from people I met while in Medjugorje in November of 2002.

The parishioners of Medjugorje are all Croats. If discussion with the folks of Medjugorje ever turns to nationalities or ethnicity they always let it be well known that they are Croatian. And that they are a peaceful people of Catholic faith.

Our host was Martin Ilic who owns and operates Hotel Martin. His hotel is very nice and modern, 40 rooms big and quite successful. At a very reasonable rate he offers a two person room with private bath and serves breakfast and dinner every day. Martin is a nice man who by all appearances is well regarded in the community. My impression is that he is a good husband to his lovely wife, Marijana, and good father to his two daughters, Enis and Antel, ages 13 and 8 respectively. The Ilic's are conversant in English[5] and since Martin runs his hotel like a B & B we were with them every day and able to interact with them frequently. As an added bonus, in my mind, since it was off-season, so to speak, Jebb and I were the only guests in the hotel. Consequently, we felt more as guests of the family than just hotel guests. But, I think Martin attempts to have all his guests feel that way. There seemed to be peace in Martin's household. Perhaps some insight into this is revealed in the following. One day I said to Martin, "You are a very blessed man." With a knowing look in his eye and slow nod of his head, he responded, "Yes. I know I am very

---

[5] Which is why our travel arranger, Paul Millard of Morning Star Ministries, set us up at Martin's.

blessed." My impression is that is the way all the parishioners of Medjugorje feel.

In Medjugorje the children all attend parochial school and then high school in Citluk, a larger town ten minutes away from Medjugorje. Many, if not all, of the parochial students walk to school unescorted. I watched them leave from their houses about 7:15 AM every weekday morning and head up the street with their backpacks hanging on their shoulders. Usually, they were paired. But occasionally a group of four or so could be seen. Most noticeable is that they always seemed to be in conversation with one speaking and the other listening. No jumble of raucous vocal intercourse. No yelling and screaming, except of course when the little, pudgy neighborhood dog chased the girls just, I think, to hear them scream. He certainly was not intent on biting them. But, for the most part the children were quite well behaved and appeared to be not at all self-absorbed and selfish. To the contrary, they are most human and realistic. Compared to the Orange County, California children I see everyday, the Medjugorje children appear to be far less beguiled by worldly charm and materialism.

Now, that is just my impression of the children. Who knows what happens when they arrive at school or when they are out of public view. And Antel, the eight year old daughter of our hosts, Martin and Marijana Ilic, did, on Saturday, go shopping in Mostar with her mother where she got a new pair of boots. But as I wiled away some time in the front courtyard of Hotel Martin on Sunday afternoon, Antel came walking up the drive by herself and she had her new boots on. I asked her where she had been. She simply said, "church" and smiled pleasantly. Likewise, one evening I was again sitting in the courtyard after dinner (alright, I confess I am a pipe smoker) and Enis, the Ilic's thirteen year old daughter came walking up the drive by herself and I asked her where she had been. "Church." She did explain that it was part of a school program. And she did have on a nice down-filled parka as it is cold in the evening in late November. In fact all the Ilics were always nicely dressed. On Wednesday we asked if there was cake for dessert. Enis said sweetly and politely, "No, we fast on Wednesday." My purpose here is to attempt to show by a few examples that the children, who are a reflection of their parents, are by all appearances neither austere nor overindulgent, involved in their church and rather pleasant human beings. By the way, Wednesday and Friday fast is what Gospa recommends.

Now on the other side of fast is feast, right? The food at Martin's was delicious. He was emphatic and made sure we knew that all his food was home-cooked. And it was. Chicken, beef, pork, fish, omelettes, crepes, you name it. It was a culinary experience of the first order (I too like to cook and bake).

His cook is a young law student named Daniella. She is from Mostar where she attends college. On occasion Marijana Ilic would fill in for Daniella when she had classes. But for the most part, Daniella stayed at the hotel so that in between meal preparations for breakfast and dinner at 7:30 PM she could study. She also provided the maid services for our room. On Saturday night, after dinner, I happened to overtake her as I walked to the Eucharistic Adoration Service at the church. She said she was going out for the night. I thought she was off for a party. A few minutes later, while waiting for Jebb in the plaza in front of St. James, I saw her and another young woman walking arm in arm up to the church. They too were going to Eucharistic Adoration! And then afterwards I think they went out because she looked and said she did not feel well Sunday morning. But, maybe she just had a little virus or something. I did not pursue it with her.

As it turned out, my greatest exposure to Medjugorje culture was through our taxi driver, Jure Soldo. Jure picked us up at the airport in Split and took us in his mustard yellow Mercedes 240D, standard shift transmission, to Medjugorje.

For a number of years I had a 240D which is the mid-size Mercedes Benz sedan of the early 80's with a diesel engine. Jure's car was much quieter, ran much smoother and was more powerful than mine. Strange.

From Split we traveled south down the coast of the Adriatic Sea and turned inland at Makarska, climbed up the coastal Dalmatian Mountains, traveled along the tops of the mountains and then dropped down into the western extreme of the Duvno Plains beginning the descent at Vrgorac. We motored generally east through Ljubuški and Cerno to Medjugorje. He made the trip in two hours and forty-five minutes taking what I would call the 'back way' because the road was narrow, winding and absent any real traffic or populated areas until we arrived at Ljubuški. In this way Jure avoided afternoon traffic congestion through the town of Grude and others along the main and much improved route from Split to Ljubuški. Eight days later, on our return, we followed this main route, but, it was at three o'clock in the morning and there was obviously no traffic.

Jure's English is not real good. When I saw him at the airport holding up a sign with my name on it, I said, "Martin?" He responded affirmatively and so over the course of our ride to Medjugorje I thought he was our host, Martin Ilic, and did not find out differently until we arrived at the hotel where Martin met us. Jure must have thought I was asking for 'Martin' Hotel. Anyway, he was a gracious driver and answered as best he could the questions Jebb and I asked of him. He often told us the Croatian word for this or that. When he dropped us at the hotel he gave me his business card and I thought he said that the taxi driver on the card, Jure Soldo, was his cousin. But, no, later in the week when I asked Martin to call Jure Soldo for a taxi ride to Jakov Colo's house I found out that Jure was Jure! When I explained it to Jure, I think he understood, we all laughed together about it. He is a very friendly guy with a good sense of humor and not overly talkative.

On my last day in Medjugorje, Jure and I spent the whole morning together. I called for him to take me to the Franciscan Monastery Museum at Humac next to Ljubuški and to the waterfalls of Kravica. We arrived at the museum a half hour before it opened so we wandered around the monastery grounds, checked out the chickens and the garden and looked in on the old church of Humac built in 1869. The church exterior is plain concrete with no ornamentation but the interior is quite dramatic, especially the huge painting on the reredos behind the altar.

In the museum were displayed Roman and Byzantine artifacts mentioned above and the Humac Plaque mentioned below. It was all quite interesting and after my tour at the invitation of a jovial Franciscan Friar I celebrated a toast with him by tossing down some concoction the friars apparently made themselves. It *did* have a jolt and the bottle contained what looked like a varietal sample of herbs.

After Humac we went to the Kravica waterfalls and then back to Medjugorje and over to Srebrenica in the hamlet of Miletina. There I was looking for ruins of a Roman basilica. I thought ruins were there but we could find none. Apparently, it is just considered *likely* by historians that there was an early basilica there. But what I did see in the church cemetery is the beautiful marble capped sepulcher of Martin Ilic's father. Jure pointed it out to me.

Leaving Srebrenica we drove about a mile north to Solde which is the neighborhood where Jure lives. He showed me his vegetable garden, fruit trees, chickens and his hunting dogs. He invited me in to meet his wife and youngest daughter. He has three children - two daughters and a son who is the oldest. He is very proud of his children. We ate Japanese apples and had a drink of schnapps. Jure's daughter speaks English very well and helped the course of conversation between us. She is 18 years old, in her last year of high school and waiting to obtain her driver's license. The minimum age for a driver's license there is 18.

All in all it was a very interesting and enjoyable morning for which I am ever grateful of Jure's hospitality.

Later in the afternoon that same day, I talked with a lovely lady, married, mother of two young children, who when she was a girl went to school with Marija Pavlovic - Lunetti in Mostar. Her name is Lillian and she works in the Veritas souvenir shop. She lives in Mostar and commutes to work in Medjugorje. I asked her about how things were now after the war. She said good here in Medjugorje but not so good in Mostar. That city is apparently, literally, divided right down the middle with Croats living on one side and Bosnian Muslims on the other. Evidently there is tension. For instance, she said the schools are controlled by Muslims and they insist that "Muslim" language be taught and spoken in the schools. The Croats do not want their children learning "Muslim" language.[6] They want their children to learn to read and write Croatian. She says the Croats cannot understand the Serbs and the Muslims. "They like to kill. We are peaceful." I asked why she doesn't relocate to somewhere like Split. "All my family is in Mostar. Besides it is too expensive in Split." "How about Ljubuški?" I ask. "No work there. At least in Mostar my husband has work." She feels very blessed to have the job in Medjugorje. Her husband is an electrician in Mostar and earns $220 a month. Their apartment costs $100 a month. She and her brother take care of their elderly mother who has her own small house. Every day, she, her husband and her children pray the rosary together.

My impression was that in relation to the pilgrims most of the parishioners keep to themselves but are friendly and courteous if addressed. They seem to be unpretentious and unassuming but not shy. Even the roughest looking fellow was immediately ready to help or offer service when the need was apparent. There is a feeling of quiet confidence

---

[6] I presume she meant some dialect of Arabic. I did not ask.

that seems to be imbued among the people. It is a humble confidence void of any bravado whatsoever. They seem to go about their business as needed without a lot of fanfare. The pace is slow but busy (which is what I noticed in all of my European stops). I cannot say they are stoics and they are not aloof. But, they do not intrude. I never saw or personally experienced any show of resentment or disgust or ridicule or whispers or looks or mockery or felt like anyone was talking about me or any other pilgrim. No one stared at me and watched my every move as if they were plotting how to separate me from my money. And I went into the community alone beyond the usual pilgrimage locale. I suppose such a good nature quickly develops if the community is to peacefully tolerate twenty years of over a million visitors a year trampling through and about their village. Of course, the pilgrims have brought a considerable economic gain to the region. But I do not think that is why the millions of pilgrims are so accepted. It goes deeper than that. Much deeper.

Religion:

The eminent Protestant church historian, Philip Schaff, reports that Justin Martyr, writing about 150 A.D., said: "There is no people, Greek or barbarian, or of any other race, by whatsoever appellation or manners they may be distinguished, however ignorant of arts or agriculture, whether they dwell in tents or wander about in covered wagons – among whom prayers and thanksgivings are not offered in the name of the crucified Jesus to the Father and

Creator of all things."[7] With this testimony it is safe to assume there were at least a few Christians sowing the seeds of the Gospel in western Herzegovina when the Church was in its infancy. Undoubtedly, some crossed the Adriatic Sea from Rome and others came across the hinterland from Greece. In fact, it is traditionally maintained that on his third missionary journey (circa 53/54-58 A.D.) St. Paul crossed the Balkan Peninsula and traveled to the city of Dyrrachium on the Adriatic Sea coast which is the modern city of Durrës in the country of Albania. Durrës is located about 250 miles south of Medjugorje. As St. Paul was a most successful evangelist, it, therefore, is quite likely that in the natural course of trade and travel Christians were in Brotnjo before the end of the 1st century.

Although remains of early Christian churches in Herzegovina may not date back to the 1st century, they certainly date to the 2nd and 3rd centuries. The martyrdom of Bishop Venantius that occurred in the Duvno range in the third century is historically recorded as is the ancient Diocese of Duvno that was active in the 6th century.[8] In fact, it is very interesting to me to note that at the time in which the Croats came to western Herzegovina in the third decade of the 7th century is about the same time that the Croatian people adopted Christianity, which is the middle of the 7th century.[9] It is traditionally believed that the first King of Croatia was crowned in the Duvno Plain.[10] Could it be that

---

[7] Philip Schaff, *History Of The Christian Church Volume II, Ante-Nicene Christianity*, pg. 22, Wm. B. Erdmans Publishing Company, Grand Rapids, MI, ©1910 by Charles Scribner's Sons, ISBN 0-8028-8048-7, Reprinted 1994.

[8] Jakov Bubalo's article, *The Church In Herzegovina, printed in Medugorje Today* © 1990 by Sonnehaus Verlag Jelenko Rastic, Medjugorje Publishing Group, ISBN 3-924902-03-8.

[9] Loc.cit., Rastic, Lauko and Horvatic: article *There Where Our Lady Speaks Croatian,* printed in *Medugorje Today*

[10] Ibid.

the Croatian people and Christianity were destined to merge in western Herzegovina? Since the 7th century the Croatian Catholic faith of western Herzegovina has been unshakeable in spite of all the war and suffering down through the centuries.

Although today, except for along the Adriatic coast, there is little standing, if any, of ancient or medieval church structures, it is quite certain there was a tenth/eleventh century church of St. Michael the Archangel located in the vicinity of Humac – close by Medjugorje. The church was built by Uskrsimir, son of Bret and his wife Pavica. This is testified to by the Plaque of Humac which dates from that period. The Plaque of Humac is a stone monument about eight inches thick that measures approximately two feet high by three feet wide. Writing is carved in the stone of the plaque. "... [It] in itself is of considerable importance, being as it is one of the oldest monuments bearing a Croatian language text – it is certainly the oldest example in Herzegovina. It is written in the Croatian variation of Cirilica – Bosancica (the Bosnian Cyrillic script) and includes some letters from the old Croatian Glagoljica script."[11]

For the most part, Herzegovina during the 12th through mid-15th centuries was governed by the Princes of Hum. Under their protection the Church enjoyed relative peace and grew as the people grew. One of the more famous Princes of Hum was Stipan Vukcic Kosaca. Pope Nicholas V gave him the title of Herzeg of Saba. Ruins of one of his fortified cities can be seen at Ljubuški.

In the early 1400's, through Providence, the sons of Saint Francis of Assisi arrived in Herzegovina. The Franciscan fathers worked hard for and with the people, gave much strength to their faith and sound direction for their spiritual lives. Churches were built, parishes established and

---

[11] Ibid.

the gospel spread throughout the land. But, it was short-lived because the Turks arrived in Bosnia in 1463 and in just a few years Herzegovina too was overrun. Thus began four centuries of persecution of Christ in the land of Hum. The Muslim Turkish invaders utterly destroyed all physical evidence of Christianity in Brotnjo but the Spirit they can never kill. The Franciscans did not flee even as they were hunted down and murdered by the Turks. The priests were hidden by the people and Holy Mass was celebrated in secret places, often in secluded glens and mountain hideaways. For over three centuries Jesus prevailed in this way through the Marian devotion of the Franciscan fathers tending to the flock of Christ in Herzegovina. And through all the generations of persecution and suffering the people remained strong in their Catholic faith.

Finally, with the rout of the Turks from Herzegovina, in the last quarter of the 19th Century the people breathed a sigh of relief as the yoke of terror and persecution was thrown off their necks. They survived the test of faith by suffering through those long years. Under the pastoral care of the Franciscan fathers they persevered in the faith and passed on to each subsequent generation Jesus and Mary, living, loving and active.

The parish of Medjugorje was founded by the sons of St. Francis in 1892 and in 1897 the parish built the church of St. Jacob. However, this church was built on unstable ground and was no longer serviceable by 1937 when construction on the present St. James church of Medjugorje was begun. Due to war delays and post-WWII poverty, the church was not completed until 1969 which was just in time. For twelve years later Our Lady appeared there in that place between the mountains. The rocky and thorny slopes of Podbrdo would from that time on never be the same.

In 1933 the parishioners hauled up to the top of Križevac by hand and donkey all the lumber, steel, cement, sand, gravel and water needed to build a concrete cross and base. The little mountain rises 1,510 feet above sea level and the cross another 30 feet beyond the top. This cross can be seen with the naked eye from anywhere in the five hamlets of the Medjugorje parish. It was built to honor the 1,933rd anniversary of Our Lord's birth and the 1,900th anniversary of his death and resurrection.[12] After the cross was built and blessed, for a time, there was peace for the faithful in Medjugorje and western Herzegovina. But not for long.

World War II came to the land followed by the Communist regime of Tito. Again, the people suffered the loss of family and priests. One Franciscan father was killed in the Medjugorje parish office. Another 68 throughout western Herzegovina were martyred. Still the people remained strong in the Catholic faith and patiently waited for the Lord to change the direction things were going. But, little did they suspect that he would do it so dramatically. For on June 24, 1981, the Blessed Virgin Mary appeared and remains with the parish to this day. By her own testimony Our Lady said she chose the parish of Medjugorje for the site of her last apparitions in this way because of the faith of the people.[13]

---

[12] This is the cross appearing on the cover of this book. It was refurbished this year in celebration of its 70th anniversary. Photo is from www.medjugorje.hr

[13] Following is the content of an e-mail communication to me from my friend Patrick Newman who was a guest at Jakov Colo's house in Medjugorje in November 2002: *A recurring theme while talking with Jakov was that there are many misinterpretations out there, and he expressed strong feelings about stating what Mary says so that they are not adding to, or taking away from what she is saying. One of the questions I asked him was, "is this the last time Mary will appear on earth?" I followed by saying that that's what one of the messages says in the book* Our Lady Speaks *(a book that organizes the messages by subject). He said that there are many misinterpretations out there, and that this is not what she has said. He said that it's the last time she will come in this way. This could mean many things, like it's the last time she will be appearing to young people to have them spread her message.*

Perhaps over a century past, a sign of what was to come was given. Jakov Bubalo writes:

> The old Herzegovian chronicler, Fra Petar Bakula, recorded 120 years ago that many people had made frequent claims of having seen a very strong red light, and who said that they were convinced that the light revealed some great treasure. Were not the ancient seers of Medugorje true and real prophets when they claimed that the light revealed hidden treasure? Is there any greater treasure from merciful Heaven than that which today in Medugorje is bestowing its kisses on this Earth? Are there more priceless riches to be obtained than the Heavenly Mother Mary being a friend to all her earthly children?[14]

The fruit of the faith of the people of Medjugorje and her pilgrims, even more solid now than ever, is well stated by Dr. Ljudevit Rupcic:

> In Medugorje, people do not settle accounts with others but with themselves. They do not point a besmirched finger at others, but at themselves. Their precious contribution to peace is their own reorientation towards values that are permanent and immutable – towards God and love.[15]

---

[14] Loc. cit, *Medugorje Today* pg. 74
[15] Ibid., article by Dr. Ljudevit Rupcic, pg. 78

This is the contagion at Medjugorje. This is what Our Blessed Mother brings to the place between the mountains. It is the starting point on the way of peace. And the people of Medjugorje and her pilgrims are blessed with this peace that surpasses understanding.

Saint James Church in Medjugorje
Photo compliments of Information center "MIR" Medjugorje

Statue of Our Lady with Tyrolean Cross in background on Apparition Hill. Photo by JMD Arnold

Holy Mass on Križevac – Feast of Exaltation of the Holy Cross, September 14, 2003. Photo courtesy of Information Center "MIR" Medjugorje

Parishioners and Pilgrims on Apparition Hill.
Photo courtesy of Information Center "MIR" Medjugorje

The Parish center of Medjugorje looking northwest from Apparition Hill. The twin spires of St. James Church can be seen in the center. Photo by JMD Arnold.

Typical rural scene along path from Medjugorje center through Bijakovi ci to Apparition Hill (Podbrdo). On the first day of the appearance of Our Lady, Milka, Marijana and Vicka went to gather the sheep when they saw Gospa with the Baby Jesus waving to them from Podbrdo. Notice the vineyards beyond the sheep. Photo by JMD Arnold.

Martin and Mirjana Ilic's hotel located two blocks north of St. James Church. Martin has planted the beginnings of a small park in front of the hotel for a place of restful reflection. Photo by JMD Arnold.

"Resurrection" by Andrej Ajdic. Photo by Romilio Castillo.

Medjugorje
Miracles

So far in this book, the phenomenon of Medjugorje and some information of the place have been presented. Before addressing the most important grace of Medjugorje - the messages of Our Lady - I think it is good to briefly examine some of the miracles that occur there.

First, however, we do well to recall that in the history of salvation God has always sent messengers to his people. In the times of the Old Testament they were prophets. By the inspiration of the Holy Spirit the prophets expressed the word of God to the people that revealed God's commands, desires, pleasure and displeasure with them.[1] The prophets' words were usually accompanied by miracles that God worked through them to authenticate them as prophets of God and to show the majesty of God. Biblical testimony abundantly illustrates this as does the Church teaching and interpretation of the Biblical representation of the Old Testament prophets.

---

[1] See *Catechism Of The Catholic Church,* paragraphs 64 and 201.

Remember the famous story of Elijah and the prophets of Baal recorded at 1 Kings 18:21-40? Elijah's prayer at verses 36 and 37 is: "'Lord, God of Abraham, Isaac, and Israel, let it be known this day that you are God in Israel and that I am your servant and have done all these things by your command. Answer me, LORD! Answer me, that this people may know that you, LORD, are God and that you have brought them back to their senses.'" The Lord answered by sending fire from heaven that consumed the water-saturated log pile that Elijah built at the command of God. And the prophets of Baal were routed.

The last and greatest prophet was John the Baptizer.[2] He was the herald of the time of fulfillment of God's promise to send a Messiah. Of the prophetesses, Mary is the purest.[3]

With the incarnation of God in Jesus come to earth everything changes. From the day of the Lord's baptism in the Jordan River to this very day it is by the power of his name that all things are done and communicated to and through the people of God. The New Testament book *Acts of the Apostles*, among other things, tells of the miracles accomplished through the Apostles in the name of Jesus.[4] And down through the centuries the Church has been blessed with those whom she recognizes as particularly exemplar of the power of the name of Jesus in holiness. These last messengers we call Saints who too have miracles accompanying their acts and exhortations. In fact, one of the standards for canonization is the requirement of miracles.

As John Paul II says, *the saints have always been the source and origin of renewal in the most difficult moments in the Church's history.*[5] Surely a big part of the force or

---

[2] Ibid. paragraphs 523 and 719.
[3] Ibid. paragraph 64
[4] Ibid. paragraph 434
[5] Ibid. paragraph 828, quoting John Paul II.

momentum of renewal referred to by the Holy Father is the miracles associated with the Saints. And the Queen of Saints, our Blessed Mother Mary, is no less gifted than they. So, in my mind, it makes sense that she would, by the grace of God, bring miracles to Medjugorje as an accompaniment to her messages. Just as there are special graces or charisms given to some for the common good of the Church that involve the gift of miracles[6] so Our Lady brings miracles with her to Medjugorje.

I call the continuing events in Medjugorje miracles because I can think of no other word to better describe in general what they really are. However, I have strong suspicion that to the heavenly host the nature of these miracles is of rather routine occurrence. But for us here on earth they are undoubtedly signs from heaven. They accompany our Blessed Mother's messages to help strengthen our faith so we may believe she brings us messages from heaven and to induce us to earnestly follow her instructions and recommendations.

Just as our Lord backed up his words with miracles - such as when he was in Capernaum and asked which was easier to do, to say your sins are forgiven or to say rise and walk, and at the command of the Lord the paralytic got up from his stretcher and walked, thus proving Jesus' *authority*[7] to forgive sins – I also believe the miracles of Medjugorje show in stark reality that Our Lady is authorized by God Almighty to bring her message in a dramatic way today.[8] As

---

[6] Ibid. paragraph 2003

[7] The Gospel According to Matthew, Chapter 9, verses 1-8, Mark 2:10 and Luke 5:24. See *Catechism Of The Catholic Church,* paragraphs 581 and 582.

[8] According to Ivan Dragicevic in a talk he gave at the Mission Basilica, San Juan Capistrano, California on February 20, 2003, Our Lady said she was sent by Jesus. See also *Catechism Of The Catholic Church,* paragraphs 967 to 970 and 975.

the perfect Christian, she never does anything without permission from God.

Just as the Apostles gave testimony of the miracles they saw at the hands of our Lord Jesus and the miracles worked through their own hands, it is prudent for us, today, to testify of what we have seen. Therefore, frankly, this third chapter is written in the hope that the reader will gain an appreciation for what must truly be supernatural events occurring in Medjugorje and for the vital importance of Mary's messages.

Eucharistic Sun:

Although, in my mind, Our Lady's appearance alone is miracle aplenty, there is more. The signs and wonders discussed below did not happen at first, but certainly within the first two months of Our Lady's apparitions at Medjugorje the miracles began.

The entry for August 3, 1981, at 6:30 p.m., in the diary of Stipe Cavar in part reads as follows: "On the mountain, we (about 3,000 people) see HOW THE CROSS SPINS, and THE SUN could be seen as if it were A HOST and a light with a spectrum of various colors surrounds it."[9]

How it happened for me is like this: Jebb and I arrived in Medjugorje at exactly 4:55 pm on Tuesday, November 19, 2002. Upon arrival we dropped our bags and

---

[9] Stipe Cavar, *The First Months Of The Apparitions In Medjugorje,* 2000, Ziral: book 121; Special Edition, Medjugorje, BIH. As of the date of his publication, and presumably still, Mr. Cavar is an electronics engineer, consultant for computer science and electronics at the Educational Institute for the Croatian Republic, professor of computer science at the secondary school in Citluk and the Information Technology Director for MIR, Official Information Center for the Shrine of Peace in Medjugorje. See www.Medjugorje.hr

immediately headed for St. James to participate in the 5:00 pm Rosary - Joyful and Sorrowful Mysteries. Croatian Mass was at 6:00 pm followed by the Glorious Mysteries. Thereafter, we returned to the hotel for dinner. Wednesday, November 20, was our first full day in Medjugorje.

We began the day's activities with a stroll around the Shrine grounds and spent some time at the Resurrection Cross as we waited for the English Mass to begin at 10:00 am. After Mass we walked through the fields and vineyards to Apparition Hill (the hill in the area known as Podbrdo where Our Lady first appeared to the children). There, on the stony hillside, we located a blue/gray cross we thought was the cross placed at the spot of Our Lady's first appearance. However, as we discovered later, that was only a cross placed there by some pilgrims and not the marker we thought. As we ascended and descended the hill on the northeast side we did not even see the statue and cross that mark the actual spot. Nevertheless, we prayed a rosary and then descended. We spent quite a bit of time looking around Bijakovici and found the place of the blue cross where Ivan's prayer group meets in the summer. After that we leisurely strolled back to town.

Both while walking to and from Apparition Hill, at least three to four times, I glanced at the sun to see if it was doing anything. We, of course, heard about the 'spinning sun' before arriving in Medjugorje. So, naturally, I was hoping to see the phenomena. But it was not to be for us at that time.

We had some time to kill before the Sacrament of Reconciliation at 5:00 pm, so back in town we looked around the souvenir shops for a little while. On the east side of the road leading up to St. James Church there is a solid concentration of souvenir shops and restaurants that extends for probably three to four hundred feet or more. On the west side are restaurants and hospitality homes in a far less dense arrangement. By about 3:30 pm we decided to take some refreshment at Restaurant Italiano. It was warm enough to sit on the covered patio so we took a table there. Except for one table of three young women, who were locals, we were the only ones there. About five young men, also Croatian, were in the bar area watching a soccer game on television.

As we sat there on that patio, sipping our beer, I began to reflect on the events of the day. Such thought confirmed and concluded what had been a growing feeling of disappointment. The problem was there had been no 'events of the day'. Nothing was happening. No feelings of deep spirituality or peace were coming over me; no thoughtful or insightful realizations, no miracles. Nothing. And the first day was just about over. I said to Jebb, "We could be at any tourist trap in the world and it would be no different than what we see here. I am beginning to wonder why I came." He said he was kind of feeling the same way. So, there we were in Medjugorje crying in our beer, thinking about going home, when I glanced over my right shoulder at the sun sitting low in the west. Calmly I said to Jebb, "There it is."

He saw it. I saw it. All the years of struggling to keep the faith, the ups and the downs, were in an instant vindicated. Beyond the mundane, God was giving extraordinary visual evidence of his majesty. The sight of it is simply humbling.

We stood and gazed at this miracle for at least five minutes. Then we took pictures. After the photographs we returned to gazing at the sun until it dropped below the rooftops. That was probably another good five minutes or more. It was amazing. We were not blinded. Our eyesight was not affected in any way as far as we know and we can still see just fine today.

What we saw I can best describe as a burning fireball of normal sun that was covered over by a warm, butter colored, apparently translucent disc. It looked much like a gigantic communion wafer or host. Encircling the disc was a distinct, narrow ring inside of which were splashes of blue, red orange, purple, yellow and green that spun around the disc in alternating clockwise and counter-clockwise directions like a neon light. I suppose that is where the term 'spinning sun' is derived. Plus, the whole affair pulsates rapidly – almost vibrates. Behind it the corona of the sun spread out in a fusion of red orange like a backdrop.

After witnessing that miracle I headed for the confessional to reconcile with God and receive absolution for my lack of faith because I was disappointed and discouraged instead of trustful and patient. The reason I was feeling that way is because I dearly wanted to bring home testimony of some kind. My desire was for an experience of the divine, even the smallest interior stirring to share with everyone back home. Don't get me wrong. I am not a miracle chaser. In fact, I only decided to go to Medjugorje because I felt compelled. I put it off for well over a year. Finally, though, I responded to the call. Thanks be to Mary.

But I do think that the miracles occur in Medjugorje at least in part for testimonial purposes. I didn't think I was going to be so blessed. What a surprise. Every day that the sun was out while I was in Medjugorje I saw the Miracle of the Eucharistic Sun. In fact, as I am told, by shall we say Medjugorje veterans, anyone receiving this gift from Our Lady brings it home with them. And I have. I can look at the sun here in the U.S.A. and see the Miracle of the Eucharistic Sun. As the sun is rising in the east and as it is falling in the west are the times when I see it best.

As I reflect on this particular phenomenon I arrive at the conclusion that it is not a physical change of the sun that occurs. The photographs we took revealed a normal looking sun. Other photographs I have seen show the same thing. Obviously, if the sun were actually to change or be eclipsed by some sort of cover there would be huge consequence to the solar system of which our planet Earth is a part. Over the last twenty-two years as far as we know there have been no abnormal solar affects on earth. Plus, except for those involved in the miracle, the sun presents normally to those otherwise observing it. Therefore, the miracle described above must be particular to the individual experiencing it while the same for all who see it. Others I know who have experienced the Miracle of the Eucharistic Sun basically give the same description.

I do not think it is an illusion or other psychological event because all else remains normal. While we were gazing at this astounding sight Jebb and I communicated normally. We were aware of our surroundings. Our peripheral vision remained the same. In fact all our sensory perceptions were unchanged. Somehow divine intervention occurs so that a protective shield with, presumably, physical properties is placed between the sun and the eyes of the beholder. That is the best explanation I can give of it.

I believe the shape of the shield as that of a communion host is incredibly significant. It confirms 1.) that Jesus comes to us everyday throughout the whole world in the Holy Eucharist; 2.) that if we will trust him he can and will protect us from all spiritual harm; 3.) that he is the authority over heaven and earth; and 4.) for those who may wonder or doubt, Jesus really is present in body and blood in the consecrated communion host.

The symbolism in the Lord's use of the sun to give this silent message is enormous. The sun is a daily event. The Church's perpetual recommendation to come to Holy Communion at Mass every day is I think confirmed by this sign and is therefore more fully appreciated. The sun is the central object in the solar system. Jesus in the Holy Eucharist is always at the center of the Church's orientation and concentration. And in the same way he must be with us personally and individually. Jesus in the Eucharist is the source and summit of Christian life.[10] It is up to us to receive him. The sun gives the earth the nourishment it

---

[10] *Catechism,* loc. cit., paragraphs 1324-1327.

needs to sustain biological life. Spiritual Life and the nourishment to sustain it are what our Lord offers us in the Holy Eucharist. He eternally *means* what he said in the Gospel according to John at Chapter 6 verses 35-58.

The sun is a gargantuan thermonuclear furnace that produces pure white light. If a person looks directly at the sun and fixes their gaze for more than as little as perhaps fifteen seconds, retina damage will occur. The direct light of the sun passing through the lens of the eye creates the same result as focusing sunlight through a magnifying glass on a piece of paper. The paper begins to burn. And so will the retinas of the eyes. Yet, to one who observes the Miracle of the Eucharistic Sun there is no such damage. Thus, the Lord demonstrates that if we trust him and do not fear even the sun's potential to injure, he will protect us. I think such message can be transferred to all aspects of life.[11] As we shall see later this is very important in the scheme of things Our Lady asks of us.

The fact that this miracle occurs as I and others describe it – some kind of intervention or suspension of natural law – demonstrates, in vivid real time, our Lord's authority over his creation. I know my words fall short of recreating for the reader the full impact of the thing. And I apologize for that. About all I can say is that I now have an intense sympathy for the disciples in the boat on the Sea of Galilee when Jesus calmed the storm. I have a far better sense of the awe experienced by the Hebrews when the waters of the Red Sea parted. Like them, and many others who see the Miracle of the Eucharistic Sun, I am a witness to an extraordinary act of God brought to us and given by our

---

[11] Here, I am sensitive to some who may say I promote irresponsibility. In view of that, I hereby warn all readers to not try and make the miracle happen. Do not look at the sun in search of the miracle. Sun gazing produces serious and permanent eye damage. If you are meant to receive the gift of witnessing the Miracle of the Eucharistic Sun you will know in a glance. So far as I know, it first happens **ONLY** in Medjugorje.

Blessed Mother Mary. From the moment I first saw it, an indescribable calm came over me and inner peace began to grow in me like I never felt before.

The appearance of this miracle in an unmistakable likeness to the typical host of Holy Communion (a thin, round wafer of unleavened wheat bread) is, in my mind and heart, highly symbolic of the *real presence* of Jesus, body, blood, soul and divinity in the Holy Eucharist or consecrated host.[12] Such symbolism of the real presence was further substantiated for me some weeks after I returned from Medjugorje as told to me by my friend Pat.

Earlier, at English Mass, 10:00am, the same Wednesday, Jebb and I met Patrick Newman from Denver, Colorado. He too had just recently arrived in Medjugorje. He was with a small, organized pilgrimage group that was staying at Jakov Colo's house. Since he stayed with his group and we went our separate way we did not necessarily do things together. But we met each morning at Mass. On Thursday we told him of our experience of the Miracle of the Eucharistic Sun. He had not seen it and by the time we left, early the following Tuesday morning, he still had not seen it. And such was the case with many people we talked with there in Medjugorje.

Still, Pat, so inwardly moved by his experience of Medjugorje, decided to remain there an extra week and did not depart with his group. He continued to stay at Jakov's house. Jebb and I could not stay, so we exchanged contact information with Patrick and departed for home.

A couple of weeks after we returned I received an e-mail from Pat that briefly related his experiences during his extended stay in Medjugorje. It was for both Jebb and me.

---

[12] By real presence I mean transubstantiation. See The Gospel According to John, Chapter 6:22-58; The Gospel According to Matthew, Chapter 26:26-29; *Catechism,* loc. cit., paragraphs 1374-1377.

Some months later I asked him to provide a little more detail. Here is what he had to say in his own words:

> I had a very interesting experience while I was on Cross Mountain. I was with our group, which was nine people, except that one in our group was struggling and at the 3rd station [Stations of the Cross] she asked that the rest of us go ahead. Her name is Adrienne and she is a 74 year old Haitian woman that had a career in the US as a Teacher and a Librarian. Adrienne had just been in the hospital the week before, but she recovered quickly which she attributed to God intending for her to make this pilgrimage. She came to Medjugorje with her 81 year old sister Jane, a former college professor. These women were a tremendous amount of fun to be around. They alternate between speaking French and English, and they are very expressive and good humored.
>
> At the top of Cross Mountain our group of nine dispersed for about ½ an hour and then began to regroup to make the journey back down the mountain. At that time members of our group began pointing to the sky – the miracle of the sun was in full effect. We could look directly at the sun, it was perfectly round like a disc or a host, and it appeared to be throbbing. We were also seeing colors fill the sky. We would see one color at a time, and it would start out faint and gradually become bolder and bolder. The colors we saw were yellow, red and blue. If you looked down at white tennis shoes you would see the

reflection of the color that was present in the sky. The leader of our group said that the sun always represents Jesus and the colors represent Mary, and they come together. My understandin g is that during the miracle of the sun, sometimes the sun spins and sometimes it throbs. The throbbing sun that we witnessed represents the heart of Jesus. It was hard to fathom that we were witnessing something so awesome and clearly supernatural.

During our descent we were surprised to find Adrienne at the 12th station kneeling on the rocks, crying as she was praying hands-in-hands with a young Croatian woman. It appeared to me that the young Croatian woman was praying in tongues, and was then able to interpret the prayers which were messages from Jesus to Adrienne. For example the young woman said that Jesus said that Adrienne needed to forgive herself. This was a tremendously emotional experience for Adrienne. When the prayer was done they stood and we proceeded together to the next station. The young woman – Dajana (pronounced Dianna) - and Adrienne would pray in a similar fashion at each station.

When we reached the top of Cross Mountain Dajana went by herself and knelt next to the cross and placed her right hand on the base of the cross and began to pray by herself. Twenty minutes later we regrouped and Dajana asked if I wanted to pray with her. I said sure. She asked me to kneel and place my hand on the base of the cross – she said this is a very powerful cross. She held my other hand. She began to pray in tongues, and then began interpreting the messages she was getting from Jesus. I felt that these messages were coming to me from Jesus, they were deeply personal and intimate, and even though the messages weren't all necessarily what I would want to hear they were what I needed to hear. She said that "Jesus says that you have many problems and he is the only one that can help you solve them." "He says that the only way you can enter into heaven is with a cross." "He is asking if you want to turn your heart over to him right now." I responded by saying yes. "The Mother Mary asks why you don't cry, this will purify you?" I felt my eyes well up, but tears didn't flow. "Jesus says that you must not just go to mass on Sunday, but everyday." "Jesus says you need to pray for yourself, your family, and your friends." "Jesus says you need to pray all of the time." "Jesus says you are my son, my baby, my sweetie." This message in particular I found to be very personal and intimate. She continued: "Jesus says he loves you." "Jesus asks why you do not believe." "Jesus says look at him, look at the sun." I looked up at the unusually bright sun, and saw the miracle of the sun once again. It looked like a bright throbbing disk or host. Honestly, I thought of Moses on the mountain – it was surreal. She went on with her interpretations saying "Jesus is saying that from deep in the bottom of your heart you do not truly

> believe." "Do you remember how happy you were as a child and how you believed in me?" When she said this I recognized that this was true. I had come to Medjugorje largely because I wanted to regain my faith in God.[13]

I think there are a couple of very noteworthy indicators to recognize in Pat's testimony. The first has to do with authenticity. Please note that Dajana is a person whom Pat never heard of, seen or met before. She gives him messages, privately, that are "deeply personal and intimate." Is she a gypsy fortune teller? Not likely. Recall what Pat said about the woman, Adrienne, in his group. Did Dajana ask for money or imply that she should be paid? No. Is she just a young woman who is fantasizing that she has a particular chrism? If that were the case how would she know the amazingly relevant, personal and intimate things that only Pat in his heart of hearts knows? Was she briefed by someone at Jakov's house and sent there to ply Pat. That is a real stretch of imagination. No, by all accounts I believe it is self-evident that Dajana is truly a gifted servant of the Lord. And Pat was blessed by Our Lady who arranged for the two of them to meet.

The second noteworthy item is that through Dajana our Lord Jesus told Pat to *look at me; look at the sun.* When Pat turned and looked, he immediately saw the Miracle of the Eucharistic Sun. What did the Lord mean by what he said? In my mind it can only point to the symbolism I have already suggested. For us here on earth today, Jesus is the

---

[13] Because that night of the same day Pat wrote down everything he was told by Jesus through Dajana he is able to quote in such detail what was said to him.

Holy Eucharist. As he promised, he is with us unto the end of the age – physically and spiritually.[14]

Star Cross:

Wednesday morning, our first morning in Medjugorje, I awoke at about four o'clock. Unable to return to sleep, I bundled up and went out to the veranda of my room just to sit and enjoy the morning silence. There were a few clouds in the night sky and I noticed right off that the planet Venus appearing low in the east over and just to the north of Podbrdo (Apparition Hill) was extremely bright and larger than I had ever seen before. Plus there were rays of light emanating from it in a sort of spiral like a pinwheel. I thought that was interesting but took no further notice of it.

The next morning I again awoke at about four and went to the veranda. The same scene presented itself except this time Venus took on a very decided change of shape in that it had a dim cross superimposed over it with an aura around the hub of the cross from which rays emanated. Now that was very interesting. I told Jebb about it that day and he asked me to wake him up if I saw it in the morning. Well, the next morning was a rainy Friday so there was no seeing the star.

Saturday morning, however, since the rainstorm moved out during the night the sky was cloudless and the air fresh and clean. I looked up to the big star. It was shaped like the Bethlehem cross we see on Christmas cards. I removed my glasses and looked again. What I saw then was, instead, a bright, distinct, simple cross of light suspended in

---

[14] See the Gospel According to Matthew 28:20; *Catechism,* loc. cit., paragraphs 1324 and 1357.

the sky where the Bethlehem star had been. The shape was like that we see everyday minus the corpus. The cross – the age old emblem of Christ – in bright, white light hovered over Medjugorje in the eastern sky about 20 degrees up just to the north of Apparition Hill. I could just about cover from my sight the whole cross with the palm of my hand. In adoration and gratitude I gazed at it for several minutes and then I remembered Jebb.

I tapped on Jebb's window and in a few minutes he came out to see … the Christmas card star. Try as I would I could not see the cross of light. All that was showing was the type of Bethlehem star. Still, Jebb was amazed to see that. But after that the mornings were all cloudy and we never had opportunity to see it again.

Now, lest one might think we were hallucinating – remember Lillian, who I mentioned in the previous chapter who works in the souvenir shop? Well, on the day I was talking with her, I mentioned the star cross. She exclaimed that lots of people had seen it and that the photo shop right next door had developed many pictures of it taken by pilgrims. She remarked that no one of the pictures seemed to be exactly alike. The star cross had many slightly different variations.

I don't recall any headline astronomical news about planet Venus changing appearances during our stay in Medjugorje. Therefore, I can only conclude that, since along with us others in Medjugorje saw the star cross, this appearance was specific to Medjugorje and not the rest of the world. Thus, again, it was a sign from heaven. A sign I take to mean that - just as we make the sign of the cross when we bless ourselves or the priest blesses the gifts at the altar or religious articles or any such blessing – God gives his visible sign of blessing on Medjugorje in the same form of a cross.

Although I did not realize it at the time, in thinking about it later, for me it was an answer to prayer of many years ago in a time of difficulty. The problem disappeared way back then but my request was not granted until November 23, 2002, some twenty years later.

Statue of our Risen Savior:

Erected in time for the Holy Easter week celebrations of 1998, a stunning, bronze statue, titled *Resurrection*, cast by Slovenian sculptor, Andrej Ajdic, stands in a special plaza about 300 yards behind St. James Church. The dynamic of the statue is of Christ, vertically represented in cruciform, raised out of a horizontal, earthbound, cross. It stands, I would say, between 14 and 18 feet tall. It is most unique and a compelling, almost mesmeric communication of the resurrection of our Lord.

We were told that on the 20th anniversary of Our Lady's appearance at Medjugorje, June 25, 2001, water began to exude from the right knee of the statue. Frequently, it continues to do so. Both Jebb and Pat saw this miracle. I did not. Healings have been associated with the water. Our Lady shall bless as she knows best for us in the mediation of God's graces. For me, just having opportunity to experience the visual impact of the statue was blessing plenty.

The Spinning Cross:

Referring back to Stipe's diary entry for August 3rd 1981, he makes note of seeing the cross on the top of Križevac spin. I myself did not see this. There have been other phenomena related to the cross on Križevac. For instance, a friend of mine and fellow parishioner, Don Voller, who made three pilgrimages to Medjugorje, told me about what he saw on his first trip in the Fall of 1997.

From the window in the room where he was staying he had a clear, unobstructed view of Križevac. Early one morning well before sunrise he looked out through the window and was amazed to see what appeared to be pulses of fire flashing off the cross into the night sky. He said that is the best way he could describe it. I asked him if it was light pulses or fire. He said it was like pulsating flames. He was not the only one who saw this phenomenon. Two other people in his tour group saw the same thing at the same time.

There is no electrical or gas service on Križevac. Except for the cross it is a barren mountain. The only time there is ever any electricity on the mountain is on special occasions when the parishioners haul up a portable generator.

Public Apparition of Our Lady:

The entry for August 14, 1981, in the diary of Stipe Cavar reads as follows: *I and Lucija were in Medjugorje.* "From the Sivric neighborhood, all of Medjugorje sees instead of the CROSS on Križevac OUR LADY, whom one can see for about 15 minutes. Underneath Her is a snow-white pedestal. She leaves to heaven in the light, and the cross remains. (This was seen after morning Mass about 9:00 o'clock.)"[15]

The entry for September 21, 1981, reads as follows: "None of us were in Medjugorje. Tomislav says Mass. Everything is as usual. The people meet Our Lady again this evening. The people, who return home after the Rosary can see Our Lady on the bridge (Lukoc) next to the Medjugorje Center. [Stipe now records in brief how the people saw

---

[15] Loc. cit. page 48

Gospa] The people go, some sing, some pray, and a young person speaks about Our Lady, saying that there is actually nothing to all this. Suddenly, all of Medjugorje is being bathed in light and the people can see the coming of Our Lady. Surrounded by light, Our Lady is standing on the bridge among the people. Everyone can see Her, just as the children had described Her (that is, completely real). Our Lady only looks at the people, whereas the people react in different ways. Some kneel down and pray, the others scream etc. Our lady stands on the bridge for 5 minutes."[16]

The entry for October 23, 1981, reads in part: "On Wednesday, October 21st, Fr. Stanko and the others (about 60) – instead of the cross – see Our lady holding Jesus in Her arms. On Thursday, October 22, 1981, all of Medjugorje can see Our Lady also. On Friday, October 23, 1981, my father sees Our Lady (the white figure instead of the cross on Križevac) from Markotica's house, i.e. from Coka. There are about 15 people, which means that in these days almost everyone (who was fortunate) could see Our Lady."[17]

Through their Morning Star Ministry, Grace and Paul Millard set up and lead pilgrimages to Medjugorje. For the Christmas season of 1990, they were in Medjugorje. Here is what they have to say as copied from e-mail to me from Paul.

> On Christmas Eve, 1990, we were standing in line next to St James church, waiting to go to confession. We had two 7 year old girls with us who were making their first confession and communion. While I was taping them making their first confession a lady passed by and said, "Look, there is the Madonna." Not realizing what she meant I kept filming the

---

[16] Loc. cit. page 100

[17] Loc. cit. page 109

> last girl. Then Grace said, "Look, it's Our Blessed Mother." I turned and began to film Her image on Mt Krizevac. She was standing about where the fourth station was, where Jesus meets his mother. I tried to zoom in on her, but every time I tried the picture would become blurry. Two other gentlemen were filming her image also and the same thing happened to them. When they tried to zoom in their video blurred up also. She let us see just a glimpse of her. When Grace asked in her mind, "Mother is that really you?" Our Lady kind of bent her knee and nodded her head, indicating, yes, it is I your Mother. The image lasted a long time, but being human, our guide called us saying that we had to leave as we were scheduled to go see Fr. Jozo. So like little sheep, we left following our guide. There were over 50 people there who witnessed this event. Thinking back, we are amazed that we just up and left, not realizing what a gift we were being given. Since then we have been to Medjugorje over 50 times, and each time Our Lady gives us a little miracle.

I have seen the video. Others who were there took photographs. One of the photographs is particularly clear and is prominently displayed on postcards that are for sale in most of the souvenir shops in Medjugorje. Through their ministry, Paul and Grace distribute the video. A copy can be obtained by contacting them at the address in the resource section at the back of this book.

There have been many more public appearances of Our Lady in Medjugorje that are not recorded in this book. The preceding vignettes are descriptions of just a few.

However, I think that many of us experience divine supernatural events that we don't talk about – angels, inner locutions, visions, dreams, etc. If we would meditate on such events I am sure we would discover a message. Our Lord and Our Lady love us and desire our salvation more than we ourselves. They do not leave us as orphans. If we repent, turn away from sin, pursue holiness and seek it with all our heart we will experience the heavenly here on earth – some more than others.

Healings:

There have been 445 completely or fragmentarily documented miraculous healings associated with Medjugorje.[18] Father Svetozar Kraljevic, O.F.M. tells of a few in his book *The Apparitions Of Our Lady At Medjugorje* which is a history of the events of Medjugorje during the years 1981 to1983. But more recently Denis Nolan shares the story set forth below. It was posted on the www.childrenofmedjugorje.com website as part of the monthly newsletter for June, 2003. Denis has long been intimately involved with Medjugorje in book publication and radio and TV production. He and Sister Emmanuel have been called by Our Lady to an apostolate which one can read about in their books: *Medjugorje: The 90's The Triumph of the Heart (Revised and Updated)* by Sr. Emmanuel and *Medjugorje: A Time For Truth And A Time For Action* by Denis (order from the website stated above).

As of the date of this writing, when the Nolans were last in Medjugorje (June, 2003) with Sister Emmanuel they were fortunate to meet a couple from South Africa. Over coffee they talked. Here is what Denis shares with us which,

[18] Information Center "MIR" Medjugorje, www.medjugorje.hr

by the way, is not that unusual for those who know Medjugorje.

> Veronica and Alex visited us in Medjugorje this week too. They have come from South Africa every year since 1998 just to give thanks and praise to God. My wife, Cathy and I had never heard Veronica's story… and so over a cup of coffee Sr. Emmanuel suggested they share it with us!
>
> For 22 years Veronica had been blind. Her retinas were damaged, and she has been unable to see. Veronica has always prayed to Jesus and Our Lady, and her faith is strong. One night in August 1998, while in pain, she began to pray. All of a sudden she saw Jesus standing before her beckoning to her with his arms outstretched. He showed her a panorama: a village, a mountain with a big cross on top, small shops and houses along the street, a large church with two steeples and inside, on the third stain glass window, the Blessed Mother. "I said to Jesus, 'I don't know where this place is.' Jesus just looked at me and smiled and said, 'Medjugorje!' "
>
> In the morning she told her husband, Alex, everything she had seen and that Jesus had called the place Medjugorje. They phoned their travel agent, who had helped them visit many Marian shrines, and asked him if he knew of such a place. The agent had never heard of it. They were perplexed. A few days later they were surprised to learn how to get there from a friend who had just returned from a pilgrimage!

Upon arriving in the village, Alex said he knew exactly where everything was because Veronica had described it so well from her vision - the post office, the bridge, the church.... as they drove down the road every building was just as it had appeared to Veronica! They went to hear Vicka speak on the steps of the blue house. There were so many pilgrims that Alex and Veronica were squashed in the back of the group. As Vicka talked, Alex noticed that she was gazing at Veronica. Alex told her: "She is looking at you!" Then Veronica heard, "She's waving at you! She's smiling at you!" Then, when Vicka had finished speaking, Alex said, "She's coming down and walking toward you!" "She's right in front of you!" Then Vicka placed her hand over Veronica's eyes and prayed. When Vicka removed her hand, one eye was completely healed and Veronica could see!

Leaping for joy and dancing in the street Veronica cried out in thanksgiving! She, who was blind, could see! To this day she's filled with such joy at the love of God that she can't resist reaching out and loving all those around her.

The next day after the healing, Veronica and Alex attended a talk by Fr. Svet in the yellow building behind the church. During his talk, to Veronica's surprise a picture of the Gospa on the front wall came alive. A silence spread over the room (everyone, it seemed, knew something was happening). Then Veronica saw that Our Lady was holding something deep blue in her hands. It was the continent of Africa! What could this mean? They prayed. Hearing Sr. Emmanuel speak the following day it became clear. They were being called to spread Our Lady's messages in Africa! As a little branch of Children of Medjugorje they have since spread thousands of audiotapes in South Africa and are spearheading an edition of Sr. Emmanuel's book, "Medjugorje, The 90's" in Zulu!

There are many more such stories associated with healings in Medjugorje. I would have to say that the experience of Veronica and Alex is not unusual.

Frankly, I think the Church is just as blessed by miracles now as it was in the beginning. Miracles always have purpose. They are not just for show. Ultimately, the impact of Medjugorje is probably even greater than, for example, the miracle worked through St. Peter at Joppa:

Now in Joppa there was a disciple named Tabitha (which translated in Greek is called Dorcas). She was completely occupied with good deeds and almsgiving. Now during those days she fell sick and died, so after washing her, they laid [her] out in a room upstairs. Since Lydda was near Joppa, the disciples, hearing that Peter was there, sent two men to him, with the request, "Please come to us without delay." So Peter got up and went with them. When he arrived, they took him to the room upstairs where all the widows came to him weeping and showing him the tunics and cloaks that Dorcas had made while she was with them. Peter sent them all out and knelt down and prayed. Then he turned to her body, he said, "Tabitha, rise up." She opened her eyes, saw Peter, and sat up. He gave her his hand and raised her up and when he had called the holy ones and the widows, he presented her alive. This became known all over Joppa, and many came to believe in the Lord. (Acts 9:36-42)

We can see that among other things the miracle at Joppa was intended to bring many to believe in the Lord. By comparison, there were far fewer people in Joppa then than those who come to Medjugorje and Joppa was a one-time event.

By 1997 it was estimated that as of then 20,000,000 pilgrims came to Medjugorje.[19] At a pace of a million visitors a year to Medjugorje that number has probably increased to over 25 million to date. Of those 25 million there are untold millions of stories of conversion to Christianity, faith renewal or faith increase. I would say that is impact. And what brings that impact in Medjugorje is the combination of the visual miracles and the pervasive, overwhelming sense of complete inner peace one experiences in Medjugorje. Yes, the Queen of Peace smiles upon and blesses Medjugorje.

[19] Janice T. Connell, *The Apparitions of the Blessed Mother at Medjugorje*, 1992, 1997, St. Martin's Press, New York, page 13.

Our Lady, Queen of Peace, appears in public apparition standing on the slopes of Križevac, December 24, 1990. This is the image that appeared in Paul Millard's video.

Medjugorje Message

PEACE

As I said in the previous chapter, after experiencing for the first time the Miracle of the Eucharistic Sun I went immediately to sacramental confession. After that, we went to the Meditation Cross on the west side of St. James and prayed a Rosary. Then, after dinner, at 9 pm we went back to St. James for Adoration of the Blessed Sacrament.

At St. James the priests bring down among the people the lunette containing the Blessed Sacrament.[1] They hold it high and turn solemnly from side to side so all may see. I could feel the blessing coming from the body and blood of our Lord. It is very moving and stirs the heart to near palpitation. Jebb too was blessed and said later that it was like Jesus was walking among us giving his holy blessing. Remarkably, from then on, the feeling of peace seemed to intensify. It is an inner peace that for me continued to grow stronger and more assured as each day passed and then fixed itself securely and permanently in my heart on the flight home. My thoughts on that long flight back were mixed and have clarified since then in many ways. Now, some six

---

[1] The monstrance is far too large to bring around to the people.

months later, in response to our Blessed Mother's request, I share them with you, the reader.

Preliminary Discussion

As I reflect on the things of Medjugorje I saw, heard and read about, I come to a basic conclusion. My premise is that Medjugorje, fundamentally, ***is a sign to the world from God***[2]. It is God's intervention in the history of man for the 20th and 21st Centuries. It is probably the most significant divine intervention since our Lord came and went from Earth and since Our Lady's Assumption. The sign is that of a heavenly messenger, sent by Jesus,[3] the Blessed Virgin Mary, who pleads for renewal in the Church and society and shows us the way to receive the graces from the Holy Spirit to effect renewal.[4] The renewal she talks of is about the way of personal peace.

Medjugorje is first and foremost about Jesus Christ.[5] Indeed from time to time a star like that of Bethlehem shines bright and bold in the eastern sky over Medjugorje showing itself sometimes as we typically see on Christmas cards and sometimes as a pure and simple, well-defined cross. And the Miracle of the Sun is extraordinarily symbolic as the Eucharistic Host miraculously covers the sun and blocks its eye-burning rays so that one may gaze at this wonder for as

---

[2] Fr. Tomislav Pervan, O.F.M., Fr. Ivan Sesar, et al., *Medjugorje*, pg. 78, Informativni centar "Mir" Medugorje, 2002, ISBN 9958-775-14-X

[3] According to Ivan Dragicevic in a talk given at the Mission Basilica, San Juan Capistrano, California on February 20, 2003, Our Lady said she was sent by Jesus.

[4] Ibid., Fr. Tomislav Pervan, pg. 79

[5] Jakov Colo stated the same in a talk to pilgrims, November 22, 2002, in Medjugorje. I was present for that brief talk.

long as one desires without any eye damage.[6] Clearly this Miracle of the Sun as a sign from God calls us to Eucharistic Adoration and visually supports Gospa's[7] ardent recommendation for daily Mass. And the apparition of Our Lady appearing publicly at the base of Cross Mountain (Križevac) for rare video and still photography demonstrates her desire for us to take up our own cross, follow Jesus and meditate on the Stations of the Cross to help us in that endeavor.

Those are just a few of the many signs that have come from Medjugorje since June of 1981. However, more significant is that of the millions of pilgrims who travel to Medjugorje and either find faith, renew or increase their faith. They either discover the meaning of their lives, expand and/or confirm their previous understanding of life. Somehow their hearts are affected by the Holy Spirit. Medjugorje is a new Pentecost. And just as at the first Pentecost when the disciples "... were all filled with the holy Spirit and began to speak in different tongues, as the Spirit enabled them to proclaim..." and the witnesses said, "'...we hear them speaking in our own tongues of the mighty acts of God.' They were all astounded and bewildered, and said to one another, 'What does this mean?'"[8] I too am compelled to ask, what is the meaning of this sign from God given in Medjugorje?

---

[6] I have personally witnessed both these miracles in Medjugorje. See the chapter on Medjugorje Miracles for detailed descriptions of these and other miracles occurring at Medjugorje.

[7] Gospa is Croatian for "Our Lady".

[8] Acts 2:4 and 11b-12.

Gospa's first message

"Peace, peace, peace and only peace!" Our Lady speaks on the third day of her visitation, June 26, 1981. She also repeated twice: *"Peace must rule between man and God and among the people."*[9] Our Lady came to Medjugorje and added to her litany of titles: Queen of Peace. Obviously, if Gospa, as the Queen of Peace, is pleading for peace then peace must be wanting. Otherwise, why would she implore us to seek peace? But what peace is she talking about? And if peace is absent then there must be conflict. What conflict?

First, it is clear to me that, as our heavenly mother, her primary concern is for us, as her children, to be *at peace* with God. She tells the world: "*You cannot have peace if your heart is not at peace with God.*"[10] And as I think about it, I find that is the question. Am I personally at peace with God or am I in conflict with God? Just because everything seems to be going pretty good does not mean I am at peace with God. To be at peace with God means to give up the fight and surrender to God. But someone may say, 'What are you talking about? I am not fighting God.' I am sure most of us believe we do not fight against God. The problem for me and most everyone, however, is that we are predominantly focused on our own self interests instead of those of God and that automatically puts us in conflict with God. By nature, because of our selfishness, our desires are contrary to the heart and mind God desires for us. We do not love the Lord our God with *all* our mind and heart, body and soul. He is not the one we love above all else. He is not top priority in our daily lives.

---

[9] Fr. Ljudevit Rupcic, O.F.M., Fr. Ivan Sesar, et al., *Medjugorje*, pg. 15, Informativni centar "Mir" Medugorje, 2002, ISBN 9958-775-14-X

[10] Contained within Our Lady's message on the 16th anniversary of her coming to Medjugorje, June 25, 1997.

I think we take all too lightly what the Gospel tells us. What Jesus says, as recorded by the Apostles, leaves me with the distinct impression, even conviction, that he is very serious and means exactly what he says. So that when he says - *"Whoever wishes to come after me must deny himself, take up his cross and follow me. For whoever wishes to save his life will lose it, but whoever loses his life for my sake will find it."*[11] – I think we need to really take *him* seriously and be very concerned about a declaration such as that just quoted. Some things to consider are set forth below.

Conflict with God

Because we possess the knowledge of good and evil, right and wrong, and are free to choose, we often make daily choices that are directly opposed to our Creator's desires for us. Worse, we take up a lifestyle and view of life and the world that is largely influenced by our culture and less influenced by the teachings and admonitions of the Church. For example, consider the first of the Ten Commandments: "You shall have no other gods besides me."[12]

Our response to this commandment is usually one of two. We either strive to live daily with no other god before God or live as practical atheists. By the latter, I mean we may say we believe in God but our actions reveal (A) a trust that relies on people and things far more than faith in the Eternal God, (B) a desire for the things of the world over a desire for the things of heaven and (C) that we really spend very little time praying to God, thinking about God or serving God. The Church describes atheism as follows:

> 2124 The name "atheism" covers many very different phenomena. One common form is

[11] The Gospel According to Matthew, Chapter 16: 24b-25.
[12] Exodus 20:3

the practical materialism which restricts its needs and aspirations to space and time. Atheistic humanism falsely considers man to be "an end to himself, and the sole maker, with supreme control, of his own history." Another form of contemporary atheism looks for the liberation of man through economic and social liberation. "It holds that religion, of its very nature, thwarts such emancipation by raising man's hopes in a future life, thus both deceiving him and discouraging him from working for a better form of life on earth."

2125 Since it rejects or denies the existence of God, atheism is a sin against the virtue of religion. The imputabilitv of this offense can be significantly diminished in virtue of the intentions and the circumstances. "Believers can have more than a little to do with the rise of atheism. To the extent that they are careless about their instruction in the faith, or present its teaching falsely, or even fail in their religious, moral, or social life, they must be said to conceal rather than to reveal the true nature of God and of religion."

2126 Atheism is often based on a false conception of human autonomy, exaggerated to the point of refusing any dependence on God. Yet, "to acknowledge God is in no way to oppose the dignity of man, since such dignity is grounded and brought to perfection in God…" "For the Church knows full well

> that her message is in harmony with the most secret desires of the human heart."[13]

With such description in mind we can discuss a few things that bring us into conflict with God and hinder if not prevent daily devotion to the things of God. First, is the problem common to all of us. If we have property and wealth we think ourselves secure and happy. This, however, by experience and Gospel testimony is proven to be a fallacy. We all know stories of which we have read or heard about how so and so was rich but not happy, even depressed, or paranoid about losing wealth. So many of us say, "I don't want to be rich, I just want to be comfortable." But, if this is so, why then do we buy lottery tickets, scratch our way up the corporate ladder, or think up ways to make more money? The consensus among us is that we should always try to get a better job that pays more money so we can buy a better house, better car, clothes, toys, go more places, do more things, take more exotic holidays or vacations and by all means procure a well-funded retirement plan. I think that even the most dedicated professional or scientist who might otherwise be unconcerned with such materialism is still at least to some degree influenced and participatory.

I know people who are rich and by all outward appearances are happy and even proclaim themselves so. Then in the next breath express their worry over the economy, world political and social conditions, or a drop in the price of this or that. Why? In my mind it is because once they experience and sustain the sensual and material pleasures their wealth affords them they are scared to death of losing their wealth and privilege. Who would want to live with that kind of nagging fear? Sad to say, the fear probably does not become known until one is financially wealthy. We are not afraid of losing it until we have it. So as an

[13] Loc. cit. *Catechism*, paragraphs 2124 to 2126, footnotes excluded.

unknown, the fear of losing it is hidden in a smoke screen and is not a barrier to seeking wealth. All too often we more or less say, "I wouldn't have that problem if I were rich." How foolish we are. Should we not rather pray to God that he would keep us humble and poor? The pursuit of material gain beyond that which provides for our necessities sucks us in to a vortex of ever increasing desire for more. I think in our hearts we know that is true but we rationalize the fact and come up with all kinds of excuses to appease our consciences.

Now, practically, how does materialism bring us into conflict with God? Well, the following comes to mind. First off, obviously, if we buy goods, services and entertainment beyond what we reasonably need, we spend money on ourselves that could otherwise be used to help alleviate the physical suffering and religious/spiritual poverty of others. If we allow materialism, in the sense just mentioned, to carry us along our merry way without thought or deed done for others, how are we denying ourselves? We are not. And that brings us into conflict with God.

Second, we come to rely heavily on our ability to earn and buy. We know that if we educate ourselves and work hard in a relatively free society we will likely increase our income and be able to buy more. And that is what we desire. Some work harder at it than others. But we all want more. Thus, our time and effort is expended attempting to or dreaming about having more. The result is that we forget about God and he becomes a very low priority if at all. And that brings us into conflict with God.

Third, the fruits of our materialistic labor and the pursuit thereof take us away from time we could be spending with God personally and in church. We say, "I don't have time for morning devotions. I have to get ready for work or I have to get the kids ready for school and then run errands, etc." Or, "I am too tired to pray. I think I will just watch television." Or, "I don't have time to pray. I have to get this or that ready for this or that." Or "This or that team is playing on TV. I can't pray now." Or "I am going to this or that sports or special event on Sunday. I can't go to church." And so it goes on endlessly.

We are in an age when the things of God are secondary to the first things of our materialistic desires. I think that brings us into conflict with God because we lose conscious sight of our real dependency on God for everything. We don't think about him much or pray more than a quick prayer before bed. We skip church frequently. We say things like "I'm a good person. I'll make it to heaven," and then our thoughts turn to our own selfish desires. And we, the creature, expect the Creator to honor that. On the contrary, here is what our Mother who visits from heaven has to say:

"Dear children! You are absorbed with material things, but in the material you lose everything that God wishes to give you. I call you, dear children, to pray for the gifts of the Holy Spirit which are necessary for you now in order to be able to give witness to my presence here and to all that I am giving you. Dear children, let go to me so I can lead you completely. Don't be absorbed with material things. Thank you for having responded to my call." (April 17, 1986)

And here is what Our Lord has to say in the Gospel according to Luke:

"...There was a rich man whose land produced a bountiful harvest. He asked himself, 'What shall I do, for I do not have space to store my harvest?' And he said, 'This is what I shall do: I shall tear down my barns and build larger ones. There I shall store all my grain and other goods and I shall say to myself, Now as for you, you have so many good things stored up for many years, rest, eat, drink, be merry!' But

God said to him, 'You fool! This night your life will be demanded of you; and the things you have prepared, to whom will they belong?' Thus it will be for the one who stores up treasure for himself but is not rich in what matters to God."

He said to His disciples, "Therefore I tell you, do not worry about your life and what you will eat, or about your body and what you will wear. For life is more than food and the body more than clothing. ...Can any of you by worrying add a moment to your life-span? If even the smallest things are beyond your control, why are you anxious about the rest? ...As for you, do not seek what you are to eat and what you are to drink and do not worry anymore. All the nations of the world seek for these things, and your Father knows that you need them. Instead, seek His kingdom, and these things will be given you besides. Do not be afraid any longer, little flock, for your Father is pleased to give you the kingdom. Sell your belongings and give alms. Provide money bags for yourselves that do not wear out, an inexhaustible treasure in heaven that no thief can reach nor moth destroy. For where your treasure is, there also will your heart be. (Luke 12:16-34)

It seems pretty clear to me that God desires for our hearts to be devoted and directed toward the things of heaven over the things of the earth. This is emphasized by St. Paul who wrote in his letter to the congregation at Colossae:

If then you were raised with Christ, [through Baptism] *seek what is above, where Christ is seated at the right hand of God. Think of what is above, not what is on earth. For you have died, and your life is hidden with Christ in God. When Christ your life appears, then you too will appear with him in glory.* (Colossians 3:1-4)

How abundantly we are in conflict with God when we are absorbed by materialism. The influence of worldly opinion and our own selfish desires are heavy upon us. Certainly it would be of benefit to examine ourselves and bring in to the light the location of our treasure. Is it on earth or in heaven? Our Blessed Mother desires the best for us and offers us the way to relocate our treasure.

Now, someone may say, "We still have to live in this world." And that is so. But the question in my mind is how do we live? How do we live so that we do not come into conflict with God? I believe it again comes down to where our treasure is located. Who or what do we like? How does the allocation of our time and energy reveal the desires of our hearts? How seriously do we take the admonition of St. John the Evangelist?

Do not love the world or the things in the world. If anyone loves the world, the love of the Father is not in him. For all that is in the world, sensual lust, enticement for the eyes and a pretentious life, is not from the Father but is from the world. (1 John 2:15-16)

I think we know, deep down, that we all far too much chase after the things of the world. The allurement is so very great. In contemporary context, probably more so than ever before, it is a constant struggle for the Christian to seek first the Kingdom of God, especially for us living in the developed countries. Yet, we must if we are to avoid conflict with God. We must surrender ourselves and constantly seek to work for Jesus first and the rest will all fall into place.

Another basic problem that brings us into conflict with God is our inherent sense of self-righteousness. Even though we may not think so, don't we really act like we know the best way for things to be done? Or what is the best policy and attitude toward people and things? I think even the most stringent pacifist cannot escape this universal character trait. It is what drives our concept of personal justice and injustice. Actually, it seems to me that we are all our own little judges. I know I am. We set the standard and judge others by that standard. I believe we either completely fool ourselves or are unwilling and afraid to admit that we are self-righteous by nature.

Every time we say that someone is stupid or an idiot or a moron I think we place ourselves in jeopardy of hellfire (see Matthew 5:22). By making such judgments, no matter how idiotic someone or something may seem to us, we actually unthinkingly assume the place of God. And then when we presume to correct someone we make ourselves hypocrites, as Jesus tells us:

"Why do you notice the splinter in your brother's eye, but do not perceive the wooden beam in your own eye? How can you say to your brother, 'Let me remove that splinter from your eye,' while the wooden beam is in your eye? You hypocrite, remove the wooden beam from your eye first; then you will see clearly to remove the splinter from your brother's eye." (Matthew 7:3-5)

I think it is easy for such self-righteousness to slip into bigotries of all sorts. History is no doubt full of stories about those who were of noble intent but somehow went afoul of their altruism because they thought that only they knew the way of righteousness. But our Blessed Mother Mary constantly repeats to us: "Seek ye first the Kingdom of God and his righteousness."

It is especially dangerous when we take it upon ourselves to prescribe the righteousness of God instead of submitting to the dogma of the Church which has preserved the teaching of the Apostles who were taught by the Righteous One, Jesus. To have independent views of who God is and who humanity is or to say something like "I have my own religion" brings us into conflict with God because he has revealed the truth he desires to be observed through the Sacred Scriptures and Tradition of the Church.

There are, of course, many other evils that bring us into conflict with God. But, I believe more than anything else the worst is indifference. Although the thought nagged at me for many years before my pilgrimage to Medjugorje – that is to what extent do I *really* know God and how much do I *really* sacrifice to serve him – I can honestly say that since Medjugorje I now have vastly more confidence and far less indifference. Allow me to explain.

We are all born into this world with a high degree of insensibility about the supernatural. Because I cannot recall my experience in my biological mother's womb or the event of my birth I cannot say exactly what my sensibility about God was when I came into this world. But there is this that I can rely upon. I was born a sinner. With King David, the ancient monarch of the Hebrew people and the writer of many of the Psalms of the Bible, I attest that I "...was born guilty, a sinner, even as my mother conceived me" (Psalm 51:7). I was, as is everyone, born naturally a child in the lineage of Adam and Eve. As I learned to speak I learned a little about God from my parents and later from Sunday school – basically that God is and that he is all powerful. So I had an impression of God. Fortunately, when I was eleven years old, my parents facilitated my baptism which brought about my rebirth in the Spirit. At the moment of my baptism, even though I did not know it, I was supernaturally transferred to the mystical body of Christ, the Church. Part of the effect of my baptism was to increase my sensibility about God, again unbeknownst to me. In other words my natural insensibility decreased and my awareness of God and responsiveness to God increased. However, I admit, not by much.

After my baptism it was my parent's and the Church's responsibility to nurture me in the faith. And then when I was of age it became my own responsibility to pursue and follow the teachings of the Church. Well, for me, this did not happen and I am convinced it does not as well for many more millions of children today. The Church is ready and willing but far too many parents are not. The consequence of which is of course an indifference about God. And that indifference carried through to my adolescent and adult life.

Until I was thirty years old I paid no or at least very little attention to the things of God. The only time I prayed was when I was in trouble. Sure, I was married in a church and two of our four children were baptized,[14] all of which I went along with as part of my wife's, Diane, program. She was a little more religious than me. But for the most part, almost entirely, we lived without attention to God. I don't know what Diane was praying or if she was praying. I know I was not. We never went to church. The only time we talked about God, let alone do anything, was at parties when lathered up in alcohol influenced discussions. As to thoughts of God? Seldom, if ever. We had no Bible in the house. We didn't own one. In fact, before I was thirty years old the only Bible I ever had was absconded by my little sister and I never missed it. It is a nice little King James Bible given to me by my grandmother. I have it now. Anyway, the point is that we were so busy with *our lives* that we had no time or desire for God. That is indifference toward God and it is the way of the world.

Indifference also, I believe, comes in differing degrees that we may never really think about. Our Lady describes it as being lukewarm. I am sure we often fool ourselves into thinking we are good Christians because we

---

[14] We are foster parents to two orphaned boys who came into our family when they were eleven and fourteen years old. We all live here in Orange County and are very much a family. However, neither Rick nor Gary to date have requested baptism.

think we do no one harm, go to church, and pray a little each day. But the question is to whom does our heart belong?

When our Blessed Mother speaks about being lukewarm I think she has in mind the Lord's admonition in the vision given to the Apostle John recorded in The Book Of Revelation, Chapter 3, verses 14b to 22.

"'The Amen, the faithful and true witness, the source of God's creation, says this: [15] "I know your works; I know that you are neither cold nor hot. I wish you were either cold or hot. [16] So, because you are lukewarm, neither hot nor cold, I will spit you out of my mouth. [17] For you say, 'I am rich and affluent and have no need of anything,' and yet do not realize that you are wretched, pitiable, poor, blind, and naked. [18] I advise you to buy from me gold refined by fire so that you may be rich, and white garments to put on so that your shameful nakedness may not be exposed, and buy ointment to smear on your eyes so that you may see. [19] Those whom I love, I reprove and chastise. Be earnest, therefore, and repent.

[20] " ' "Behold, I stand at the door and knock. If anyone hears my voice and opens the door, (then) I will enter his house and dine with him, and he with me. [21] I will give the victor the right to sit with me on my throne, as I myself first won the victory and sit with my Father on his throne.

[22] " ' "Whoever has ears ought to hear what the Spirit says to the churches." ' "

To help illustrate what I am saying I would like to relate part of the content of a talk I heard from one of the parish priests while we were in Medjugorje. His name is Fr. Svetozar Kraljevic O.F.M. Father Svet, as he is lovingly referred to in Medjugorje, gave this analogy: A life without God is a life that is like a man that comes and goes every day from his house and waves to his neighbors when he happens to see them. They wave back. He knows they exist and they know he exists but they never become friends. They never sit down and have coffee together and talk. They never share concerns with one another. And so it goes day in and day out year after year. Much like we are with God. He is over there and I am over here. We seldom meet with him. But he desires to be with us always.

It is a self evident truth that the majority of humanity is law abiding. I am sure many people think they are not bad people. Therefore, they will make it to heaven – so they think. Now, I am surely not one to say one way or the other. But this I do know. By just obeying the national and societal laws, minding one's own business and being nice to people while remaining indifferent to God is self defeating. I believe God is after our hearts. As the Lord said, where our treasure is there too are our hearts. But, how we give our hearts to God and the way we devote our time, effort and money for God is not open to individual interpretation. As Fr. Svet said, to attempt to come to God and obtain his graces in a way not prescribed by God is like stealing from God. We have heard it before and I am sure it is true. Although he will not refuse them, I don't think God wants just Sunday saints. Furthermore, as far as being a so called good person in the eyes of world and societal opinion, I am sure we would do well to consider the following.

In the seventh chapter of the Gospel according to John, Jesus makes a startling declaration. On one occasion when Jesus was in Galilee his brothers[15] attempted to convince him to go public and show himself to the world by going up to Jerusalem for the annual Feast of Tabernacles. They apparently reasoned that Jesus should be doing his miraculous works at a place where he could obtain maximum exposure and thereby his fame would spread over the whole world. Jesus responds: "My time is not yet here, but the time is always right for you. The world cannot hate you, but it

[15] Actually more likely cousins or half brothers.

hates me, because I testify that its works are evil." In the context of what I have so far stated about conflict with God I think it is rather remarkable that in the passage just quoted, Jesus, without reservation, explicitly states that the works or ways of the world are evil. I then ask myself, 'why would I follow the way of the world if it is evil?' No. With all my heart I desire to follow Jesus. But, how do I do that? Well, Our Lady says that we must be converted and the first step in conversion is surrender to God.

Surrender To God

The Holy Mother of God says the following:

"Dear children! I am calling you to a complete surrender to God. I am calling you to great joy and peace which only God can give. I am with you and I intercede for you every day before God. I call you, little children, to listen to me and to live the messages that I am giving you. Already for years you are invited to holiness but you are still far away. I am blessing you. Thank you for having responded to my call." (March 25, 1989)

"Dear children! I am calling you to a complete surrender to God. Let everything that you possess be in the hands of God. Only in that way shall you have joy in your heart. Little children, rejoice in everything that you have. Give thanks to God because everything is God's gift to you. That way in your life you shall be able to give thanks for everything and discover God in everything even in the smallest flower. Thank you for having responded to my call." (April 25, 1989)

"Dear children! I invite you now to be open to God. See, children, how nature is opening herself and is giving life and fruits. In the same way I invite you to live with God and to

surrender completely to him. Children, I am with you and I want to introduce you continuously to the joy of life. I desire that everyone may discover the joy and love which can be found only in God and which only God can give. God doesn't want anything from you only your surrender. Therefore, children, decide seriously for God because everything else passes away. Only God doesn't pass away. Pray to be able to discover the greatness and joy of life which God gives you. Thank you for having responded to my call." (May 25, 1989)

I don't know about you, but when I read those messages (and many others like them) for the first time I was seriously affected. I continue to be soul-stirred every time I read them. They go right to the heart of the matter. Mary, who stands before the Eternal Father in Heaven, tells us we must surrender to God.

Ever had that nagging feeling that you need to do something but you keep putting it off and it continues to nag at you until you've done what you needed to do? For many years I had the feeling that I needed to surrender, completely, to the Lord. I read the Bible every day and I am sure by that reading and the applied grace of God given to me by our Blessed Mother I felt the need. Oh, I would say in my prayers that I surrender, but I knew I was still holding back. I did not turn everything over to God. I relied on myself. I rationalized that God gave me the gift of who I am and I should use that gift - which, by the way, I thought was pretty good. The problem was I really had little peace. Any peace I thought I had proved to be elusive and temporary. Things would go good for awhile and then they would go bad. As I came to know myself better and recognized my sin I realized I wasn't as good and capable as I thought I was. I came face to face with my sinner self. I wasn't the peacemaker I thought I was. It was not until I began to really surrender to God that I began to experience real peace. I found out that it requires a full submission of our will to the will of God. If it is the tendency of our makeup to battle against any threat to our individualism, our pride, I am convinced we shall only be at peace with God when we accept defeat.

To illustrate the importance of complete surrender as a condition for peace we can look at examples of armed conflict. The end of World War II came when Germany and Japan surrendered. Germany *unconditionally surrendered* to the allied forces and Japan *unconditionally surrendered* to the U.S. forces. Thus ended the most stupendous and destructive war in human history and relative peace prevailed thereafter. Europe was rebuilt under the Marshall Plan and Japan evolved into an economic giant. Not counting the Russian situation, Germany became an ally of the allied nations fighting against her and Japan a strong U.S. ally.

By contrast, in the Korean War an armistice was signed. That is, a truce was called and there were certain conditions each side agreed to abide by as part of the armistice. But there was no surrender by either side. Neither side admitted defeat. The consequence is that whereas Germany and Japan submitted and became allies of their former enemies, North Korea did not and there is still conflict to this very day – fifty years later.

In the same way, I am sure there are no armistice deals to be had with God. It is unconditional surrender to him that he desires and nothing less if we are to have peace with God. And as I said, from Our Lady's messages, the Bible and Church teaching, it is clear that we *first* need to surrender if we are to convert our way of thinking and living, change our heart's desires and have peace with God. I have learned there can be no holding back. Our beliefs, our value system, our thoughts, our actions, our whole view of life and the world must conform to the way of Jesus Christ, the Lord, as taught by his Apostles, preserved and taught by the Church. That requires conversion every day.

Conversion

To speak of conversion is in the same breath to talk about transformation. I believe that when Our Lady refers to conversion she is calling for the complete transformation of our hearts, minds, souls and bodies. She desires to lead us to and in a life of holiness.

"Dear children! Today again I am calling you to pray with your whole heart and day by day to change your life. Especially, dear children, I am calling that by your prayers and sacrifices you begin to live in holiness, because I desire that each one of you who has been to this fountain of grace will come to Paradise with the special gift which you shall give me, and that is holiness. Therefore, dear children, pray and daily change your life in order to become fully holy. I shall always be close to you. Thank you for having responded to my call." (November 13, 1986)

In his first pastoral epistle Saint Peter writes:

"... gird up the loins of your mind, live soberly, and set your hopes completely on the grace to be brought to you at the revelation of Jesus Christ. Like obedient children, do not act in compliance with the desires of your former ignorance but, as he who called you is holy, be holy yourselves in every aspect of your conduct, for it is written, "Be holy because I (am) holy." (1 Peter 1:13-16).

This is the objective of the Christian life. As stated in the *Catechism*:

"In the waters of Baptism, we have been 'washed ... sanctified ... justified in the name of the Lord Jesus Christ and in the Spirit of our God.' Our Father calls us to holiness in the whole of our life, and since 'he is the source of [our] life in Christ Jesus, who became for us wisdom from God, and ... sanctification,' both his glory and our life depend on the hallowing of his name in us and by us. Such is the urgency in our first petition." [16]

So, I ask myself, what is all this they are talking about? Immediately what comes to mind is what Father Svet said in Medjugorje. He used a term I cannot recall ever hearing prior to that day. Of course the significance of my familiarity with the term could be relevant or irrelevant. However, I am not exactly a Biblical, theological and church history slouch. Intellectually I understood very well what he was saying. Many times I taught the subject myself. But when I heard this 'new' term I was really moved inwardly. It seemed like for many years I groped about as if in a room dimly lit. Then, with the speaking of a few words the impact of my head knowledge filled my heart. The room became fully illuminated, so to speak. Many times I have read the relevant passages of Sacred Scripture. Many sermons I have heard on the subject and many books I have read. All of which prove to me that far too often we read right over the message contained in Sacred Scripture and never really get it. Or at least I didn't. The full weight and depth of meaning somehow fails to penetrate our inner being and move us to heartfelt understanding of the message. But, this is not so in Medjugorje. The message in Medjugorje breaks through like sunbeams through the clouds. So, what did Father Svet say?

---

[16] *Catechism*, paragraph 2813 referring to the first petition of the Lord's Prayer or Our Father where we begin by saying 'Our father ... hallowed [holy] be your name.'

He talked about Christ in us and called it the 'incarnated life.'

The Incarnated Life

When we speak of the Incarnation we are talking about the union of divinity with humanity in Jesus. St. John, the Evangelist, in the prologue of his gospel refers to Jesus as the Word who was in the beginning, was with God and was God (John 1:1). Further down, he writes: "*And the Word became flesh and made his dwelling among us, and we saw his glory, the glory as of the Father's only Son, full of grace and truth.*" (John 1:14) He, the Son of God, assumed a human nature and became fully man and fully God.[17] That is the Incarnation as I understand it.

The *Catechism* answers the question of why did the Word become flesh. Referring to Sacred Scripture and to Saints Irenaeus, Athanasius and Thomas Aquinas, the magisterium of the Church teaches that the Word became flesh:

(i) "in order to save us by reconciling us with God," (ii) "so that we might know God's love," (iii) "to be our model of holiness," and (iv) "... to make us *'partakers of the divine nature'*: [2 Peter 1:4] 'For this is why the Word became man, and the Son of God became man: so that man, by entering into communion with the Word and thus receiving divine sonship, might become a son of God.' 'For the Son of God became man so that we might become God' 'The only-begotten Son of God, wanting to make us sharers in his divinity, assumed our nature, so that he, made man, might make men gods.'"[18]

---

[17] *Catechism*, paragraph 461.
[18] Ibid., paragraphs 456-460.

So, in essence, what the Church has always taught is that because of Jesus' Incarnation, through the Word and Sacrament, by faith we are actually incarnated by Jesus. It only remains for us to realize this, allow it to penetrate the very substance of our being and live it! And that is the key. Live the Incarnated Life. I repeat. Live the Incarnated Life. As Fr. Svet said, the Incarnated Life is the life where God dwells. It is the life that loves Jesus. It is the life that has responded to God's love. It is the life filled with the resurrected Christ.

I believe that all who live the Incarnated Life are the ones who are truly at peace with God. This is what the Blessed Virgin Mary is teaching at her school in Medjugorje. It is why she comes to Medjugorje; to lead us to Jesus which she knows is the only way to peace.

"Dear children, this is the reason for my presence among you for such a long time: to lead you to Jesus. I want to save you and, through you, to save the whole world. Many people now live without faith; some don't even want to hear about Jesus, and yet they still want peace and fulfillment! Children this is the reason why I need your prayer: Prayer is the only way to save the human race." (July 30, 1987 – one of the last messages to the locutionists).[19]

I know from experience to the degree which I respond to God's love is the degree to which I live the Incarnated Life. In the Incarnated Life Jesus and our Blessed Mother are always there. I often was not.

---

[19] Taken from Father Richard J. Beyer's book *Medjugorje Day By Day*, ©1993 by Ave Maria Press, Notre Dame, IN, 46556 USA, page August 19.

Compartmentalization

The reason I was often not there, I have come to realize, is because, like most everyone, I compartmentalized my life's activities. Let me explain.

I draw six squares on a piece of paper evenly spaced in two vertical columns of three squares per column. Then I draw one square centered over and with the same spacing at the head of the two columns. In this square I write the word God. In the remaining six squares I write in one the word family; in another, the word work; in another, the word church. Then recreation, self and home in the other squares so that I end up with one of the foregoing words in one of the six boxes. I then record a week of activity by starting on a Sunday. I draw a line from home to church and from church to God because I worshipped God at church. Then I put a line from church to recreation because I went to brunch after church. Then I make one from recreation to home and then from home to recreation because I watched a football game on television. The kids come over for dinner so now I draw a line to family and so on. Then on Monday I follow the same routine with a line from home to work. By Saturday the spaces in between the six boxes are filled almost solid with lines crisscrossing between the six lower boxes. But there is still just one line going up to God.

What I see graphically is that I put God in his own compartment and left him there while I went through a weekly routine that excluded God. Not only did I not include him, I spent very little time with him as illustrated by the one lonely line going up to the God square. My only contact with God was on Sunday. Whereas that is the case with compartmentalized living, Incarnated living involves God in everything. God not only desires but actually is, even though we may not be aware of it, in the center of all our activity. As St. Paul told the philosophers in Athens, Greece: "'... it is he [God] who gives to everyone life and breath and everything. He made from one the whole human race to dwell on the entire surface of the earth, and he fixed the ordered seasons and the boundaries of their regions, so that people might seek God, even perhaps grope for him and find him, though indeed he is not far from any one of us. For 'In him we live and move and have our being...'" (Acts 17: 25b-28a).

It seems rather clear to me that our living, movement and our very being are ordered by God. But until I was converted and *really* responded to God's love, I never lived like I really believed it. Now, I prioritize my activities so that I spend time every day with Jesus and Mary and that can also be graphically represented.

To draw a diagram of the incarnated life, I soften the squares by using ovals instead of squares and arrange them in a circle around a circle with God written in it. Now with God in the center I can draw a line from one activity oval to another and each line goes through God. Of course I can go outside the boundary of the ovals and connect them. But then that would not be representative of the Incarnated life. In fact it may represent what many, many of us do. That is, like I did, say we believe in God but live like practical atheists. We actually live a life that circumnavigates encounter with God. Conversely, the Incarnated life eagerly seeks encounter with God every day. The incarnated life diagram has many, many lines that touch the God circle. And that, we are told, is the essence of conversion. The conversion that puts us at peace with God is a radical change in values. It decides the locus of our hearts which, as already stated, is where also the things we treasure or value are located.

As we know, we learn our values as we grow from childhood into adulthood. Sad to say, for the overwhelming majority of humanity the values we learn are in opposition to the virtues the Lord desires for us to pursue. Even that which we think to be good may not be so good - we went over some of that ground in the discussion regarding conflict with God. Any compilation of Bible doctrine will make very clear the virtues God desires of us. We surely would do well also to read and take to heart paragraphs 1426 to 1439 of the *Catechism*. For example, paragraph 1431 reads as follows:

"Interior repentance is a radical reorientation of our whole life, a return, a conversion to God with all our heart, and an end of sin, a turning away from evil, with repugnance toward the evil actions we have committed. At the same time it entails the desire and resolution to change one's life, with hope in God's mercy and trust in the help of his grace."

I think it is imperative to recognize that there are three influences upon us that exert powerful temptation to sin. They are the world, the flesh and the devil. The world or the system of values held by the secular consensus condones that which is evil. So since everybody else is doing and not condemning that which is actually evil we fall into the trap of thinking it is all right for us to do too. Our own selfish desires, sensual and material, (the flesh) encourage us to throw off virtue and live for the pleasurable, immediate moment. And Satan is right in the middle of it all surreptitiously masking the evil so that our consciences are lulled into thinking there is nothing wrong with what we are doing or how we think about things or what value we place on this or that. The result is: unbridled desire (sex, money, power, adultery, boats, RV's, shopping, fashion, extravagance, bigger and more lavish houses, more expensive cars, expensive dining, trips, cruises, etc.). The consequence is: indifference toward God, self-righteous prejudices and bigotry, excessive material consumption, abortion, divorce, crime, etc. that destroy peace. I am sure the only way to convert and overcome our own evil desires is by faith in Jesus Christ.

Faith

If we can agree that the dynamic of faith basically means trust in someone or something we can, I think, easily see that we humans are fundamentally people of faith. If that is so, then the question regarding our personal peace boils down to: in whom or what do we have faith? Who or what do I trust and what will it get me? Well, don't we really live our lives trusting in this or that? In my mind we do. For instance, consider mundane faith.

Mundane Faith

Common or mundane faith, by which we are all occupied, virtually controls our daily lives. For example, everyday, mundane faith is exercised in something as simple as arranging with a friend to meet somewhere at a specific time and place for coffee, lunch or whatever. In the agreement for the meeting each person trusts that the other will be at the appointed place and time. However, there may be some small measure of uncertainty dependent on the parties involved. But, for the most part, once a pact, as it were, is made, the expectation is that each will arrive as agreed. If one or the other fails to show, then the one present at the meeting place, assuming that person is themselves punctual, will likely account the other person's absence to a delay caused by traffic, baby-sitter or whatever. Thus, mundane faith persists. Only when some insincere excuse is offered by the person who never showed up, is mundane faith broken. All kinds of doubts creep into the mind of the offended person and trust is weakened. So, when the next meeting is arranged there is probably a little less confidence that it will actually take place. And so on it goes. I trust him or her and likewise I trust him or her less. Isn't this the way it is?

The example above is applied to everything in life. Our daily functions are largely based on expectations derived from mundane faith. Such things as waking in the morning, a reliable alarm clock, water from the tap, clothes in the closet, food in the pantry, a car that starts, gas at the pump, etc. are all things that we trust will not fail – even though we know they do. The list is endless and to some small or large degree they involve reliance on other people, seen and unseen. Why, even driving on the freeway involves trust. We trust that as we hurtle down the road at 70 miles an hour the guy in front of us is not going to slam on the brakes so we are not rear-ended by the guy behind us. But... we know that it happens - a lot. Yet, we get out there every day and in some measure trust that it will not. Otherwise why would we do it? Because we want to get where we are going? Yes. And if we did not have some measure of faith we probably would not take the risk. We could say that we hope it will not happen. But, do we really think that every time we go out? No. We trust that it won't because we rely on other people to use good sense and drive safely. So there is risk in the confidence we have in others - people we do not even know. It is part of society discussed at length by sociologists. If we had the time and the inclination we could no doubt sit down and make a detailed list of a week's worth of daily activities and find that many, if not all, of the activities involved trusting someone or something to do or not do something. So, who or what are we going to trust?

Christian Faith

Generally we trust in what we think we know. This raises a question in my mind. Is what we think we know adequate for faith or trust in God? I ask the question because so much of what we do depends on our trust or what we believe.

In Medjugorje the answer is readily available. In the last 22 years Our Lady has made daily visits to Earth from Heaven and delivered in that period of time over 300 messages for worldwide publication. Humble, studious and thoughtful Franciscan priests such as Father Svetozar Kraljevic O.F.M. serve at Medjugorje. Fr. Svet talks with the visionaries who see Our Blessed Mother. He studies the messages. He applies his theological training. He prays heartfelt prayers. The Holy Spirit speaks to his heart and he listens. I have set forth below a few paragraphs from his book *The Apparitions Of Our Lady At Medjugorje* (loc. cit.). Personally, I think what he writes pretty well answers the question I posed above.

> Mirjana[20] once said: "God cannot take it anymore!" This is very simple human talk, but it was said with transcendental, divine knowledge. It is Mirjana's expression of what she sees in the world, but it proceeds from God's experience with man as God revealed it to her (about you and me). Thus her words must be taken seriously. God is greatly displeased with our sinful behavior, and "without faith, it is impossible to please him" (Heb 11:6).
>
> "This is the work of God: have faith in the One he sent" (Jn 6:29). Faith is a gift [[21]]

---

[20] Visionary Mirjana Dragicevic-Soldo

[21] It is critically important to remember that a gift is only complete when accepted. A gift rejected or ignored fails to convey the intended benefit. So the gift of faith from God must also be ***accepted*** by us for us to realize the benefit. It begins at Baptism. When a gift is refused the giver's feelings are usually hurt, are they not? The joy of giving is erased in a

from God, but faith has vanished in many people. God holds no place in many hearts, and the results are inevitable. The soul and the spirit are impoverished, the mind is confused, meaning and goals are lost and confounded [even though one might not think so]. The past is bloody and sad; the future is bleak. Our Lady, however, has come to waken our slumbering souls and spirits, to waken our faith in the One whom he [the Father] sent.

The Word of God first came into our world in his creation of man "in his image" (Gen 1:27). In freedom, the first man decided to disobey God by eating fruit from the forbidden tree; thus he turned away from God. Later, the new Word of God was incarnated and came into the world in the person of Jesus Christ to restore peace – the initial unity and harmony between God and man – by being totally obedient to our Father. Now, in our time, Our Lady brings us the same Word of God, to be incarnated within us – to be as real in us as it is in her. Thus God celebrates eternal Christmas with man.

Mary has again brought the Word of God into the world so that man can say a momentous yes to the Word, as she did. Saying yes signifies personal surrender to God, in faith, for the Word of God is God himself. Somewhat as the Word, Jesus Christ was born in Mary, it can be born in us. We thereby become a new creation, as the Creator

---

flash. Imagine how God must feel when his gift of faith is ignored or rejected or his gift of human life is unwanted and aborted.

means us to. The process is a real, personal liberation whereby man does not imprison himself in himself, but willingly reinstates God as the core or the center.

When man puts himself at the center of things, his power works against him and oppresses him [again, even though we may not think so]. For him, "truth" becomes an attempt to justify his selfishness and his freedom to enslave himself, because he is unable to find the true way and the basic meaning of the world. Despite all revolutions, achievements and technical breakthroughs, and new knowledge in all fields, man is still forced to face the truth – the fact – of death. Thus life has become more tragic for him than ever before, because he has tried harder than ever before to dismiss – "account for" – the certainty of death.

The only alternative is faith in God and surrender to him (even though it is motivated by failure and desperation). God offers us his hand through Jesus and Our Lady, who brings her Son into the world again, making every new day a new Christmas, a new opportunity for conversion. God wills that every road in our lives lead to redemption, that every human effort meet the ultimate success, that every defeat and sacrifice contribute to final victory, that our death become new life.

Our Lady of Medjugorje seeks to bring us real faith, real meaning, and put us in touch with God and ourselves. [Footnotes are my own].

Summary

The message from Medjugorje is one that clearly tells of the way to have personal peace. Once a person is at peace then love and forgiveness can be truly had and given. The peace is contagious. As more and more people obtain personal peace, the family, the community, the nation and the world become peaceful. The Blessed Virgin Mary says the way to personal peace is through surrender to God, conversion and faith in Jesus. All other perceived ways are illusion.

Not too many years ago there was an expression I heard often enough. I don't hear it much anymore. You too may remember hearing it: "It takes two to tangle." The moral, of course, is that if just one person is willing to tangle and the other is not, there will be no dispute or altercation. I have learned the incarnated life of peace enables one to truly turn the other cheek and disengage or not engage at all to avoid conflict. Whereas many societies promote competition and confrontation the incarnated society promotes peace through personal humility and holiness.

Long ago, Saint Paul, inspired by the Holy Spirit, summed it up in his epistle to the Church in Ephesus:

So I declare and testify in the Lord that you must no longer live as the Gentiles do, in the futility of their minds; [18] darkened in understanding, alienated from the life of God because of their ignorance, because of their hardness of heart, [19] they have become callous and have handed themselves over to licentiousness for the practice of every kind of impurity to excess. [20] That is not how you learned Christ, [21] assuming that you have heard of him and were taught in him, as truth is in Jesus, [22] that you should put away the old self of your former way of life, corrupted through deceitful desires, [23] and be renewed in the spirit of your minds, [24] and put on the new self, created in God's way in righteousness and holiness of truth. (Ephesians 4:17-24).

So as we flew from Zagreb, Croatia to Frankfurt, Germany I stared out the window of the plane and contemplated all that I have told you so far. I did not make an act of surrender but somehow I knew it was finally complete. My conversion was now in high gear and my faith immensely strengthened. The peace that surpasses understanding is permanently lodged in my inner being. I truly trust everything to our Blessed Mother. Worries over money, the future, retirement provisions, my family, the state of things in general, are gone. No longer do I feel wronged by people and situations. My sense of justice rests in the confidence that even in the smallest of things Jesus knows all and handles all. I do not need to interfere. I do not need to make anything right. I do not need to make things happen. He will take care of it. I am in the care of the Queen of Peace, our Mother, and that is all that matters. She will by the grace of God guide me and teach me what I need to know and what I need to do to please her son, our brother and Lord, Jesus, which is pleasing to the Eternal Father. All I need to do is act on her advice. She confirms many things to me. Working in the background, unseen, she helps me every day. Like never before, I am at peace with God.

In my experience and from testimony of others I find that conversion usually begins as a spiritual awakening and then becomes a daily process. We begin a journey that starts with our baptism. Then we are instructed and mature in the faith. But we are often weak and prone to wander into dangerous territory. We lose peace and long to regain it. Even the peace of Medjugorje is under constant assault by the world, the flesh and the devil. We need help in the battle. Where can we find it? Who will show us the way to conversion and peace?

"Why do you not put your trust in me? I know that you have been praying for a long time, but truly, surrender yourself. Abandon your concerns to Jesus. Listen to what he says in the gospel: 'And who among you, through his anxiety, is able to add a single cubit to the length of his life?'" (Message to one of the locutionists, October 30, 1983, taken from Fr. Richard J. Beyer's book *Medjugorje Day By Day*, June 9).

"Dear children! Today I call you to prepare your hearts for these days when the Lord particularly desires to purify you from all the sins of your past. ***You, dear children, are not able by yourselves, therefore I am here to help you.*** *You pray, dear children! Only that way shall you be able to recognize all the evil that is in you and surrender it to the Lord so the Lord may completely purify your hearts. Therefore, dear children, pray without ceasing and prepare your hearts in penance and fasting. Thank you for having responded to my call."* (December 4, 1986, emphasis mine).

Five Little Stones

Our Lady gives us five little stones as weapons to conquer our Goliath. Here she is referring to the Bible story of the shepherd boy David's victory over the Philistine giant, Goliath, when he slew Goliath with a slingshot. I think that by analogy she compares our giant to conquer as our sin brought about by our succumbing to the world, the flesh and the devil. Meaning that by using the five little stones she gives us we can overcome our Goliath. We can resist the world, the flesh and the devil, convert and be at peace with God.

In Medjugorje one will find in virtually every souvenir shop prayer cards that list the five little stones. They are meant to remind us to devote ourselves every day to the practices Our Lady from Heaven teaches us. She is our Mother and as the best mother possible she instructs us because she is deeply concerned about her children's welfare. The five endeavors, if we apply ourselves with heartfelt devotion, will change our lives for the better. There are millions of witnesses who will testify to this truth. I am but one of them. The five little stones are prayer, Holy Mass, Bible, fasting and Sacramental Confession.

Prayer

Of all her messages given through the Medjugorje visionaries and locutionists the most repeated request of our Blessed Mother Mary is for prayer. She is always recommending prayer. More than once she simply said "Pray, pray, pray!"

"Dear children! Today I am calling you all to prayer. Without prayer, dear children, you are not able to experience either God, or me or the graces which I am giving you. Therefore, my call to you is that the beginning and end of your day always be prayer. Dear children, I wish to lead you daily more and more in prayer, but you are not able to grow because you do not desire it. My call, dear children, is that for you prayer be in the first place. Thank you for having responded to my call." (July 3, 1986)

"Dear children! My call to you is that your prayer be the joy of an encounter with the Lord. I am not able to guide you as long as you yourselves do not experience joy in prayer. From day to day I desire to lead you more and more in prayer, but I do not wish to force you. Thank you for having responded to my call." (August 14, 1986)

By the two preceding messages alone we can see that prayer is the way we experience God, our dear Mother and receive the graces she brings to us from God our Father. It logically follows then that if we want to live the Incarnated Life and have peace with God we must pray. I repeat. We must pray. And we must pray a lot – every single day. The Teaching Magisterium of the Church has always exhorted the faithful to prayer.

With all prayer and supplication, pray at every opportunity in the Spirit. To that end, be watchful with all perseverance and supplication for all the holy ones. (Ephesians 6:18)

Have no anxiety at all, but in everything, by prayer and petition, with thanksgiving, make your requests known to God. (Philippians 4:6)

...For the eyes of the Lord are on the righteous and his ears turned to their prayer, but the face of the Lord is against evildoers." (1 Peter 3:12)

Prayer in the events of each day and each moment is one of the secrets of the kingdom revealed to "little children," to the servants of Christ, to the poor of the Beatitudes. It is right and good to pray so that the coming of the kingdom of justice and peace may influence the march of history, but it is just as important to bring the help of prayer into humble, everyday situations; all forms of prayer can be the leaven to which the Lord compares the kingdom. (*Catechism* paragraph 2660)

Because of Mary's singular cooperation with the action of the Holy Spirit, the Church loves to pray in communion with the Virgin Mary, to magnify with her the great things the Lord has done for her, and to entrust supplications and praises to her. (*Catechism* paragraph 2682)[1]

I really believe one must truly feel deep down in their heart that the Incarnated Life is a life of prayer. It is a life where we spend much time directly with our Mother and the Holy Trinity and where we always present our thoughts to God no matter what we may be up to. The important thing is

---

[1] In fact the whole Fourth Part of the *Catechism* is devoted to Christian prayer.

to be constantly aware that God is with us. Our Mother Mary is always with us watching over us. We needn't ask them to be with us. They ALWAYS are with us. We are the ones who need to take time to focus on them in prayer every day and have experiences with them.

I am sure we all know that if we really love someone we want to spend as much time as we can with that person. We arrange our schedules so we can be with the one we love. That is one of, if not the major, reasons why we get married. So we can live together and be together more than if we were living separately. It follows then that if we really love Jesus and our Blessed Mother we will do all we can to spend time with them in prayer. It seems to me that if we are surrendered to God we will gladly give two or three hours a day to be with Jesus and Our Lady in prayer, at Mass and adoration. As the *Catechism* says "the Church loves to pray in communion with the Virgin Mary."

How should we pray? Our Lady answers the question for us:

"*Dear children! Also today I call you to prayer. Renew your personal prayer, and in a special way pray to the Holy Spirit to help you pray with the heart...* " (May 25, 2003).

She repeatedly advises us to pray with our hearts. Her consistency in this strong recommendation is seen throughout her messages. On March 1, 1984, Our Lady began weekly messages for the Medjugorje parish and for the world. In the message for August 11, 1984, she said: "*Pray with the heart and surrender yourselves to Jesus in prayer.*" So, from 1984 to the present time she has been telling the whole of humanity to pray to God with all their heart. That, to me, means to pray in a meaningful way from the bottom of my heart.

We all have heard someone say or probably said ourselves that our heart was not in this or that. Consequently we did a poor job of this or that. We were not motivated. Conversely, when our heart is in what we are doing we are motivated, it is a joy and we do it well. Our dear Mother knows us through and through and she wants us to be genuine with Jesus. I understand her to mean that for that to be accomplished we must really have our heart in our prayers. She wants us to feel the impact of the words we pray. Therefore, she asks for prayer with the heart so that the words are contemplated mentally and assimilated to the soul.

At his talk on February 20, 2003, at the Mission Basilica in San Juan Capistrano, California, Ivan Dragicevic said that Our Lady says that if we want to pray better we should pray more. To pray more is a personal decision we make out of love for God. To pray better is a grace. We receive the grace if we pray more. That seems pretty straight forward to me. It is readily apparent that quality and quantity are extremely important in our prayer lives. I think the Lord desires a serious daily time commitment to prayer. One might ask why so much prayer? Our Lady answers:

"Dear children! I still need your prayers. You wonder why all these prayers? Look around you, dear children, and you will see how greatly sin has dominated the world. Pray, therefore, that Jesus conquers. Thank you for having responded to my call." (September 13, 1984).

The next question in my mind would be what should we pray?

In her messages Our Lady talks about the prayers at Holy Mass and the Our Father, Hail Mary and Glory Be. She says all prayers are pleasing to God but she specifically asks all her children to pray the Rosary.

Rosary

We might ask why our Blessed Mother asks us to pray the Rosary. I really do not need to know why she asks this. It is enough that our Heavenly Messenger, Queen and Mother, requests it of her children. Yet, I think it is probably of some value to at least look at a few things. First are a few of Our Lady's messages.

"God has sent me among you so that I may help you. If you so wish, grasp for the rosary. Even the rosary alone can work miracles in the world and in your lives." (January 25, 1997).

"I call all priests and religious brothers and sisters to pray the rosary and to teach others to pray. The rosary, little children, is especially dear to me. Through the rosary open your heart to me and I am able to help you. Thank you for having responded to my call." (August 25, 1997).

"Dear children! Also today, I call you to prayer. Little children, prayer works miracles. When you are tired and sick and you do not know the meaning of your life, take the Rosary and pray; pray until prayer becomes for you a joyful meeting with your Savior. I am with you, little children, and I intercede and pray for you. Thank you for having responded to my call." (April 25, 2001).

Second, we do well, I think, to study the Holy Father's letter, *Rosarium Virginis Mariae, On The Most Holy Rosary*. John Paul II sends out this letter in the 25th year of his Pontificate and declares October 2002 to October 2003 to be the year of the Rosary. In the Conclusion of the letter he states that he willingly entrusts to the power of the Rosary prayer "the cause of peace in the world and the cause of the family." He writes:

The grave challenges confronting the world at the start of this new Millennium lead us to think that only an intervention from on high, capable of guiding the hearts of those living in situations of conflict and those governing the destinies of nations, can give reason to hope for a brighter future.

The Rosary is by nature a prayer for peace, since it consists in the contemplation of Christ, the Prince of Peace, the one who is "our peace" (Eph 2:14). Anyone who assimilates the mystery of Christ – and this is clearly the goal of the Rosary – learns the secret of peace and makes it his life's project. Moreover, by virtue of its meditative character, with the tranquil succession of *Hail Marys,* the Rosary has a peaceful effect on those who pray it, disposing them to receive and experience in their innermost depths, and to spread around them, that true peace which is the special gift of the Risen Lord (cf. Jn 14:27; 20:21).

The Rosary is also a prayer for peace because of the fruits of charity which it produces. When prayed well in a truly meditative way, the Rosary leads to an encounter with Christ in his mysteries and so cannot fail to draw attention to the face of Christ in others, especially in the most afflicted. How could one possibly contemplate the mystery of the child of Bethlehem, in the joyful mysteries, without experiencing the desire to welcome, defend and promote life, and to shoulder the burdens of suffering children all over the world? How could one possibly follow in the footsteps of Christ the Revealer, in the mysteries of light, without resolving to bear witness to his "Beatitudes" in daily life? And how could one contemplate Christ carrying the cross and Christ crucified, without feeling the need to act as a "Simon of Cyrene" for our brothers and sisters weighed down by grief or crushed by despair? Finally, how could one possibly gaze upon the glory of the risen Christ or of Mary Queen of Heaven, without yearning to make this world more beautiful, more just, more closely conformed to God's plan?

In a word, by focusing our eyes on Christ, the Rosary also makes us peacemakers in the world. By its nature as an insistent choral petition in harmony with Christ's invitation to "pray ceaselessly" (Lk 18:1), the Rosary allows us to hope that, even today, the difficult "battle" for peace can be won. Far from offering an escape from the problems of the world, the Rosary obliges us to see them with responsible and generous eyes, and obtains for us the strength to face them with the certainty of God's help and the firm intention of bearing witness in every situation to "love, which binds everything together in perfect harmony" (Col 3:14).

Dear brothers and sisters! A prayer so easy and yet so rich deserves to be rediscovered by the Christian community. Let us do so, especially this year, as a means of confirming the direction outlined in my Apostolic Letter *Novo Millennio Ineuente,* from which the pastoral plans of so many particular Churches have drawn inspiration as they look to the immediate future.

I turn particularly to you, my dear brother bishops, priests and deacons, and to you, pastoral agents in your different ministries: through your own personal experience of the beauty of the Rosary, may you come to promote it with conviction.

I also place my trust in you, theologians: by your sage and rigorous reflection, rooted in the word of God and sensitive to the lived experience of the Christian people, may you help them to discover the Biblical foundations, the spiritual riches and the pastoral value of this traditional prayer.

I count on you, consecrated men and women, called in a particular way to contemplate the face of Christ at the school of Mary.

I look to all of you, brothers and sisters of every state of life, to you, Christian families, to you, the sick and the elderly, and to you, young people: *confidently take up the Rosary once again.* Rediscover the Rosary in the light of Scripture, in harmony with the liturgy, and in the context of your daily lives.

One would think that the Holy Father's Apostolic exhortation would be sufficient to drive us all to the Rosary. But just in case a little motivation is needed we might want to consider the promises the Blessed Virgin Mary gave to Saint Dominic when she instituted the Rosary prayer.

Janice Connell writes in her book, *The Visions of the Children:*

> The Blessed Mother has reminded the pilgrims frequently to study the fifteen promises made by her to Saint Dominic, to whom she was sent in the early thirteenth century with the first rosary, when times were dark and fraught with moral weakness. Those promises are:
>
> 1. To all those who will recite my rosary devoutly, I promise my special protection and very great graces.
> 2. Those who will persevere in the recitation of my rosary shall receive some signal grace.
> 3. The rosary shall be a very powerful armor against hell; it shall destroy vice, deliver from sin, and shall dispel heresy.
> 4. The rosary shall make virtue and good works flourish, and shall obtain for souls the most abundant divine mercies; it shall substitute in hearts love of God for love of the world, elevate them to desire heavenly and eternal goods. Oh, that souls would sanctify themselves by this means!
> 5. Those who trust themselves to me through the rosary shall not perish.
> 6. Those who recite my rosary piously, considering its mysteries, shall not be overwhelmed by misfortune, nor die a bad death. The sinner shall be converted; the

just shall grow in grace and become worthy of eternal life.

7. Those truly devoted to my rosary shall not die without the consolations of the Church, or without grace.
8. Those who will recite my rosary shall find during their life and their death the light of God, the fullness of His grace, and shall share in the merits of the blessed.
9. I will deliver very promptly from purgatory the souls devoted to my rosary.
10. The true children of my rosary shall enjoy great joy in heaven.
11. What you ask through my rosary, you shall obtain.
12. Those who propagate my rosary shall obtain through me aid in all their necessities.
13. I have obtained from my Son that all those who pray the rosary shall have for their brethren in life and death the saints in heaven.
14. Those who recite my rosary faithfully are all my beloved children, who are the brothers and sisters of Jesus Christ.
15. Devotion to my rosary is a special sign of predestination. [2]

I find that to contemplate the Rosary virtues while praying the Rosary and heartfelt concentration on the words of the prayers (Queen of the Holy Rosary, Apostle's Creed, Our Father, Glory Be, Oh My Jesus, Hail Mary, Hail Holy

---

[2] Janice M. Connell, *The Visions Of The Children,* Revised Edition, page 202ff, © 1992, 1997, St. Martin's Press, New York, ISBN 0-312-18204-X.

Queen and Oh My God) bring me into meditative prayer. They set me in what we today call a zone, so to speak. It is the realm of the mystical. It is a spiritual involvement in the life, death and resurrection of our Lord Jesus with particular reference to his Mother and our Mother, Mary. That which I find significant includes but is not limited to the following:

Joyous Mysteries

The Annunciation – Luke 1:26ff. – The Archangel Gabriel is sent by God to Mary and tells her that she will be the mother of the Son of God. She responds by humbly accepting the decree of the Almighty. She could have said that she would rather not. No, instead she says to Gabriel, "Behold, I am the handmaiden of the Lord. May it be done to me according to your word." So, through my Rosary I ask our Blessed Mother to teach me and help me increase in humility.

The Visitation – Luke 1:39ff. – Pregnant Mary denied herself and traveled probably somewhere close to 100 miles either on foot, donkey or donkey-cart to arrive at the house of her elderly, pregnant relative, Elizabeth. Mary stayed with Elizabeth for three months and helped her care for her household. In that we see Our Lady's spirit of fraternal charity. So, through my Rosary I ask our Blessed Mother to teach me and help me increase in fraternal charity.

The Nativity – Luke 2:1ff. – I am sure most every mother can recall that special feeling of consuming love when their child is born. But for Mary, overshadowed by the Holy Spirit, and bringing forth from her womb the Infant Jesus, Son of God, it must have been overwhelming love she felt for her son. And in that we see Our Lady's love for God. So, through my Rosary I ask our Blessed Mother to teach me and help me increase in love for God.

The Presentation – Luke 2:22ff. – Now, knowing that her Son is God in the flesh and she the Mother of God, she nevertheless obeys the Mosaic Law and presents the Infant

Jesus at the Temple in Jerusalem. He is consecrated unto God and Mary entrusts her one and only child entirely to God. In that we see Our Lady's spirit of sacrifice. So, through my Rosary I ask our Blessed Mother to teach me and help me increase in sacrifice.

The Reunion – Luke 2:41ff. – In the thirteenth year of his Incarnation for three days Mary was separated from Jesus. Imagine the anxiety she suffered when after the first day she realized Jesus was missing. Ever suffered the temporary loss of a child? I have. It is pure, indescribable mental and emotional torture. I can only imagine the agony in the permanent loss of a child. And so in such a state Mary searches for her son, Jesus, for three days without stopping until she finds him. In that, we see her zeal for our Lord. So, through my Rosary I ask our Blessed Mother to teach me and help me increase in zeal for her son, our brother and Lord, Jesus.

The Luminous Mysteries

The Baptism Of Jesus – Matthew 3:13ff. – Jesus submits to Baptism at the hands of John the Baptizer. By this Jesus institutes the Sacrament of Baptism and sets the example that all Christians must be baptized. So, through my Rosary I ask our Blessed Mother to teach me and help me remain faithful to my baptismal vows.

The Wedding At Cana – John 2:1ff. – Here we see Jesus reveal his power and hear his mother tell the servants to "do whatever he tells you." So, through my Rosary I ask our Blessed Mother to teach me and help me increase in daily obedience to her son, our brother and Lord, Jesus.

The Proclamation Of The Kingdom And The Invitation To Conversion – Mark 1:14-15 – Here, what more can I do? I surrender, kneel before my King and through my Rosary ask our Blessed Mother to teach me and help me convert daily.

The Transfiguration – Mark 9:2ff. – Saint Peter is so overcome by the glory of the Lord and the appearance of Moses and Elijah that he wants them to stay there forever! That is why I think he offered to set up tents for them. Who wouldn't be so over-awed? Is that not our desire – to be with the Lord in his glory? I think so. So, through my Rosary I ask our Blessed Mother to teach me and help me always to press close to her Immaculate Heart so I may some day be with the Lord in his glory.

The Institution Of The Holy Eucharist – Matthew 26:26ff. – Jesus fulfills his promise to be with us until the end of the age by coming to us every day in the Holy Eucharist. For the forgiveness of my sins I must drink his blood. To have life in me I must eat his flesh (John 6:53). So, through my Rosary I ask our Blessed Mother to teach me and help me increase in love of and desire for our Lord in the Holy Eucharist.

Sorrowful Mysteries

The Agony In The Garden – Matthew 26:36ff. – Why was the Lord in such agony? I do not think it was because he feared the coming torture he would suffer. Saint Peter, who was with him in the garden, tells us that Jesus bore our sins on the cross (1Peter 2:24). Therefore, I think our Lord was stressed to the point of sweating blood because the sins of the whole world were coming upon him. And he begged the Father to take the cup of such soul scorching pain away from him. Yet, he remained true to the will of the Father. In this we can see how critical repentance is to our salvation. So, through my Rosary I ask our Blessed Mother to teach me and help me increase in daily repentance.

The Scourging At The Pillar – Matthew 27:26 – Here we see our Lord show us the importance of mortification as he himself allowed his own flogging. If the Prince of Peace submits to such mortification and sets the example can I not do likewise? So, through my Rosary I ask our Blessed

Mother to teach me and help me increase in the mortification of my sensual and material desires.

The Insulting Crown Of Thorns – John 19:1 – Such and insult to mock the King of Glory as did the Roman soldiers. Yet, our King did not retaliate. In that we see his humility and moral courage. So, through my Rosary I ask our Blessed Mother to teach me and help me increase in humility and moral courage.

The Burden Of The Cross – John 19:16-17 – As Jesus struggled up the Via Dolorosa, with his cross on his back, destined for execution at Golgotha, a death he freely accepted, he was met by Mary along the way. Her heart was pierced by a sword of sorrow at the sight of her son patiently bearing the burden of that heavy cross. Yet, it is the Lord's patience in suffering that we admire and desire. So, through my Rosary I ask our Blessed Mother to teach me and help me increase in patience in all things.

The Crucifixion – John 19:23ff. – Despite the immense physical pain, mental anguish and torment of soul, Jesus nevertheless persevered to the final end to show irrefutably his love for all of humanity and to provide for our redemption. So, through my Rosary I ask our Blessed Mother to teach me and help me increase in love for all people and to persevere in the faith.

The Glorious Mysteries

The Resurrection – John 20:1ff. – It is from our Risen Lord that we receive faith in him (v.29). As Saint Paul wrote "...if Christ has not been raised, your faith is vain; you are still in your sins." (1 Cor 15:17). So, through my Rosary I ask our Blessed Mother to teach me and help me increase in faith in her son, our brother and Lord, Jesus.

The Ascension – Luke 24:50ff. and Acts 1:6ff. – By Jesus ascending back to heaven he went to prepare a place in heaven for us (John 14:2-3). Therefore, to hope for heaven is a well-placed desire. So, through my Rosary I ask our

Blessed Mother to help me increase and sustain my hope to be soon in heaven.

The Descent Of The Holy Spirit – Acts 2:1ff. – When the Holy Spirit descended upon Our Lady, the Apostles and all the disciples in Jerusalem on the day of Pentecost we see how they were filled with zeal for Jesus. So, through my Rosary I ask our Blessed Mother to teach, inspire and help me increase in zeal for her son, our brother and Lord, Jesus.

The Assumption Of Mary – *Catechism* paragraph 966 – The Assumption of Mary, body and soul, is the holy and happy departure from this world of our dear Mother. Following her example we too can dare to hope for a holy and happy death. So, through my Rosary I ask our Blessed Mother to help me achieve a holy and happy death.

The Coronation Of Mary – Pope Pius XII, November 1, 1954 – The Church celebrates the Memorial of the "Queenship of Mary" every August 22. Imagine Our Lady arriving in heaven. There she is lovingly greeted by the Holy Trinity and the Eternal Father crowns her Queen of Heaven. What divine love is lavished upon her, our dear Mother. So, through my Rosary I ask our Blessed Mother to teach me and help me increase in love for her.

I find that the wonder of the Rosary prayer grows ever more wonderfully the more I pray the Rosary. I can testify to you, in all humility, that of the 15 promises our Blessed Mother gives to those who devote themselves to her Rosary I know I have and am realizing six. My life has changed. I am actually able to live the virtues I pray for through the Rosary. I believe I am experiencing the Incarnated Life. I am being converted.

The Rosary prayer is a powerful weapon in the battle against the world, the flesh and the devil. It is a mighty little stone. It is a gift from our dear Mother. I pray that more and more people would accept her gift and employ it every day.

Holy Mass

There are two parts of the Mass. They are the Liturgy of the Word and the Liturgy of the Eucharist. Contained within both are the prayers of the Mass. Included in prayer is our singing. St. Augustine somewhere wrote, "He who sings prays twice." So, essentially we come to Holy Mass for three basic reasons. We come to pray together, to receive Jesus in word and sacrament and to offer ourselves as participants in the Sacrifice of Christ. This is our worship. Our Lady knows the benefit we receive and that is why she encourages us to attend Mass every day.

"Dear children! I wish to call you to a living of the Holy Mass. There are many of you who have sensed the beauty of the Holy Mass, but there are also those who come unwillingly. I have chosen you, dear children, but Jesus gives you His graces in the Mass. Therefore, consciously live the Holy Mass and let your coming to it be a joyful one. Come to it with love and make the Mass your own. Thank you for having responded to my call." (April 3, 1986).

"Always have God's love within you, for without this love you cannot convert yourselves completely. Let the rosary be in your hands in memory of Jesus. Dear children, strive to enter more deeply into the Mass as you should." (*Medjugorje Day By Day,* June 12, loc. cit.)

"My children, I wish that the holy Mass would be the day's gift to you. Attend it, wish for it to begin. Jesus gives himself to you at the Mass. Therefore, look forward to that moment, for then you are cleansed." (*Medjugorje Day By Day,* July 10, loc. cit.)

Jesus said to them, "Amen, amen, I say to you, unless you eat the flesh of the Son of Man and drink his blood, you do not have life within you. [54] Whoever eats my flesh and drinks my blood has eternal life, and I will raise him on the last day. [55] For my flesh is true food, and my blood is true drink. [56] Whoever eats my flesh and drinks my blood remains in me and I in him. [57] Just as the living Father sent me and I have life because of the Father, so also the one who feeds on me will have life because of me. John 6:53-57.

Then he took the bread, said the blessing, broke it, and gave it to them, saying, "This is my body, which will be given for you; do this in memory of me." Luke 22:19

Then he took a cup, gave thanks, and gave it to them, saying, "Drink from it, all of you, [28] for this is my blood of the covenant, which will be shed on behalf of many for the forgiveness of sins. Matthew 26:27-28

I urge you therefore, brothers, by the mercies of God, to offer your bodies as a living sacrifice, holy and pleasing to God, your spiritual worship. Romans 12:1

Communion with the Body and Blood of Christ increases the communicant's union with the Lord, forgives his venial sins, and preserves him from grave sins. Since receiving this sacrament strengthens the bonds of charity between the communicant and Christ, it also reinforces the unity of the Church as the Mystical Body of Christ. (*Catechism,* paragraph 1416).

Having passed form this world to the Father, Christ gives us in the Eucharist the pledge of glory with him. Participation in the Holy Sacrifice identifies us with his Heart, sustains our strength along the pilgrimage of this life, makes us long for eternal life, and unites us even now to the Church in heaven, the Blessed Virgin Mary, and all the saints. (*Catechism,* paragraph 1419).

The liturgy is the work of the whole Christ, head and body. Our high priest celebrates it unceasingly in the heavenly liturgy, with the holy Mother of God, the apostles, all the saints, and the multitude of those who have already entered the kingdom. (*Catechism*, paragraph 1187).

The Liturgy of the Word is an integral part of the celebration. The meaning of the celebration is expressed by the Word of God which is proclaimed and by the response of faith to it. (*Catechism*, paragraph 1190).

Song and music are closely connected with the liturgical action. The criteria for their proper use are the beauty expressive of prayer, the unanimous participation of the assembly, and the sacred character of the celebration. (*Catechism*, paragraph 1191).

Jebb and I get together at least a couple of times a month. Not infrequently we remark on how amazed we are that since we have been attending daily Mass and praying the Rosary every day, our incidence of little personal sins has fallen off dramatically. Those sins that we had for years habitually committed have all but vanished. Personally, I confess, I was for many years unable to conquer certain sins no matter how hard I tried. Now, Jesus cleanses me and strengthens me through Holy Mass and the Holy Rosary so that I am no longer a slave to my sin but, truly and dynamically, a new creation. I owe it all to our Blessed Mother who took me by the hand, spiritually, and showed me what to do. I look forward every day to Mass. It is the highlight of my day. Often on Sundays I will sing in the choir at 9 o'clock Mass and stay for 11o'clock Mass to receive Communion.

The Medjugorje parish celebrates an evening Mass in the Croatian language every day. A morning Mass is celebrated Monday through Saturday and on Sunday pupil Masses are in the morning and the main Croatian Mass at 11 am. The parishioners gather one hour before the evening Masses and pray the Joyful and Sorrowful Mysteries of the Rosary. After Mass they remain and pray the Glorious Mysteries. On Thursday they pray the Luminous Mysteries. At every Croatian Mass I attended there was standing room only and on Sunday I estimate there were at least another 1,000 parishioners seated on benches outside the church. The Mass is broadcast through loudspeakers and the priests bring Holy Communion to those seated outside. Also on Sunday afternoon the parish gathers together and en mass ascends Apparition Hill while praying the Rosary. A priest leads the Rosary and so everyone can hear the broadcasts on a portable loudspeaker. When the currents are favorable the Rosary prayers can then be heard floating in the air over the whole parish. Every Friday afternoon the parish ascends Cross Mountain and prays the Way of the Cross together. Adoration of Jesus in the Most Blessed Sacrament is every Wednesday, Thursday and Saturday at 9:00 pm and 10:00 pm in the summer. Again the church is packed at every service with standing room only in a church that can seat about a thousand people.

Croatian pilgrim daily Masses are celebrated at 1:00 pm during the summer and during winter only on Saturdays. Other language Masses are celebrated in the mornings during the week and some on Sunday afternoon.

It is abundantly clear that the Medjugorje parishioners take Our Lady's messages to heart and that, I think, is why she is able to sustain an Oasis of Peace in Medjugorje.

The Mass is the most holy event of the day. Every day the same miracle occurs throughout the whole world probably somewhere between 400,000 and a 1,000,000 or so times. The bread and wine is changed into the body and blood, soul and divinity of Jesus. The King of heaven and earth comes to us for our good. I am sure that the greatest desire of God is for us to receive his son. That is why our Blessed Mother asks us to come to Holy Mass every day. She says:

"Dear children! God wants to make you holy. Therefore, through me He is inviting you to complete surrender. Let holy mass be your life. Understand that the church is God's palace, the place in which I gather you and want to show you the way to God. Come and pray. Neither look at others nor slander them, but rather, let your life be a testimony on the way of holiness. Churches deserve respect and are set apart as holy because God, who became man, dwells in them day and night. Therefore, little children, believe and pray that the Father increase your faith, and then ask for whatever you need. I am with you and I am rejoicing because of your conversion and I am protecting you with my motherly mantle. Thank you for having responded to my call." (April 25, 1988).

"The Mass is the greatest prayer to God. You will never be able to comprehend its importance. That is why you must be perfect and humble at Mass, and should prepare yourselves beforehand." (*Medjugorje Day by Day,* February 17, loc. cit.).

What can be compared to one Holy Communion? A vast fortune? What price would I pay for one Holy Communion? I would pay with my life for one Holy Communion. Thanks be to God for the gift of Jesus given every day.

Bible

The Bible contains the information we need to absorb so we can learn how to live the Incarnated Life day by day. The devout Christian life is far different from that we experience in our society outside the Church. I have no doubt that Satan's minions attempt minute by minute to convince us that there is not that much difference. However, if that were so, we would sure be a vengeful lot. But no, the Bible clearly sets forth a doctrine of forgiveness. That is why the Church teaching so emphasizes mercy and forgiveness. The secular culture demands retribution. We Christians know no such thing. We only know love. Where did we learn that? Well, from the successors of the Apostles, our Bishops, as they gently guide us in the interpretation of the Bible and from the Holy Spirit who bears witness to our hearts and minds as we read the Bible. Our Blessed Mother knows this and that is why she asks us to read the Bible every day.

"Dear children! Today I call on you to read the Bible every day in your homes and let it be in a visible place so as always to encourage you to read it and to pray. Thank you for having responded to my call." (October 18, 1984).

"... from infancy you have known (the) sacred scriptures, which are capable of giving you wisdom for salvation through faith in Christ Jesus. [16] All scripture is inspired by God and is useful for teaching, for refutation, for correction, and for training in righteousness, [17] so that one who belongs to God may be competent, equipped for every good work." (2 Tim. 3:15-17).

The Church "forcefully and specifically exhorts all the Christian faithful ... to learn 'the surpassing knowledge of Jesus Christ' (Phil 3:8) by frequent reading of the divine Scriptures....Let them remember, however, that prayer should accompany the reading of Sacred Scripture, so that a dialogue takes place between God and man. For 'we speak to him when we pray; we listen to him when we read the divine oracles.'" (*Catechism,* paragraph 2653).

Fasting

There are two ancient documents in the Church Archives. One is known as *Didache* (an Anglicized spelling of the Greek word pronounced did-a-kay. It means teaching). The other is the *Apostolic Constitutions.* Some scholars date the *Didache* as early as 80 AD. Others say more probably around 120 to 200 AD. The *Apostolic Constitutions* also have various scholars assigning different dates. But most agree that, except for the *Canons* at the end, the *Constitutions* are most likely Second to Third Century AD writings. Both the *Didache* and the *Apostolic Constitutions* provide summary information of the teachings of the twelve Apostles. It is significant to note that in both these extra-biblical Church writings of antiquity it is stated that the Church fasts on Wednesdays and Fridays.[3] Of equal interest is that Our Lady, today, recommends that we fast on Wednesdays and Fridays.

The ancient authors of the early Church documents mentioned above state that the reason to fast on Wednesday and Fridays is sacrificial. They say that on Wednesday the

---

[3] *Ante-Nicene Fathers, Volume 7*, pages 379, 445 and 469, Drs. Roberts and Donaldson, Editors, Hendrickson Publishers, Peabody, MA, Reprint June 1995, originally published in the USA by the Christian Literature Publishing Company, 1886, ISBN 1-56563-089-0

Lord was betrayed and condemned and, of course, on Friday he suffered the crucifixion. Therefore, if the Lord could make such sacrifice for us, we should honor him, remember his sacrifice and make our sacrifice by fasting on the appointed days.

It, now, seems strange to me that the whole Body of Christian believers has apparently lost its conviction for fasting. There can be no doubt that our Lord embraced fasting. He specifically refers to fasting in his Sermon on the Mount recorded in the Gospel According To Matthew. The whole Bible is replete with references to prayer and fasting. In fact, the order of presentation of the Lord's teaching in Matthew Chapter 6 is I think not to go unnoticed. Jesus begins by talking about almsgiving, then prayer, then the Lord's Prayer, followed by teaching on fasting. Then he exhorts us to store up treasure in heaven, tells us that the eye is the lamp of the body, reminds us that we cannot serve God and money and then points us to dependence on God alone. Most of the dynamics of the spiritual life are wrapped up in this one chapter and fasting is right in the middle paired with prayer.

Believe it or not, Our Lady says that wars and the natural order can be changed by prayer and fasting. On July 21, 1982, the first years of her apparitions, she said:

"The best fast is on bread and water. Through fasting and prayer, one can stop wars, one can suspend the laws of nature. Charity cannot replace fasting. Those who are not able to fast can sometimes replace it with prayer, charity, and a confession; but everyone, except the sick, must fast." (*Medjugorje Day by Day*, February 5, loc. cit.).

The testimony of Medjugorje related to the fall of Communism and the Yugoslav Civil War of 1992 – 1995 are proof enough of Our Lady's declaration. For interesting reading on the subject see Janice Connell's book, *The Visions Of The Children.*

Fasting also helps us discipline ourselves. If we can overcome our desire for food and regularly deny ourselves the satisfaction of eating we find that we can overcome many other sensual desires – even addictions. However, to be successful this self-discipline must be practiced secretly and with devotion and love for God.

"When you fast, do not look gloomy like the hypocrites. They neglect their appearance, so that they may appear to others to be fasting. Amen, I say to you, they have received their reward. [17] But when you fast, anoint your head and wash your face, [18] so that you may not appear to be fasting, except to your Father who is hidden. And your Father who sees what is hidden will repay you. (Matthew 6:16-18)

The interior penance of the Christian can be expressed in many and various ways. Scripture and the Fathers insist above all on three forms, fasting, prayer and almsgiving, which expresses conversion in relation to oneself, to God and to others. (*Catechism*, paragraph 1434)

Confession

Medjugorje has more than once been called the confessional of the world. Thousands line up at the confessionals to celebrate the Sacrament of Reconciliation. It is no wonder when you consider that most everyone who goes on pilgrimage to Medjugorje feels the presence of the Holy. In such presence there is an overwhelming desire to get clean inside. And that is the issue.

"I am happy because you have begun to receive the sacrament of reconciliation on a monthly basis. This is good for the whole world."

"Do not go to confession only through habit, to remain the same afterwards. No, that is not good. Confession should invigorate your faith; it should refresh you and bring you closer to Jesus. If confession does not mean anything to you, truly, you will be converted with great difficulty.

One must invite people to go to confession each month, especially the first Saturday. Here I have not spoken about it yet.... Do what I have told you. There are numerous who do not observe it. Monthly confession will be a remedy for the church in the West. One must convey this message to the West.[4]

For me Sacramental Confession is essential to the Incarnated Life. Certainly there is absolutely no one who can go a whole month without somehow wounding the Sacred Heart of Jesus. That for me is reason enough. I need to receive absolution for the hurt I cause my Lord. But what keeps us away from celebrating the Sacrament of Reconciliation? Pride, shame, embarrassment? Perhaps. Telling our deepest, darkest secret to another human being?

Once I apologized to the priest for having to hear the despicable thing I did. He reminded me that it was not about him or me but about God and his forgiveness. And so someone might say, "Well then why do I have to go to a priest to confess? Can't I just confess directly to God?" I answer: now that the Scriptures have become more open to

---

[4] This and the preceding two messages are excerpted from *Medjugorje Day By Day*, April 17, December 11 and March 11 respectively.

me,[5] a close reading of the Gospels demonstrates that it is the first disciples of Jesus who were given the authority to forgive sins in his name. Those disciples passed that authority to the bishops who authorized priests to give absolution. This for example is how the magisterium of the Church interprets Matthew 16:18 and John 20:23. Also, the Sacred Tradition substantiates this practice of the Church from its infancy. Although not then denominated as a Sacrament, the spirit of confessing before the priest was certainly a part of Church life.

For example, St. Ignatius, who was born the same year that the Lord Jesus began his public ministry, was, along with St. Polycarp, a disciple of St. John the Apostle. He was bishop of Antioch where he voluntarily presented himself to Trajan, confessed himself a Christian and was immediately sentenced to die in the Circus at Rome. On his trip to Rome he stopped in Smyrna (in present day Turkey), the see of Polycarp, where he wrote four epistles. In his epistle to the Ephesians he writes: "It is therefore befitting that you should in every way glorify Jesus Christ, who hath glorified you, that by a unanimous obedience 'ye may be perfectly joined together in the same mind, and in the same judgment, and may all speak the same thing concerning the same thing,' and that, being subject to the bishop and the presbytery, ye may in all respects be sanctified."[6] St. Ignatius carried this same theme throughout the four epistles. It is, therefore, in my mind, sound reasoning to conclude that if everything was to be done subject to the bishop and the priests then certainly the penitent would have been heard by the priest and absolved of sin by the priest. This had to have

---

[5] By more open I mean that things make more sense to me now because I submit to the *interpretive authority* of the teaching magisterium of the one holy and apostolic Catholic Church that has been in full, uninterrupted communion with Jesus Christ for nearly two thousand years.

[6] *Ante-Nicene Fathers Vol. 1*, page 50, loc. cit.

been instituted by St. John, the Apostle, because it is what Saints Ignatius and Polycarp were teaching. Also, I would think it highly likely that St. Ignatius asked St. Polycarp to review the epistle before it was sent out so they would be in agreement.

Furthermore, again the *Apostolic Constitutions*, established way back then, perhaps as early as 150 to 200 AD, the practice of the Sacrament of Reconciliation, although it was not known by that name. I set forth below a direct quote from Book II, Section III of *Constitutions Of The Holy Apostles.* The Section is entitled *How The Bishop Is To Treat The Innocent, The Guilty, And The Penitent.*

> OF REPENTANCE, THE MANNER OF IT, AND RULES ABOUT IT
>
> XVI. When thou seest the offender, with severity command him to be cast out; and as he is going out, let the deacons also treat him with severity, and then let them go and seek for him, and detain him out of the Church; and when they come in, let them entreat thee for him. For our Savior Himself entreated His Father for those who had sinned, as it is written in the Gospel: "Father, forgive them; for they know not what they do." Then order the offender to come in; and if upon examination thou findest that he is penitent, and fit to be received at all into the Church when thou hast afflicted him his days of fasting, according to the degree of his offense — as two, three, five, or seven weeks — so set him at liberty, and speak such things to him as are fit to be said in way of reproof, instruction, and exhortation to a sinner for his reformation, that so he may continue privately in his

> humility, and pray to God to be merciful to him, saying: "If Thou, O Lord, shouldest mark iniquities, O Lord, who should stand? For with Thee there is propitiation." Of this sort of declaration is that which is said in the book of Genesis to Cain: "Thou hast sinned; be quiet;" that is, do not go on in sin. For that a sinner ought to be ashamed for his own sin, that oracle of God delivered to Moses concerning Miriam is a sufficient proof, when he prayed that she might be forgiven. For says God to him: "If her father had spit in her face, should she not be ashamed? Let her be shut out of the camp seven days, and afterwards let her come in again." We therefore ought to do so with offenders, when they profess their repentance, — namely, to separate them some determinate time, according to the proportion of their offense, and afterwards, like fathers to children, receive them again upon their repentance. [7]

It is clear to me that the Church has from its very early beginnings come to the Sacrament of Reconciliation before a priest. Of course, today, the celebration of the Sacrament is nowhere near as severe as it was then. Then, the concentration was on the love of God in his justice. Now, the concentration is on the love of God in his mercy.

Our Lady recommends Sacramental Confession for us whenever we feel the need but no less than monthly. Although she says we are cleansed at the Mass, she still calls for monthly confession. We might wonder why both? I think the *Catechism* answers the question for us.

---

[7] *Ante-Nicene Fathers, Vol. 7*, page 402, loc. cit.

Without being strictly necessary, confession of everyday faults (venial sins) is nevertheless strongly recommended by the Church. Indeed the regular confession of our venial sins helps us form our conscience, fight against evil tendencies, let ourselves be healed by Christ and progress in the life of the Spirit. By receiving more frequently through this sacrament the gift of the Father's mercy, we are spurred to be merciful as he is merciful:[footnote inserted here is to compare to Lk 6:36]

> *Whoever confesses his sins...is already working with God. God indicts your sins; if you also indict them, you are joined with God. Man and sinner are, so to speak, two realities: when you hear "man" – this is what God has made; when you hear "sinner" - this is what man himself has made. Destroy what you have made, so that God may save what he has made....When you begin to abhor what you have made, it is then that your good works are beginning, since you are accusing yourself of your evil works. The beginning of good works is the confession of evil works. You do the truth and come to the light [St. Augustine]* (*Catechism*, paragraph 1458).

So, as for me, I will listen to Our Blessed Mother, and come to Sacramental Confession every month. For I know I need to if I am to pursue holiness. And, as I already said, it is my goal to become more holy. I have no desire to become more worldly.

In her desire to see us surrender to God and convert from a set of values that are driven by human culture and society to that which our Blessed Mother tells us God values, she gave us the five little stones. This is not to say that all values of human culture and society are bad. Obviously, there are many good values that we humans esteem. But when we exclude or assign low priority to heavenly values we run afoul of God.

If we will commit time, much time, to the practice of the five little stones Our Lady recommends, we will experience conversion if our hearts are open to it. Then we must stay on the path of conversion for the rest of our days here on earth. Therefore, her messages repeatedly stress the importance of prayer (especially daily rosary), Holy Mass, Bible study, fasting and sacramental confession. In fact the tone of her messages asserts vital implications for our eternal condition. She insists that we must have our spiritual lives as top priority and devotion to God as our utmost guiding principle in life. This is the same call that Jesus made for the entire world. Mary has come to help us answer the call and lead us to a strong faith in her son, our brother and Lord, Jesus.

"From the very beginning I have been conveying the messages of God to the world. It is a great pity not to believe it. Faith is essential, but one cannot compel a person to believe. Faith is the foundation from which everything else flows (First Years 12-31-81)" (*Medjugorje Day By Day*, August 27, loc. cit.)

Photograph of a statue of Our Lady located at the church in Tihalinja. I have read that the visionaries say that although it falls far short of capturing the indescribable beauty of Our Lady it looks more like her than any other they have seen. Photo by Romilio Castillo.

Mary's Love

"If you knew how much I love you, you would cry for joy!"

A thorough study of Church doctrine which is based on Sacred Scripture and Sacred Tradition will undoubtedly reveal that there are really only two different states of being for the human race: eternal life or eternal death. That is, we are actually either eternally alive or eternally dead. I say this in rather inflexible terms because I am speaking of the spirit, not of the body. The Apostles understood this and it has been passed down from bishop to bishop throughout the millennia.

Amen, amen, I say to you, whoever hears my word and believes in the one who sent me has eternal life and will not come to condemnation, but has passed from death to life. (John 5:24)

Following St. Paul, the Church has always taught that the overwhelming misery which oppresses men and their inclination toward evil and death cannot be understood apart from their connection with Adam's sin and the fact that he has transmitted to us a sin with which we are all born afflicted, a sin which is "the death of the soul." Because of this certainty of faith, the Church baptizes for the remission of sins even tiny infants who have not committed personal sin. (*Catechism,* paragraph 403).

This is somewhat mystical and maybe hard to grasp. But I think it is vitally important that we face the stark reality that we are spirits residing in biological bodies. Some day the body will forever cease to function. Our souls will go on forever. The question is: what is the condition of our soul? What is our state of being? And are we even concerned about it?

When Nicodemus came to Jesus to affirm his belief that Jesus indeed came from God he was taken aback by the Lord's response. For Nicodemus was told: *"Amen, amen, I say to you, no one can see the kingdom of God without being born from above."* (John 3:3). Nicodemus was amazed for he rightly understood what Jesus said but had difficulty accepting it. He asks: *"How can a person once grown old be born again? Surely he cannot reenter his mother's womb and be born again, can he?" Jesus answered, "Amen, amen, I say to you, no one can enter the kingdom of God without being born of water and Spirit. What is born of flesh is flesh and what is born of spirit is spirit."* (John 3:4-6).

So it is pretty clear that for one to enter the kingdom of God one must first be re-born in the spirit. One must be born of water and the Spirit. The Apostles taught that this is accomplished through Baptism with water in the name of the Father, the Son and the Holy Spirit. *One becomes a member of this people* [the Church] *not by a physical birth, but by being "born anew," a birth of "water and the Spirit," that is, by faith in Christ, and Baptism.* (*Catechism* paragraph 782).

Through the Sacrament of Baptism we pass from death to life. Our souls are participants in the death and resurrection of Jesus. We go down into the water dead and arise from the water alive. Adam's sin (Original Sin) that was transmitted to us is taken away. As Saint Paul says and the Church has forever proclaimed:

We were indeed buried with him through baptism into death, so that, just as Christ was raised from the dead by the glory of the Father, we too might live in newness of life. (Romans 6:4).

The following paragraphs of the *Catechism* bring to light what the Apostles taught and handed down to the Bishops as verified by Sacred Scripture and Sacred Tradition.

1263 *By Baptism all sins are forgiven, original sin and all personal sins, as well as all punishment for sin. In those who have been [so] reborn nothing remains that would impede their entry into the Kingdom of God, neither Adam's sin, nor personal sin, nor the consequences of sin, the gravest of which is separation from God.*
1265 *Baptism not only purifies from all sins, but also makes the neophyte "a new creature," an adopted son of God, who has become a "partaker of the divine nature," member of Christ and co-heir with him, and a temple of the Holy Spirit.*
1266 *The Most Holy Trinity gives the baptized sanctifying grace, the grace of justification:*
- enabling them to believe in God, to hope in him, and to love him through the theological virtues;
- giving them the power to live and act under the prompting of the Holy Spirit through the gifts of the Holy Spirit;
- allowing them to grow in goodness through the moral virtues.
Thus the whole organism of the Christian's supernatural life has its roots in Baptism. (*Catechism,* paragraphs 1263, 1265 and 1266).

This is the great gift from God given through Jesus and made possible by his incarnation, life, death, resurrection and ascension. It is only ours to receive by coming to the waters of Baptism and faith. We who are baptized have all of the aforesaid available to us. Our Blessed Mother knows all this far better than we do. She desires our salvation far more than we do ourselves. I think she wants us to realize our state of being, to be at peace, to be happy and to love the Lord our God with all our hearts, minds and bodies and to love our neighbors. It is only we ourselves who tarnish the gift by abuse. We fall away from the life of love that God, who is love, desires for us, his children, to live. That is why, I think, our Mother and Queen, who loves us dearly, is calling us to convert, trust God and to live the Incarnated Life of love. She wants us to live a life devoted to our Father who loves us. She wants us to actually live what we say we believe. She wants us every day to reap the benefit of our Baptism. That is why she calls us to live her messages. She wants us to voluntarily seek purity so that our involuntary purgation will be minimized if not eliminated. She knows what she is talking about.

In the face of evil, injustice and hardship she is full of courage because she is the Mother of God. She is the Mother of the Church and loves all of us, her children, so much that if we could be with her like the Medjugorje visionaries we would, like them, cry for joy. I don't know about you, but I pray that I can draw on her spiritual strength and her trust in God to inspire me so that I may know how to overcome all the obstacles that I encounter in this world.

Dear children! I am calling everyone [sic] *of you to start living in God's love. Dear children, you are ready to commit sin, and to put yourselves in the hand of Satan without reflecting. I call on each one of you to consciously decide for God and against Satan. I am your Mother and, therefore, I want to lead you all to perfect holiness. I want each one of you to be happy here on earth and to be with me in Heaven. That is, dear children, the purpose of my coming here and it's my desire. Thank you for having responded to my call."* May 25, 1987.

Of all the personages we encounter in the whole Bible there is only one who is called "favored one" (full of grace). This is the greeting the Archangel Gabriel gave to Mary. He told her she found favor with God. She is full of God's grace. It is clear in the content of her many messages given in our time in Medjugorje that she desires to impart to us the graces of God so we may live the Incarnated Life.

The Incarnated Life is a life of love. Holiness is born of love. Our Blessed Mother Mary comes to us at the pleasure of God to teach us about love. She takes us, her children, by the hand and walks us to Church. It is the Church whose Prophet, Priest and King, Jesus, established. It is Mary's School of Love. I believe she is, today, exercising her God-given freedom to intercede for us like never before because she loves us so much and we love so little.

I am learning about love because I enrolled in Our Lady's school. She holds class in Medjugorje. One of her best pupils and teacher's aid is Father Slavko Barbaric. I speak of him in the present tense because although he departed this earth November 24, 2000, I feel he is still with us in spirit and in his writings. He was in his 55th year when on Križevac, after the Stations of the Cross, his body fell over and quit working.

Father Barbaric is one of the most loved priests in Medjugorje. He held a Doctor of Religious Pedagogy degree and was a licensed psychotherapist. His body and soul were devoted to the work Our Lady calls us to in her messages. He lived the Incarnated Life. His was a life in Medjugorje that was a living witness to the fruits of love. He wrote many books on the subject – mostly as aids to understanding and applying Our Lady's call. I wish to close my story by sharing with you several excerpts from his book *In the School of Love.*[1] I am sure I will read this book many times more over the remaining course of my days here on earth.

> When I love, I have time, I have patience, I am attentive and I am vulnerable. But when I do not love, then I lose my temper and I do not have time and things make me tired and angry. Therefore, the state of love is, at the same time, a way to peace, to understanding and to forgiveness. A state of no-love is the path to destruction. We can preserve our inner peace and remain rested only if we love. We live in a constant rat race. If people loved, many would be saved from psychological illnesses, and in a great part, from many physical illnesses. The way of love is the way of life! [Page 18]

> The one who loves is always in a personal meeting with the one he loves….to love means to yearn to know the loved one more and more. He who loves God learns about Him more and more, and loves Him all the more. [Page 22]

> He who has no time for prayer does not love God and is not growing in God's presence. [Page 23]

---

[1] Father Slavko Barbaric, *In the School of Love*, ©Zupni ured Medugorje, 2000, Informativni Centar "Mir" Medugorje, Medugorje, B-H

Human happiness is unthinkable without peace in the heart. Peace gives birth to a deep security and the heart is joyful. A joyful heart is open to love, and love increases joy and peace. Peace, love and joy are certainly the deepest desires of every human heart. Therefore, a human being tries to do everything to achieve that peace which gives birth to joy and which, in turn, increases love. [Page 35]

Mary is pointing out to us the divine way to this peace, joy and love. The first condition is an openness to God, for He is the spring of peace, joy and love. He is the Creator and also the Lord of our hearts. To open oneself does not mean anything more than to accept His love, to allow His love to flow into the heart with peace and, in a daily encounter with God, to allow His peace, joy and love to grow. Mary knows that our emotions and problems can become obstacles to openness to God. Therefore, She is inviting us to give Her our feelings, everything that bothers us, even things that make us happy. Because success and failure, health and illness, riches and poverty, all can become obstacles to our opening up to God. They can become fateful obstacles on the way towards peace.

Each one of us needs consolation, human and divine. If we only want peace, joy and love on a human level and by human ways, then we accept the way of betrayal and disappointment. A person enchanted by this world excludes a divine awareness in himself and prepares a stage in which he has to be disappointed. It becomes again a moment for seeking divine consolation, divine peace and love. Happy are all those who hear the offer that God, through Mary, wants to fill them with peace, joy and love, so they can open themselves to this offer and accept its conditions. [Page 36]

The more a person is free from his own self, the more he will be able to sacrifice himself for others. We begin to sacrifice ourselves when we love someone. Without love, sacrifice is impossible and unthinkable; with love, sacrifice loses its unpleasantness.
Christ has been sacrificing for us from the beginning. He gives His life and His cross as a gift to the Father for us. His action is redemptive because He did it all without pressure, but with love, freely.
Mary, in Her school, asks for prayer, fasting, confession, Holy Mass, reading of the Sacred Scriptures. She wants us to help others, to give our life for them. She asks for sacrifice, but with love. She thanks us for all our actions that are done with love. [Page 39]

Our human experience tells us and reminds us that our actions, our efforts and even our love towards others and towards God are efforts for our own gain. What we seek is recognition, a response to love, respect from others and praise. On a human level, we can understand and justify this. But we have to admit, however, that even our acts of love are clouded by selfishness, personal advancement and a desire for self-glory and sometimes by desires to control and to be in control. There is probably no other way on the human level but, by Divine Love, our actions can become free from our personal intentions and be more purified.

This kind of gift giving makes us happy, even when our life is in question. He who expects immediate payment, reward, success, or recognition will be a burden to himself because he has to succeed and be recognized, and to others because others are expected, either out of regard or out of fear, to give praise. This kind of person is like a beggar or hired worker who runs after daily success or daily reward. At that point, a person can either free himself so that whatever he does gives glory to God, or he can enslave and bind himself in his actions, looking at everything through his own glasses and never being happy or satisfied. God glorifies Himself through those who continuously cooperate with Him and who continuously serve in humility.

Mary calls us to prayer. Through prayer, we can cleanse ourselves, because prayer is meeting God. In prayer, a person learns to yield to God and to others. Without prayer, it is impossible to realize true Christian love. Without prayer, we are always in danger of taking over what does not belong to us, thus overshadowing the glory of God and torturing those around us.

Mary's role is to teach us how to love God and other people correctly. Through prayer, we receive strength to do that which we recognize as good. If we notice that we are not advancing spiritually, then that is a sign that we are not praying enough. Let us begin to pray for the Lord to purify our intentions! [Pages 59 & 60]

Mary leads us to Jesus. She cannot, in any way, bypass Christ who suffered and with whom She suffered. [Page 61] [My comment - Let us never forget that our dear Mother could do nothing as her dear son agonized on the cross. His agony was hers and hers his. She saw his divine blood spill from his Sacred Heart onto the ground, mixing with the trampled soil to become bloody mud. Blood he shed for the sins of the whole world. And when ripped off the cross he, the Holy Son of God, son of Mary, fell into her lap.]

Many people in today's world are walking the way of unrest, looking for peace but becoming even more unpeaceful. Desiring salvation, they walk farther from it. The further away we are from peace and salvation, the more anxious we become. The more anxious we are, the easier we lose the way and, instead of peace and salvation, unrest and damnation increase. God does not want us to destroy ourselves in this way. His will is our peace and our salvation because He knows that He is peace to our soul and He is life for us. He is the way for the one who is lost, the light for the one in darkness, joy to the one who mourns and He is calling all of us. [Page 106]

Whoever decides for life, decides for God, Who wants to enrich us with His peace today, tomorrow, every day and for all eternity. The goal is accepted, the way exists. We only need to start! [Page 118]

Conclusion

So, all things considered, as it turns out I found that the only obstacle to peace for me is me. All I have to do is surrender to God so that he is top priority for me each and every day. When Satan attempts to divert my thinking away from the things of God to the things of the world, I pray. When I am tempted by my own sensual and material desires, I pray. To gain strength for the battle and be cleansed by the body and blood of Jesus, I am at Holy Mass every day. To keep my thinking clear and correct, I read the Bible every day. To honour our Lord's sacrifice, I fast every Wednesday and Friday. To keep me humble and acknowledge my sinful self, I celebrate the Sacrament of Reconciliation every month. In this way, Mary's way, I am at peace with God and myself.

The peace I and many, many others have discovered is a true and lasting peace. It is the peace that allows one to be free of self and capable of a radical change in view on life. It is the peace that brings quiet, steadfast joy through love and forgiveness of others. It is the peace that fills the heart with love for Mary, the Holy Spirit, Jesus and the Eternal Father. It is the peace of God that fills one with the strength to be humble and selfless. So that instead of physically assaulting an unfaithful spouse, one can actually forgive the other's indiscretion and continue in the bond of holy matrimony. Instead of beating someone up because they did something wrong against you, like stealing your golf ball, you can forgive and not even be fazed by it. Such forgiveness is only possible through overriding love. And that is what peace brings.

For me, the peace began to seep into me when I first got serious about the five devotional practices Our Lady gives us. In Medjugorje the cup of my soul was filled with peace. Such abundance of peace brings everything into focus. God is spirit. I am spirit. I must live spiritually or I die. I pray:

O, Mary, Mother dear,
Bless and teach your child here.
To your heart, draw me near.
Whisper love in my ear.
Amen

"Dear children! Also today I call you to prayer. Little children, pray until prayer becomes a joy for you. Only in this way each of you will discover peace in the heart and your soul will be content. You will feel the need to witness to others the love that you feel in your heart and life. I am with you and intercede before God for all of you. Thank you for having responded to my call." [July 25, 2003]

"Dear children! Also today I call you to give thanks to God in your heart for all the graces which He gives you, also through the signs and colors that are in nature. God wants to draw you closer to Himself and moves you to give Him glory and thanks. Therefore, little children, I call you anew to pray, pray, pray and do not forget that I am with you. I intercede before God for each of you until your joy in Him is complete. Thank you for having responded to my call." [August 25, 2003]

"Dear children! Also today I call you to come closer to my heart. Only in this way, will you comprehend the gift of my presence here among you. I desire, little children, to lead you to the heart of my Son Jesus; but you resist and do not desire to open your hearts to prayer. Again, little children, I call you not to be deaf but to comprehend my call, which is salvation for you. Thank you for having responded to my call." [September 25, 2003]

Postscript

Our Lady's messages from Medjugorje convey the need for urgent action. She has revealed ten secrets to Mirjana, Ivanka and Jakov. When these three visionaries received the tenth secret from our Blessed Mother they ceased to have daily visions. Vicka, Marija and Ivan have been given nine secrets. They still receive daily visions and on the 25th of every month Marija receives Our Lady's message to give to the whole world.

The visionaries have not been allowed by our Blessed Mother to reveal what the secrets are until just before what they are about is to occur. However, the visionaries have been permitted to disclose that one secret involves a permanent sign of unmistakable supernatural origin. It will be preceded by two supernatural warnings. The warnings are secrets one and two that Mirjana holds and will occur in her lifetime. She is now 38 years old. The implication is that the warnings are intended to spur the world population to surrender to God.

The tenth secret is particularly horrible. It involves potential chastisements from God for the sin of the world – the rejection of Jesus. Mirjana is said to weep every time she thinks of this secret. Needless to say, she tries not to think about it much. The portent of things to come is not from the worldly perspective a good thing. In Our Lady's own words, she pleads with us:

My angel, pray for unbelievers. People will tear their hair, brother will plead with brother, they will curse their past lives lived without God. They will repent, but it will be too late. Now is the time for conversion. I have been calling you for the past four years. Pray for them. Invite everyone to pray the rosary." (*Medjugorje Day By Day*, June 18, loc. cit., a special message given August 15, 1985 – the same day the Church celebrates the Feast of the Assumption of the Blessed Virgin Mary).

Can you imagine what frustration and personal panic could cause people to tear out their hair? Or what it might be like for there to be such worldwide chaos that all one can do is plead for mercy because there is nothing else that can be done? I think the shock of divine chastisement, if it comes, will be devastating – beyond comprehension for most everybody. However, there is hope. The chastisement can be averted if people will convert – if we will surrender and obey our Maker.

Just the other day at Mass a prayer card from the Missionaries of Africa literally fell into my lap. I suppose someone put it into the missal and songbook rack in the pew. For when I reached for the songbook the prayer card fell into my lap. I would like to share with you the prayer on the card:

> O Virgin full of courage, may your spiritual strength and trust in God inspire us, so that we might know how to overcome all the obstacles that we encounter in life. Teach us to have joyful hope of the coming of God's kingdom, and of a "new heaven and a new earth." May God's Spirit deepen our

> unity and love so that the Promise made to us by your Son may reach its fulfillment at the end of time.

I prayed and fasted for three days over the meaning of this card falling into my lap. The answer I received was to include it in this book. Now someone might think that is a bit "out there." And that it may be. But if it is "out there" it is also in my heart. For I know what our Blessed Mother promises and I trust her more than I trust myself.

Finally, let me say that in the face of Our Lady's call to conversion and peace I firmly believe that, other than our Blessed Mother, we can find no better role model than His Holiness, John Paul II, Bishop Servant of the Servants of God for everlasting memory. Consider this: In a message through the Medjugorje locutionists given September 16, 1983, Our Lady said –

"In my messages, I recommend to everyone and to the Holy Father in particular, to spread the messages which I have received from my Son here at Medjugorje. I wish to entrust to the Pope, the word with which I came here: "mir" (peace), which he must spread everywhere. And here is a message which is especially for him: that he bring together the Christian people through his word and his preaching; that he spread, particularly among the young people, the messages which he has received from the Father in his prayer, with which God inspires him." (*Medjugorje Day By Day,* June 29, loc. cit.).

And what has His Holiness, John Paul II, been doing for the last twenty years? Exactly what our Blessed Mother, Mary, asked him to do.

Likewise, I am convinced that we all would be wise to heed Our Lady's advice even as she expresses it in the most recent message at the time of this writing:

"Dear children! I call you anew to consecrate yourselves to my heart and the heart of my Son Jesus. I desire, little children, to lead you all on the way of conversion and holiness. Only in this way, through you, we can lead all the more souls on the way of salvation. Do not delay, little children, but say with all your heart: 'I want to help Jesus and Mary that all the more brothers and sisters may come to know the way of holiness.' In this way, you will feel the contentment of being friends of Jesus. Thank you for having responded to my call." [October 25, 2003]

"It is not enough to discover Christ – you must bring him to others! The world today is one great mission land, even in countries of longstanding Christian tradition."

Pope John Paul II

Appendix One

St. Paul's Epistle To The Romans Chapters 8 and 12

<u>Romans 8:1-39</u>

Hence, now there is no condemnation for those who are in Christ Jesus. [2] For the law of the spirit of life in Christ Jesus has freed you from the law of sin and death. [3] For what the law, weakened by the flesh, was powerless to do, this God has done: by sending his own Son in the likeness of sinful flesh and for the sake of sin, he condemned sin in the flesh, [4] so that the righteous decree of the law might be fulfilled in us, who live not according to the flesh but according to the spirit. [5] For those who live according to the flesh are concerned with the things of the flesh, but those who live according to the spirit with the things of the spirit. [6] The concern of the flesh is death, but the concern of the spirit is life and peace. [7] For the concern of the flesh is hostility toward God; it does not submit to the law of God, nor can it; [8] and those who are in the flesh cannot please God. [9] But you are not in the flesh; on the contrary, you are in the spirit, if only the Spirit of God dwells in you. Whoever does not have the Spirit of Christ does not belong to him. [10] But if Christ is in you, although the body is dead because of sin, the spirit is alive because of righteousness. [11] If the Spirit of the one who raised Jesus from the dead dwells in you, the one who raised Christ from the dead will give life to your mortal bodies also, through his Spirit that dwells in you. [12] Consequently, brothers, we are not debtors to the flesh, to live according to the flesh. [13] For if you live according to the flesh, you will die, but if by the spirit you put to death the deeds of the body, you will live.

[14] For those who are led by the Spirit of God are children of God. [15] For you did not receive a spirit of slavery to fall back into fear, but you received a spirit of adoption, through which we cry, "Abba, Father!" [16] The Spirit itself bears witness with our spirit that we are children of God, [17] and if children, then heirs, heirs of God and joint heirs with Christ, if only we suffer with him so that we may also be glorified with him.

[18] I consider that the sufferings of this present time are as nothing compared with the glory to be revealed for us. [19] For creation awaits with eager expectation the revelation of the children of God; [20] for creation was made subject to futility, not of its own accord but because of the one who subjected it, in hope [21] that creation itself would be set free from slavery to corruption and share in the glorious freedom of the children of God. [22] We know that all creation is groaning in labor pains even until now; [23] and not only that, but we ourselves, who have the firstfruits of the Spirit, we also groan within ourselves as we wait for adoption, the redemption of our bodies. [24] For in hope we were saved. Now hope that sees for itself is not hope. For

who hopes for what one sees? [25] But if we hope for what we do not see, we wait with endurance.

[26] In the same way, the Spirit too comes to the aid of our weakness; for we do not know how to pray as we ought, but the Spirit itself intercedes with inexpressible groanings. [27] And the one who searches hearts knows what is the intention of the Spirit, because it intercedes for the holy ones according to God's will.

[28] We know that all things work for good for those who love God, who are called according to his purpose. [29] For those he foreknew he also predestined to be conformed to the image of his Son, so that he might be the firstborn among many brothers. [30] And those he predestined he also called; and those he called he also justified; and those he justified he also glorified.

[31] What then shall we say to this? If God is for us, who can be against us? [32] He who did not spare his own Son but handed him over for us all, how will he not also give us everything else along with him? [33] Who will bring a charge against God's chosen ones? It is God who acquits us. [34] Who will condemn? It is Christ (Jesus) who died, rather, was raised, who also is at the right hand of God, who indeed intercedes for us. [35] What will separate us from the love of Christ? Will anguish, or distress, or persecution, or famine, or nakedness, or peril, or the sword? [36] As it is written:

"For your sake we are being slain all the day;
we are looked upon as sheep to be slaughtered."

[37] No, in all these things we conquer overwhelmingly through him who loved us. [38] For I am convinced that neither death, nor life, nor angels, nor principalities, nor present things, nor future things, nor powers, [39] nor height, nor depth, nor any other creature will be able to separate us from the love of God in Christ Jesus our Lord.

Romans 12:1-21

I urge you therefore, brothers, by the mercies of God, to offer your bodies as a living sacrifice, holy and pleasing to God, your spiritual worship. [2] Do not conform yourselves to this age but be transformed by the renewal of your mind, that you may discern what is the will of God, what is good and pleasing and perfect.

[3] For by the grace given to me I tell everyone among you not to think of himself more highly than one ought to think, but to think soberly, each according to the measure of faith that God has apportioned. [4] For as in one body we have many parts, and all the parts do not have the same function, [5] so we, though many, are one body in Christ and individually parts of one another. [6] Since we have gifts that differ according to the grace given to us, let us exercise them: if prophecy, in proportion to the faith; [7] if ministry, in ministering; if one is a teacher, in teaching; [8] if one exhorts, in exhortation; if one contributes, in generosity; if one is over others, with diligence; if one does acts of mercy, with cheerfulness.

[9] Let love be sincere; hate what is evil, hold on to what is good; [10] love one another with mutual affection; anticipate one another in showing honor. [11] Do not grow slack in zeal, be fervent in spirit, serve the Lord. [12] Rejoice in hope, endure in affliction, persevere in prayer. [13] Contribute to the needs of the holy ones, exercise hospitality. [14] Bless those who persecute (you), bless and do not curse them. [15] Rejoice with those who rejoice, weep with those who weep. [16] Have the same regard for one another; do not be haughty but associate with the lowly; do not be wise in your own estimation. [17] Do not repay anyone evil for evil; be concerned for what is noble in the sight of all. [18] If possible, on your part, live at peace with all. [19] Beloved, do not look for revenge but leave room for the wrath; for it is written, "Vengeance is mine, I will repay, says the Lord."

[20] Rather, "if your enemy is hungry, feed him; if he is thirsty, give him something to drink; for by so doing you will heap burning coals upon his head." [21] Do not be conquered by evil but conquer evil with good.

Appendix Two

New Testament Word Reference Guide To "Peace"

Matthew 10:12-13

As you enter a house, wish it peace. [13] If the house is worthy, let your peace come upon it; if not, let your peace return to you.

Matthew 10:34

"Do not think that I have come to bring peace upon the earth. I have come to bring not peace but the sword.

Mark 5:34

He said to her, "Daughter, your faith has saved you. Go in peace and be cured of your affliction."

Mark 9:50

Salt is good, but if salt becomes insipid, with what will you restore its flavor? Keep salt in yourselves and you will have peace with one another."

Luke 1:79

to shine on those who sit in darkness and death's shadow,
to guide our feet into the path of peace."

Luke 2:14

"Glory to God in the highest
and on earth peace to those on whom his favor rests."

Luke 2:29

"Now, Master, you may let your servant go
in peace, according to your word,

Luke 7:50

But he said to the woman, "Your faith has saved you; go in peace."

Luke 8:48

He said to her, "Daughter, your faith has saved you; go in peace."

Luke 10:5-6

Into whatever house you enter, first say, 'Peace to this household.' [6] If a peaceful person lives there, your peace will rest on him; but if not, it will return to you.

Luke 12:51

Do you think that I have come to establish peace on the earth? No, I tell you, but rather division.

Luke 14:32

But if not, while he is still far away, he will send a delegation to ask for peace terms.

Luke 19:38

They proclaimed:

"Blessed is the king who comes in the name of the Lord.
Peace in heaven and glory in the highest."

Luke 19:42

saying, "If this day you only knew what makes for peace--but now it is hidden from your eyes.

Luke 24:36

While they were still speaking about this, he stood in their midst and said to them, "Peace be with you."

John 14:27

Peace I leave with you; my peace I give to you. Not as the world gives do I give it to you. Do not let your hearts be troubled or afraid.

John 16:33

I have told you this so that you might have peace in me. In the world you will have trouble, but take courage, I have conquered the world."

John 20:19

On the evening of that first day of the week, when the doors were locked, where the disciples were, for fear of the Jews, Jesus came and stood in their midst and said to them, "Peace be with you."

John 20:21

(Jesus) said to them again, "Peace be with you. As the Father has sent me, so I send you."

John 20:26

Now a week later his disciples were again inside and Thomas was with them. Jesus came, although the doors were locked, and stood in their midst and said, "Peace be with you."

Acts 9:31

The church throughout all Judea, Galilee, and Samaria was at peace. It was being built up and walked in the fear of the Lord, and with the consolation of the holy Spirit it grew in numbers.

Acts 10:36

You know the word (that) he sent to the Israelites as he proclaimed peace through Jesus Christ, who is Lord of all,

Acts 12:20

He had long been very angry with the people of Tyre and Sidon, who now came to him in a body. After winning over Blastus, the king's chamberlain, they sued for peace because their country was supplied with food from the king's territory.

Acts 15:24

Since we have heard that some of our number (who went out) without any mandate from us have upset you with their teachings and disturbed your peace of mind,

Acts 15:33

After they had spent some time there, they were sent off with greetings of peace from the brothers to those who had commissioned them.

Acts 16:36

The jailer reported the (se) words to Paul, "The magistrates have sent orders that you be released. Now, then, come out and go in peace."

Acts 24:2
When he was called, Tertullus began to accuse him, saying, "Since we have attained much peace through you, and reforms have been accomplished in this nation through your provident care,

Romans 1:7
to all the beloved of God in Rome, called to be holy. Grace to you and peace from God our Father and the Lord Jesus Christ.

Romans 2:10
But there will be glory, honor, and peace for everyone who does good, Jew first and then Greek.

Romans 3:17
and the way of peace they know not.

Romans 5:1
Therefore, since we have been justified by faith, we have peace with God through our Lord Jesus Christ,

Romans 8:6
The concern of the flesh is death, but the concern of the spirit is life and peace.

Romans 12:18
If possible, on your part, live at peace with all.

Romans 14:17
For the kingdom of God is not a matter of food and drink, but of righteousness, peace, and joy in the holy Spirit;

Romans 14:19
Let us then pursue what leads to peace and to building up one another.

Romans 15:13
May the God of hope fill you with all joy and peace in believing, so that you may abound in hope by the power of the holy Spirit.

Romans 15:33
The God of peace be with all of you. Amen.

Romans 16:20
then the God of peace will quickly crush Satan under your feet. The grace of our Lord Jesus be with you.

1 Cor. 1:3
Grace to you and peace from God our Father and the Lord Jesus Christ.

1 Cor. 7:15
If the unbeliever separates, however, let him separate. The brother or sister is not bound in such cases; God has called you to peace.

1 Cor. 14:33
since he is not the God of disorder but of peace.
As in all the churches of the holy ones,

1 Cor. 16:11
Therefore no one should disdain him. Rather, send him on his way in peace that he may come to me, for I am expecting him with the brothers.

2 Cor. 1:2
grace to you and peace from God our Father and the Lord Jesus Christ.

2 Cor. 13:11
Finally, brothers, rejoice. Mend your ways, encourage one another, agree with one another, live in peace, and the God of love and peace will be with you.

Galatians 1:3
grace to you and peace from God our Father and the Lord Jesus Christ,

Galatians 5:22
In contrast, the fruit of the Spirit is love, joy, peace, patience, kindness, generosity, faithfulness,

Galatians 6:16
Peace and mercy be to all who follow this rule and to the Israel of God.

Ephes. 1:2
grace to you and peace from God our Father and the Lord Jesus Christ.

Ephes. 2:14-15
For he is our peace, he who made both one and broke down the dividing wall of enmity, through his flesh, [15] abolishing the law with its commandments and legal claims, that he might create in himself one new person in place of the two, thus establishing peace,

Ephes. 2:17
He came and preached peace to you who were far off and peace to those who were near,

Ephes. 4:3
striving to preserve the unity of the spirit through the bond of peace:

Ephes. 6:15
and your feet shod in readiness for the gospel of peace.

Ephes. 6:23
Peace be to the brothers, and love with faith, from God the Father and the Lord Jesus Christ.

Philip. 1:2
grace to you and peace from God our Father and the Lord Jesus Christ.

Philip. 4:7
Then the peace of God that surpasses all understanding will guard your hearts and minds in Christ Jesus.

Philip. 4:9
Keep on doing what you have learned and received and heard and seen in me. Then the God of peace will be with you.

Col. 1:2
to the holy ones and faithful brothers in Christ in Colossae: grace to you and peace from God our Father.

Col. 1:20
and through him to reconcile all things for him,
making peace by the blood of his cross
(through him), whether those on earth or those in heaven.

Col. 3:15
And let the peace of Christ control your hearts, the peace into which you were also called in one body. And be thankful.

1 Thes. 1:1
Paul, Silvanus, and Timothy to the church of the Thessalonians in God the Father and the Lord Jesus Christ: grace to you and peace.

1 Thes. 5:3
When people are saying, "Peace and security," then sudden disaster comes upon them, like labor pains upon a pregnant woman, and they will not escape.

1 Thes. 5:13
and to show esteem for them with special love on account of their work. Be at peace among yourselves.

1 Thes. 5:23
May the God of peace himself make you perfectly holy and may you entirely, spirit, soul, and body, be preserved blameless for the coming of our Lord Jesus Christ.

2 Thes. 1:2
grace to you and peace from God (our) Father and the Lord Jesus Christ.

2 Thes. 3:16
May the Lord of peace himself give you peace at all times and in every way. The Lord be with all of you.

1 Tim. 1:2
to Timothy, my true child in faith: grace, mercy, and peace from God the Father and Christ Jesus our Lord.

2 Tim. 1:2
to Timothy, my dear child: grace, mercy, and peace from God the Father and Christ Jesus our Lord.

2 Tim. 2:22
So turn from youthful desires and pursue righteousness, faith, love, and peace, along with those who call on the Lord with purity of heart.

Titus 1:4
to Titus, my true child in our common faith: grace and peace from God the Father and Christ Jesus our savior.

Philemon 1:3
Grace to you and peace from God our Father and the Lord Jesus Christ.

Hebrews 7:2
And Abraham apportioned to him "a tenth of everything." His name first means righteous king, and he was also "king of Salem," that is, king of peace.

Hebrews 11:31
By faith Rahab the harlot did not perish with the disobedient, for she had received the spies in peace.

Hebrews 12:14
Strive for peace with everyone, and for that holiness without which no one will see the Lord.

Hebrews 13:20

May the God of peace, who brought up from the dead the great shepherd of the sheep by the blood of the eternal covenant, Jesus our Lord,

James 2:16

and one of you says to them, "Go in peace, keep warm, and eat well," but you do not give them the necessities of the body, what good is it?

James 3:18

And the fruit of righteousness is sown in peace for those who cultivate peace.

1 Peter 1:2

in the foreknowledge of God the Father, through sanctification by the Spirit, for obedience and sprinkling with the blood of Jesus Christ: may grace and peace be yours in abundance.

1 Peter 3:11

must turn from evil and do good,
seek peace and follow after it.

1 Peter 5:14

Greet one another with a loving kiss. Peace to all of you who are in Christ.

2 Peter 1:2

may grace and peace be yours in abundance through knowledge of God and of Jesus our Lord.

2 Peter 3:14

Therefore, beloved, since you await these things, be eager to be found without spot or blemish before him, at peace.

2 John 1:3

Grace, mercy, and peace will be with us from God the Father and from Jesus Christ the Father's Son in truth and love.

3 John 1:14

Instead, I hope to see you soon, when we can talk face to face.

[15] Peace be with you. The friends greet you; greet the friends there each by name.

Jude 1:2

may mercy, peace, and love be yours in abundance.

Rev. 1:4

John, to the seven churches in Asia: grace to you and peace from him who is and who was and who is to come, and from the seven spirits before his throne,

Rev. 6:4

Another horse came out, a red one. Its rider was given power to take peace away from the earth, so that people would slaughter one another. And he was given a huge sword.

Appendix Three

Messages To The World
From
Blessed Virgin Mary
QUEEN OF HEAVEN AND EARTH

Beginning March 1, 1984, Our Lady gave weekly messages to the visionaries for the whole world. On January 25, 1987, she reduced the schedule to the 25th of every month. The monthly messages continue to this day. They are delivered through the visionary Marija Pavlovic-Lunetti.

1984

March 1, 1984
"Dear children! I
have chosen this parish in a special way and I wish to lead it. I am guarding it in love and I want everyone to be mine. Thank you for having responded tonight. I wish you always to be with me and my Son in ever greater numbers. I shall speak a message to you every Thursday."

March 8, 1984
"Thank you for having responded to my call! Dear children, you in the parish, be converted. This is my other wish. That way all those who shall come here shall be able to convert."

March 15,1984
"Tonight also, dear children, I am grateful to you in a special way for being here. Unceasingly adore the Most Blessed Sacrament of the Altar. I am always present when the faithful are adoring. Special graces are then being received."

March 22, 1984
"Dear children! In a special way this evening I am calling you during Lent to honor the wounds of my Son, which He received from the sins of this parish. Unite yourselves with my prayers for the parish so that His sufferings may be bearable. Thank you for having responded to my call. Try to come in ever greater numbers."

March 29, 1984
"Dear children! In a special way this evening I am calling you to perseverance in trials. Consider how the Almighty is still suffering today on account of your sins. So when sufferings come, offer them up as a sacrifice to God. Thank you for having responded to my call."

April 5, 1984
"Dear children! This evening I pray you especially to venerate the Heart of my Son, Jesus. Make reparation for the wound inflicted on the Heart of my Son. That Heart is offended by all kinds of sins. Thank you for coming this evening."

April 12, 1984
"Dear children! Today I beseech you to stop slandering and to pray for the unity of the parish, because I and my Son have a special plan for this parish. Thank you for having responded to my call."

April 19, 1984 (Holy Thursday)
"Dear children! Sympathize with me! Pray, pray, pray!"

April 26, 1984

April 30, 1984 (Monday)
Marija asked Our Lady, "Dear Madonna, why didn't you give me a message for the parish on Thursday?" Our Lady replied,
"I do not wish to force anyone to do that which he/she neither feels nor desires, even though I had special messages for the parish by which I wanted to awaken the faith of every believer. But only a really small number has accepted my Thursday messages. In the beginning there were quite a few. But its become a routine affair for them. And now recently some are asking for the message out of curiosity, and not out of faith and devotion to my Son and me."

May 10, 1984
Many of the faithful felt shaken by the last message of Our Lady. Some had the feeling that Our Lady would not give any more messages to the parish, but this evening she said, "I am speaking to you and I wish to speak further. You just listen to my instructions!"

May 17, 1984
"Dear children! Today I am very happy because there are many who want to consecrate themselves to me. Thank you. You have not made a mistake. My Son, Jesus Christ, wishes to bestow on you special graces through me. My Son is

happy because of your dedication. Thank you for having responded to my call."

May 24, 1984
"Dear children! I have told you already that I have chosen you in a special way, just the way you are. I, the Mother, love you all. And in any moment that is difficult for you, do not be afraid! Because I love you even then when you are far from me and my Son. Please, do not let my heart weep with tears of blood because of the souls who are lost in sin. Therefore, dear children, pray, pray, pray! Thank you for having responded to my call."

May 31, 1984 (Ascension Thursday)
There were many people present from abroad. Our Lady did not give a message for the parish. She told Marija that she would give a message on Saturday to be announced at the Sunday parish Mass.

June 2, 1984 (Saturday)
"Dear children! Tonight I wish to tell you during the days of this novena to pray for the outpouring of the Holy Spirit on your families and on your parish. Pray, and you shall not regret it. God will give you gifts by which you will glorify Him till the end of your life on this earth. Thank you for having responded to my call."

June 9, 1984 (Saturday)
"Dear children! Tomorrow night pray for the Spirit of Truth! Especially, you from the parish. Because you need the Spirit of Truth to be able to convey the messages just the way they are, neither adding anything to them, nor taking anything whatsoever way from them, but just the way I said them. Pray for the Holy Spirit to inspire you with the spirit of prayer, so you will pray more. I, your Mother, tell you that

you are praying little. Thank you for having responded to my call."

June 14, 1984

June 21, 1984
"Pray, pray, pray! Thank you for having responded to my call."

June 28, 1984
No message was given by Our Lady

July 12, 1984
"Dear children! These days Satan wants to frustrate my plans. Pray that his plan not be realized. I will pray my Son Jesus to give you the grace to experience the victory of Jesus in the temptations of Satan. Thank you for having responded to my call."

July 19, 1984
"Dear children! These days you have been experiencing how Satan is working. I am always with you, and don't you be afraid of temptations because God is always watching over us. Also I have given myself to you and I sympathize with you even in the smallest temptation. Thank you for having responded to my call."

July 26, 1984
"Dear children! Today also I wish to call you to persistent prayer and penance. Especially, let the young people of this parish be more active in their prayers. Thank you for having responded to my call."

August 2, 1984
"Dear children! Today I am joyful and I thank you for your prayers. Pray still more these days for the conversion of sinners. Thank you for having responded to my call."

August 9, 1984
No message was given by Our Lady

August 11, 1984 (Saturday)
"Dear children! Pray, because Satan wishes to complicate my plans still further. Pray with the heart and surrender yourselves to Jesus in prayer."

August 14, 1984 (Tuesday)
This apparition was unexpected. Ivan was praying at home. After that he started to get ready to go to Church for the evening services. By surprise Our Lady appeared to him and told him to relate to the people. "I would like the people to pray along with me these days. And to pray as much as possible! And to fast strictly on Wednesdays and Fridays, and every day to pray at least one Rosary: the joyful, sorrowful and glorious mysteries." Our Lady asked that we accept this message with a firm will. She especially requested this of the parishioners and the faithful of the surrounding places.

August 16, 1984
"Dear children! I beseech you, especially those from this parish, to live my messages and convey them to others, to whomever you meet. Thank you for having responded to my call."

August 23, 1984
"Dear children! Pray, pray!" Marija said that he also invited the people, and especially the young people, to keep order during the Mass.

August 30, 1984
"Dear children! The cross was also in God's plan when you built it. These days, especially, go on the mountain and pray before the cross. I need your prayers. Thank you for having responded to my call."

September 6, 1984
"Dear children! Without prayer there is no peace. Therefore I say to you, dear children, pray at the foot of the cross for peace. Thank you for having responded to my call."

September 13, 1984
"Dear children! I still need your prayers. You wonder why all these prayers? Look around you, dear children, and you will see how greatly sin has dominated the world. Pray, therefore, that Jesus conquers. Thank you for having responded to my call."

September 20, 1984
"Dear children! Today I call on you to begin fasting with the heart. There are many people who are fasting, but only because everyone else is fasting. It has become a custom which no one wants to stop. I ask the parish to fast out of gratitude because God has allowed me to stay this long in this parish. Dear children, fast and pray with the heart. Thank you for having responded to my call."

September 27, 1984
"Dear children! You have helped me along by your prayers to realize my plans. Keep on praying that my plans completely I request the families of the parish to pray the family rosary. Thank you for having responded to my call."

October 4, 1984
"Dear children! Today I want to tell you that again and again you make me happy by your prayer, but there are enough of those in this very parish who do not pray and my heart is saddened. Therefore pray that I can bring all your sacrifices and prayers to the Lord. Thank you for having responded to my call."

October 8, 1984 (Monday)
(Jakov was sick and received this message at home.) "Dear children, Let all the prayers you say in your homes in the evening be for the conversion of sinners because the world is in great sin. Every evening pray the rosary."

October 11, 1984
"Dear children! Thank you for dedicating all your hard work to God even now when He is testing you through the grapes you are picking. Be assured, dear children, that He loves you and, therefore, He tests you. You just always offer up all your burdens to God and do not be anxious. Thank you for having responded to my call."

October 18, 1984
"Dear children! Today I call on you to read the Bible every day in your homes and let it be in a visible place so as always to encourage you to read it and to pray. Thank you for having responded to my call."

October 25, 1984
"Dear children! Pray during this month. God allows me every day to help you with graces to defend yourselves against evil. This is my month. I want to give it to you. You just pray and God will give you the graces you are seeking. I will help along with it. Thank you for having responded to my call."

November 1, 1984
"Dear children! Today I call you to the renewal of prayer in your homes. The work in the fields is over. Now devote yourselves to prayer. Let prayer take the first place in your families. Thank you for having responded to my call."

November 8, 1984
"Dear children! You are not conscious of the messages which God is sending you through me. He is giving you great graces and you do not comprehend them. Pray to the Holy Spirit for enlightenment. If you only knew how great are the graces God is granting you, you would be praying without ceasing. Thank you for having responded to my call."

November 15, 1984
"Dear children! You are a chosen people and God has given you great graces. You are not conscious of every message which I am giving you. Now I just want to say - pray, pray, pray! I don't know what else to tell you because I love you and I want you to comprehend my love and God's love through prayer. Thank you for having responded to my call."

November 22, 1984
"Dear children! These days live all the main messages and keep rooting them in your hearts till Thursday. Thank you for having responded to my call."

November 29, 1984
"Dear children! No, you don't know how to love and you don't know how to listen with love to the words I am saying to you. Be conscious, my beloved, that I am your Mother and I have come on earth to teach you to listen out of love, to pray out of love and not compelled by the fact that you are carrying a cross. By means of the cross God is glorified

through every person. Thank you for having responded to my call."

December 6, 1984
"Dear children! These days I am calling you to family prayer. In God's Name many times I have been giving you messages, but you have not listened to me. This Christmas will be unforgettable for you only if you accept the messages which I am giving you. Dear children, don't allow that day of joy to become my most sorrowful day. Thank you for having responded to my call."

December 13, 1984
"Dear children! You know that the season of joy is getting closer, but without love you will achieve nothing. So first of all, begin to love your own family, everyone in the parish, and then you'll be able to love and accept all who are coming over here. Now let these seven days be a week when you need to learn to love. Thank you for having responded to my call."

December 20, 1984
"Dear children! Today I am inviting you to do something concrete for Jesus Christ. As a sign of dedication to Jesus I want each family of the parish to bring a single flower before that happy day. I want every member of the family to have a single flower by the crib so Jesus can come and see your dedication to Him! Thank you for having responded to my call."

December 21, 1984 (Friday)
"I want you to be a flower which will blossom for Jesus on Christmas. And a flower that will not stop blooming when Christmas is over. I want your hearts to be shepherds to Jesus."
(Message given through Jelena Vasilj.)

December 27, 1984
"Dear children! This Christmas Satan wanted in a special way to spoil God's plans. You, dear children, have discerned Satan even on Christmas day itself. But God is winning in all your hearts. So let your hearts keep on being happy. Thank you for having responded to my call."

1985

January 3, 1985
"Dear children! These days the Lord has bestowed upon you great graces. Let this week be one of thanksgiving for all the graces which God has granted you. Thank you for having responded to my call."

January 10, 1985
"Dear children! Today I want to thank you for all your sacrifices, but special thanks to those who have become dear to my heart and come here gladly are enough parishioners who are not listening to the messages, but because of those who are in a special way close to my heart, because of them I am giving messages for the parish. And I will go on giving them because I love you and I want you to spread my messages with your heart. Thank you for having responded to my call."

January 14, 1985 (Monday)
"My dear children! Satan is so strong and with all his might wants to disturb my plans which I have begun with you. You pray, just pray and don't stop for a minute! I will pray to my Son for the realization of all the plans I have begun. Be patient and constant in your prayers. And don't let Satan

discourage you. He is working hard in the world. Be on your guard!"
(Message conveyed by Vicka from Our Lady.)

January 17, 1985
"Dear children! These days Satan is working underhandedly against this parish, and you, dear children, have fallen asleep in prayer, and only some are going to Mass. Withstand the days of temptation! Thank you for having responded to my call."

January 24, 1985
"Dear children! These days you have experienced God's sweetness through the renewals which have been in this parish. Satan wants to work still more fiercely to take away your joy from each one of you. By prayer you can completely disarm him and ensure your happiness. Thank you for having responded to my call."

January 31, 1985
"Dear children! Today I wish to tell you to open your hearts to God like the spring flowers which crave for the sun. I am your Mother and I always want you to be closer to the Father and that He will always give abundant gifts to your hearts. Thank you for having responded to my call."

February 7, 1985
"Dear children! These days Satan is manifesting himself in a special way in this parish. Pray, dear children, that God's plan is brought into effect and that every work of Satan ends up for the glory of God. I have stayed with you this long so I might help you along in your trials. Thank you for having responded to my call."

February 14, 1985
"Dear children! Today is the day when I give you a message for the parish, but the whole parish is not accepting the messages and is not living them. I am saddened and I want you, dear children, to listen to me and to live my messages. Every family must pray family prayer and read the Bible! Thank you for having responded to my call."

February 21, 1985
"Dear children! From day to day I have been inviting you to renewal and prayer in the parish, but you are not accepting it. Today I am calling you for the last time! Now it's Lent and you as a parish can turn to my messages during Lent out of love. If you do not do that, I do not wish to keep on giving messages. God is permitting me that. Thank you for having responded to my call."

February 28, 1985
"Dear children! Today I call you to live the word this week: "I love God!" Dear children through love you will achieve everything and even what you think is impossible. God wants this parish to belong completely to Him. And that's what I want too. Thank you for having responded to my call."

March 7, 1985
"Dear children! Today I call you to renew prayer in your families. Dear children, encourage the very young to prayer and the children to go to Holy Mass. Thank you for having responded to my call."

March 14, 1985
"Dear children! In your life you have all experienced light and darkness. God grants to every person to recognize good and evil. I am calling you to the light which you should carry to all the people who are in darkness. People who are in

darkness daily come into your homes. Dear children, give them the light! Thank you for having responded to my call."

March 21, 1985
"Dear children! I wish to keep on giving messages and therefore today I call you to live and accept my messages! Dear children, I love you and in a special way I have chosen this parish, one more dear to me than the others, in which I have gladly remained when the Almighty sent me. Therefore I call on you - accept me, dear children, that it might go well with you. Listen to my messages! Thank you for having responded to my call."

March 24, 1985 (Sunday)
"Today I wish to call you all to confession, even if you have confessed a few days ago. I wish that you all experience my feast day within yourselves. But you cannot experience it unless you abandon yourselves completely to God. Therefore, I am inviting you all to reconciliation with God!"

March 28, 1985
"Dear children! Today I wish to call you to pray, pray, pray! In prayer you shall perceive the greatest joy and the way out of every situation that has no exit. Thank you for starting up prayer. Each individual is dear to my heart. And I thank all who have urged prayer in their families. Thank you for having responded to my call."

April 4, 1985 (Holy Thursday)
"Dear children! I thank you for having started to think more about God's glory in your hearts. Today is the day when I wished to stop giving the messages because some individuals did not accept me. The parish has been moved and I wish to keep on giving you messages as it has never been in history from the beginning of the world. Thank you for having responded to my call."

April 5, 1985 (Good Friday)
"You parishioners have a great and heavy cross, but don't be afraid to carry it. My Son is here Who will help you."
(Message given through Ivanka)

April 11, 1985
"Dear children! Today I wish to say to everyone in the parish to pray in a special way to the Holy Spirit for enlightenment. From today God wishes to test the parish in a special way in order that He might strengthen it in faith. Thank you for having responded to my call."

April 18, 1985
"Dear children! Today I thank you for every opening of your hearts. Joy overtakes me for every heart that is opened to God especially from the parish. Rejoice with me! Pray all the prayers for the opening of sinful hearts. I desire that. God desires that through me. Thank you for having responded to my call."

April 25, 1985
"Dear children! Today I wish to tell you to begin to work in your hearts as you are working in the fields. Work and change your hearts so that a new spirit from God can take its place in your hearts. Thank you for having responded to my call."

May 2, 1985
"Dear children! Today I call you to prayer with the heart, and not just from habit. Some are coming but do not wish to move ahead in prayer. Therefore, I wish to warn you like a Mother: pray that prayer prevails in your hearts in every moment. Thank you for having responded to my call."

May 9, 1985
"Dear children! No, you do not know how many graces God is giving you. You do not want to move ahead during these days when the Holy Spirit is working in a special way. Your hearts are turned toward the things of earth and they preoccupy you. Turn your hearts toward prayer and seek the Holy Spirit to be poured out on you. Thank you for having responded to my call."

May 16, 1985
"Dear children! I am calling you to a more active prayer and attendance at Holy Mass. I wish your Mass to be an experience of God. I wish especially to say to the young people: be open to the Holy Spirit because God wishes to draw you to Himself in these days when Satan is at work. Thank you for having responded to my call."

May 23, 1985
"Dear children! These days I call you especially to open your hearts to the Holy Spirit. Especially during these days the Holy Spirit is working through you. Open your hearts and surrender your life to Jesus so that He works through your hearts and strengthens you in faith. Thank you for having responded to my call."

May 30, 1985
"Dear children! I call you again to prayer with the heart. Let prayer, dear children, be your every day food in a special way when your work in the fields is so wearing you out that you cannot pray with the heart. Pray, and then you shall overcome even every weariness. Prayer will be your joy and your rest. Thank you for having responded to my call."

June 6, 1985
"Dear children! During these days people from all nations will be coming into the parish. And now I am calling you to

love: love first of all your own household members, and then you will be able to accept and love all who are coming. Thank you for having responded to my call."

June 13, 1985
"Dear children! Until the anniversary day I am calling you, the parish, to pray more and to let your prayer be a sign of surrender to God. Dear children, I know that your are all tired, but you don't know how to surrender yourselves to me. During these days surrender yourselves completely to me! Thank your for having responded to my call."

June 20, 1985
Dear children! For this Feast Day I wish to tell you to open your hearts to the Master of all hearts. Give me all your feelings and all your problems! I wish to comfort your in all your trials. I wish to fill you with peace, joy and love of God. Thank you for having responded to my call."

June 25, 1985 (Tuesday)
"I invite you to call on everyone to pray the Rosary. With the rosary you shall overcome all the adversities which Satan is trying to inflict on the Catholic Church. All you priests, pray the Rosary! Dedicate your time to the Rosary!" (This message Our Lady gave in response to the question of Marija Pavlovic: "Our Lady, what do you wish to recommend to priests?")

June 28, 1985 (Friday)
"Dear children! Today I am giving you a message through which I desire to call you to humility. These days you have felt great joy because of all the people who have come and to whom you could tell your experiences with love. Now I invite you to continue in humility and with an open heart speak to all who are coming. Thank you for having responded to my message."

July 4, 1985
"Dear children! I thank you for every sacrifice you have offered. And now I urge you to offer every sacrifice with love. I wish you, the helpless ones, to begin helping with confidence and the Lord will keep on giving to you in confidence. Thank you for having responded to my call."

July 11, 1985
"Dear children! I love the parish and with my mantle I protect it from every work of Satan. Pray that Satan retreats from the parish and from every individual who comes into the parish. In that way you shall be able to hear every call of God and answer it with your life. Thank you for having responded to my call."

July 18, 1985
"Dear children! Today I call you to place more blessed objects in your homes and that everyone put some blessed objects on their person. Bless all the objects and thus Satan will attack you less because you will have armor against him. Thank you for having responded to my call."

July 25, 1985
"Dear children! I desire to lead you, but you do not wish to listen to my messages. Today I am calling you to listen to the messages and then you will be able to live everything which God tells me to convey to you. Open yourselves to God and God will work through you and keep on giving you everything you need. Thank you for having responded to my call."

August 1, 1985
"Dear children! I wish to tell you that I have chosen this parish and that I am guarding it in my hands like a little flower that does not want to die. I call you to surrender to me so that I can keep on presenting you to God, fresh and

without sin. Satan has taken part of the plan and wants to possess it. Pray that he does not succeed in that, because I wish you for myself so I can keep on giving you to God. Thank you for having responded to my call."

August 8, 1985
"Dear children! Today I call you especially now to advance against Satan by means of prayer. Satan wants to work still more now that you know he is at work. Dear children, put on the armor for battle and with the Rosary in your hand defeat him! Thank you for having responded to my call."

August 15, 1985
"Dear children! Today I am blessing you and I wish to tell you that I love you and that I urge you to live my messages. Today I am blessing you with the solemn blessing that the Almighty grants me. Thank you for having responded to my call."

August 22, 1985
"Dear children! Today I wish to tell you that God wants to send you trials which you can overcome by prayer. God is testing you through daily chores. Now pray to peacefully withstand every trial. From everything through which God tests you come out more open to God and approach Him with love. Thank you for having responded to my call."

August 29, 1985
"Dear children! I am calling you to prayer! Especially since Satan wishes to take advantage of the yield of your vineyards. Pray that Satan does not succeed in his plan. Thank you for having responded to my call."

September 5, 1985
"Dear children! Today I thank you for all the prayers. Keep on praying all the more so that Satan will be far away from this place. Dear children, Satan's plan has failed. Pray for fulfillment of what God plans in this parish. I especially thank the young people for the sacrifices they have offered up. Thank you for having responded to my call."

September 12, 1985
"Dear children! I wish to tell you that the cross should be central these days. Pray especially before the cross from which great graces are coming. Now in your homes make a special consecration to the cross. Promise that you will neither offend Jesus nor abuse the cross. Thank you for having responded to my call."

September 19, 1985
September 20, 1985 (Friday) "Dear children! Today I invite you to live in humility all the messages which I am giving you. Do not become arrogant living the messages and saying 'I am living the messages'. If you shall bear and live the messages in your heart, everyone will feel it so that words, which serve those who do not obey, will not be necessary. For you, dear children, it is necessary to live and witness by your lives. Thank you for having responded to my call."

September 26, 1985
"Dear children! I thank you for all the prayers. Thank you for all the sacrifices. I wish to tell you, dear children, to renew the messages which I am giving you. Especially live the fast, because by fasting you will achieve and cause me the joy of the whole plan, which God is planning here in Medjugorje, being fulfilled. Thank you for having responded to my call."

October 3, 1985
"Dear children! I wish to tell you to thank God for all the graces which God has given you. For all the fruits thank the Lord and glorify him! Dear children, learn to give thanks in little things and then you will be able to give thanks also for the big things. Thank you for having responded to my call."

October 10, 1985
"Dear children! I wish also today to call you to live the messages in the parish. Especially I wish to call the youth of the parish, who are dear to me. Dear children, if you live the messages, you are living the seed of holiness. I, as the Mother, wish to call you all to holiness so that you can bestow it on others. You are a mirror to others! Thank you for having responded to my call."

October 17, 1985
"Dear children! Everything has its own time. Today I call you to start working on your own hearts. Now that all the work in the field is over, you are finding time for cleaning even the most neglected areas, but you leave your heart aside. Work more and clean with love every part of your heart. Thank you for having responded to my call."

October 24, 1985
"Dear children! From day to day I wish to clothe you in holiness, goodness, obedience and God's love, so that from day to day you become more beautiful and more prepared for your Master. Dear children, listen to and live my messages. I wish to guide you. Thank you for having responded to my call."

October 31, 1985
"Dear children! Today I wish to call you to work in the Church. I love all the same and I desire from each one to work as much as is possible. I know, dear children, that you

can, but you do not wish to because you feel small and humble in these things. You need to be courageous and with little flowers do your share for the church and for Jesus so that everyone can be satisfied. Thank you for having responded to my call."

November 7, 1985
"Dear children! I am calling you to the love of neighbor and love toward the one from whom evil comes to you. In that way with love you will be able to discern the intentions of hearts. Pray and love, dear children! By love you are able to do even that which you think is impossible. Thank you for having responded to my call."

November 14, 1985
"Dear children! I, your Mother, love you and wish to urge you to prayer. I am tireless, dear children, and I am calling you even then, when you are far away from my heart. I am a Mother, and even though I feel pain for each one who goes astray, I forgive easily and am happy for every child who returns to me. Thank you for having responded to my call."

November 21, 1985
"Dear children! I want to tell you that this season is especially for you from the parish. When it is summer, you saw that you have a lot of work. Now you don't have work in the fields, work on your own self personally! Come to Mass because this is the season given to you. Dear children, there are enough of those who come regularly despite bad weather because they love me and wish to show their love in a special way. What I want from you is to show me your love by coming to Mass, and the Lord will reward you abundantly. Thank you for having responded to my call."

November 28, 1985
"Dear children! I want to thank everyone for all you have done for me, especially the youth. I beseech you, dear children, come to prayer with awareness. In prayer you shall come to know the greatness of God. Thank you for having responded to my call."

December 5, 1985
"Dear children! I am calling you to prepare yourselves for Christmas by means of penance, prayer and works of charity. Dear children, do not look toward material things, because then you will not be able to experience Christmas. Thank you for having responded to my call."

December 12, 1985
"Dear children! For Christmas my invitation is that together we glorify Jesus. I present Him to you in a special way on that day and my invitation to you is that on that day we glorify Jesus and His nativity. Dear children, on that day pray still more and think more about Jesus. Thank you for having responded to my call."

December 19, 1985
"Dear children! Today I wish to call you to love of neighbor. The more you will to love your neighbour, the more you shall experience Jesus especially on Christmas Day. God will bestow great gifts on you if you surrender yourselves to Him. I wish in a special way on Christmas Day to give mothers my own special motherly blessing, and Jesus will bless the rest with His own blessing. Thank you for having responded to my call."

December 26, 1985
"Dear children! I wish to thank all who have listened to my messages and who on Christmas Day have lived what I said. Undefiled by sin from now on, I wish to lead you further in

love. Abandon your hearts to me! Thank you for having responded to my call!"

1986

January 2, 1986
"Dear children! I call you to decide completely for God. I beseech you, dear children, to surrender yourselves completely and you shall be able to live everything I am telling you. It shall not be difficult for you to surrender yourselves completely to God. Thank you for having responded to my call."

January 9, 1986
"Dear children! I call you by your prayers to help Jesus along in the fulfillment of all the plans which He is forming here. And offer your sacrifices to Jesus in order that everything is fulfilled the way He has planned it and that Satan can accomplish nothing. Thank you for having responded to my call."

January 16, 1986
"Dear children! Today also I am calling you to prayer. Your prayers are necessary to me so that God may be glorified through all of you. Dear children, I pray you, obey and live the Mother's invitation, because only out of love am I calling you in order that I might help you. Thank you for having responded to my call."

January 23, 1986
"Dear children! Again I call you to prayer with the heart. If you pray with the heart, dear children, the ice of your brothers will melt and every barrier shall disappear. Conversion will be easy for all who desire to accept it. That

is the gift which by prayer you must obtain for your neighbor. Thank you for having responded to my call."

January 30, 1986
"Dear children! Today I call you all to pray that God's plans for us may be realized and also everything that God desires through you! Help others to be converted, especially those who are coming to Medjugorje. Dear children, do not allow Satan to get control of your hearts, so you would be an image of Satan and not of me. I call you to pray for how you might be witnesses of my presence. Without you, God cannot bring to reality that which He desires. God has given a free will to everyone, and it's in your control. Thank you for having responded to my call."

February 6, 1986
"Dear children! This parish, which I have chosen, is special and different from others. And I am giving great graces to all who pray with the heart. Dear children, I am giving the messages first of all to the residents of the parish, and then to all the others. First of all you must accept the messages, and then the others. You shall be answerable to me and my Son, Jesus. Thank you for having responded to my call."

February 13, 1986
"Dear children! This Lent is a special incentive for you to change. Start from this moment. Turn off the television and renounce various things that are of no value. Dear children, I am calling you individually to conversion. This season is for you. Thank you for having responded to my call."

February 20, 1986
"Dear children! The second message of these Lenten days is that you renew prayer before the cross. Dear children, I am giving you special graces and Jesus is giving you special gifts from the cross. Take them and live! Reflect on Jesus'

Passion and in your life be united with Jesus! Thank you for having responded to my call."

February 27, 1986
"Dear children! In humility live the messages which I am giving you. Thank you for having responded to my call."

March 6, 1986
"Dear children! Today I call you to open yourselves more to God, so that He can work through you. The more you open yourselves, the more you receive the fruits. I wish to call you again to prayer. Thank you for having responded to my call."

March 13, 1986
"Dear children! Today I call you to live Lent by means of your little sacrifices. Thank you for every sacrifice you have brought me. Dear children, live that way continuously, and with your love help me to present the sacrifice. God will reward you for that. Thank you for having responded to my call."

March 20, 1986
"Dear children! Today I call you to approach prayer actively. You wish to live everything I am telling you, but you are not succeeding because you are not praying. Dear children, I beseech you to open yourselves and begin to pray. Prayer will be your joy. If you make a start, it won't be boring to you because you will be praying out of joy. Thank you for having responded to my call."

March 27, 1986
"Dear children! I wish to thank you for all the sacrifices and I invite you to the greatest sacrifice, the sacrifice of love. Without love, you are not able to accept either me or my Son. Without love, you cannot give an account of your experiences to others. Therefore, dear children, I call you to

begin to live love within yourselves. Thank you for having responded to my call."

April 3, 1986
"Dear children! I wish to call you to a living of the Holy Mass. There are many of you who have sensed the beauty of the Holy Mass, but there are also those who come unwillingly. I have chosen you, dear children, but Jesus gives you His graces in the Mass. Therefore, consciously live the Holy Mass and let your coming to it be a joyful one. Come to it with love and make the Mass your own. Thank you for having responded to my call."

April 10, 1986
"Dear children! I desire to call you to grow in love. A flower is not able to grow normally without water. So also you, dear children, are not able to grow without God's blessing. From day to day you need to seek His blessing so you will grow normally and perform all your actions in union with God. Thank you for having responded to my call."

April 17, 1986
"Dear children! You are absorbed with material things, but in the material you lose everything that God wishes to give you. I call you, dear children, to pray for the gifts of the Holy Spirit which are necessary for you now in order to be able to give witness to my presence here and to all that I am giving you. Dear children, let go to me so I can lead you completely. Don't be absorbed with material things. Thank you for having responded to my call."

April 24, 1986
"Dear children! Today my invitation is that you pray. Dear children, you are forgetting that you are all important. The elderly are especially important in the family. Urge them to pray. Let all the young people be an example to others by

their life and let them witness to Jesus. Dear children, I beseech you, begin to change through prayer and you will know what you need to do. Thank you for having responded to my call."

May 1, 1986
"Dear children! I beseech you to start changing your life in the family. Let the family be a harmonious flower that I wish to give to Jesus. Dear children, let every family be active in prayer for I wish that the fruits in the family be seen one day. Only that way shall I give you all, like petals, as a gift to Jesus in fulfillment of God's plans. Thank you for having responded to my call."

May 8, 1986
"Dear children! You are the ones responsible for the messages. The source of grace is here, but you, dear children, are the vessels which transport the gifts. Therefore, dear children, I am calling you to do your job with responsibility. Each one shall be responsible according to his own ability. Dear children, I am calling you to give the gifts to others with love, and not to keep them for yourselves. Thank you for having responded to my call."

May 15, 1986
"Dear children! Today I call you to give me your heart so I can change it to be like mine. You are wondering, dear children, why you cannot respond to that which I am seeking from you. You are not able to because you have not given me your heart so I can change it. You are talking but you are not doing. I call on you to do everything that I am telling you. That way I will be with you. Thank you for having responded to my call."

May 22, 1986

"Dear children! Today I wish to give you my own love. You do not know, dear children, how great my love is, and you do not know how to accept it. In various ways I wish to show it to you, but you, dear children, do not recognize it. You do not understand my words with your heart and neither are you able to comprehend my love. Dear children, accept me in your life and so you will be able to accept all I am saying to you and to which I am calling you. Thank you for having responded to my call."

May 29, 1986

"Dear children! Today my call to you is that in your life you live love toward God and neighbor. Without love, dear children, you can do nothing. Therefore, dear children, I am calling you to live in mutual love. Only in that way will you be able to love and accept both me and all those around you who are coming into your parish. Everyone will sense my love through you. Therefore, I beseech you, dear children, to start loving from today with an ardent love, the love with which I love you. Thank you for having responded to my call."

June 5, 1986

"Dear children! Today I am calling on you to decide whether or not you wish to live the messages which I am giving you. I wish you to be active in living and spreading the messages. Especially, dear children, I wish that you all be the reflection of Jesus, which will enlighten this unfaithful world walking in darkness. I wish all of you to be the light for everyone and that you give witness in the light. Dear children, you are not called to the darkness, but you are called to the light. Therefore, live the light with your own life. Thank you for having responded to my call."

June 12, 1986
"Dear children! Today I call you to begin to pray the Rosary with a living faith. That way I will be able to help you. You, dear children, wish to obtain graces, but you are not praying. I am not able to help you because you do not want to get started. Dear children, I am calling you to pray the Rosary and that your Rosary be an obligation which you shall fulfill with joy. That way you shall understand the reason I am with you this long. I desire to teach you to pray. Thank you for having responded to my call."

June 19, 1986
"Dear children! During these days my Lord is allowing me to be able to intercede more graces for you. Therefore, I wish to urge you once more to pray, dear children! Pray without ceasing! That way I will give you the joy which the Lord gives to me. With these graces, dear children, I want your sufferings to be a joy. I am your Mother and I desire to help you. Thank you for having responded to my call."

June 26, 1986
"Dear children! God is allowing me along with Himself to bring about this oasis of peace. I wish to call on you to protect it and that the oasis always be unspoiled. There are those who by their carelessness are destroying the peace and the prayer. I am inviting you to give witness and by your own life to help to preserve the peace. Thank you for having responded to my call."

July 3, 1986
"Dear children! Today I am calling you all to prayer. Without prayer, dear children, you are not able to experience either God, or me or the graces which I am giving you. Therefore, my call to you is that the beginning and end of your day always be prayer. Dear children, I wish to lead you daily more and more in prayer, but you are not able to grow

because you do not desire it. My call, dear children, is that for you prayer be in the first place. Thank you for having responded to my call."

July 10, 1986

"Dear children! Today I am calling you to holiness. Without holiness you cannot live. Therefore, with love overcome every sin and with love overcome all the difficulties which are coming to you. Dear children, I beseech you to live love within yourselves. Thank you for having responded to my call."

July 17, 1986

"Dear children! Today I am calling you to reflect upon why I am with you this long. I am the Mediatrix between you and God. Therefore, dear children, I desire to call you to live always out of love all that which God desires of you. For that reason, dear children, in your own humility live all the messages which I am giving you. Thank you for having responded to my call."

July 24, 1986

"Dear children! I rejoice because of all of you who are on the way of holiness and I beseech you, by your own testimony help those who do not know how to live in holiness. Therefore, dear children, let your family be a place where holiness is birthed. Help everyone to live in holiness, but especi ally your own family. Thank you for having responded to my call."

July 31, 1986

"Dear children! Hatred gives birth to dissensions and does not regard anyone or anything. I call you always to bring harmony and peace. Especially, dear children, in the place where you live, act with love. Let your only instrument always be love. By love turn everything into good which

Satan desires to destroy and possess. Only that way shall you be completely mine and I shall be able to help you. Thank you for having responded to my call."

August 7, 1986
"Dear children! You know that I promised you an oasis of peace, but you don't know that beside an oasis stands the desert, where Satan is lurking and wanting to tempt each one of you. Dear children, only by prayer are you able to overcome every influence of Satan in your place. I am with you, but I cannot take away your freedom. Thank you for having responded to my call."

August 14, 1986
"Dear children! My call to you is that your prayer be the joy of an encounter with the Lord. I am not able to guide you as long as you yourselves do not experience joy in prayer. From day to day I desire to lead you more and more in prayer, but I do not wish to force you. Thank you for having responded to my call."

August 21, 1986
"Dear children! I thank you for the love which you are showing me. You know, dear children, that I love you immeasurably and daily I pray the Lord to help you to understand the love which I am showing you. Therefore, you, dear children, pray, pray, pray!"

August 28, 1986
"Dear children! My call is that in everything you would be an image for others, especially in prayer and witnessing. Dear children, without you I am not able to help the world. I desire that you cooperate with me in everything, even in the smallest things. Therefore, dear children, help me by letting your prayer be from the heart and all of you surrendering completely to me. That way I shall be able to teach and lead

you on this way which I have begun with you. Thank you for having responded to my call."

September 4, 1986
"Dear children! Today again I am calling you to prayer and fasting. You know, dear children, that with your help I am able to accomplish everything and force Satan not to be seducing to evil and to remove himself from this place. Dear children, Satan is lurking for each individual. Especially in everyday affairs he wants to spread confusion among each one of you. Therefore, dear children, my call to you is that your day would be only prayer and complete surrender to God. Thank you for having responded to my call."

September 11, 1986
"Dear children! For these days while you are joyfully celebrating the cross, I desire that your cross also would be a joy for you. Especially, dear children, pray that you may be able to accept sickness and suffering with love the way Jesus accepted them. Only that way shall I be able with joy to give out to you the graces and healings which Jesus is permitting me. Thank you for having responded to my call."

September 18, 1986
"Dear children! Today again I thank you for all that you have accomplished for me in these days. Especially, dear children, I thank you in the Name of Jesus for the sacrifices which you offered in this past week. Dear children, you are forgetting that I desire sacrifices from you so I can help you and drive Satan away from you. Therefore, I am calling you again to offer sacrifices with a special reverence toward God. Thank you for having responded to my call."

September 25, 1986
"Dear children! By your own peace I am calling you to help others to see and begin to seek peace. You, dear children, are

at peace and not able to comprehend lack of peace. Therefore, I am calling you, so that by your prayer and your life you help to destroy everything that is evil in people and uncover the deception that Satan makes use of. You pray that the truth prevails in all hearts. Thank you for having responded to my call."

October 2, 1986
"Dear children! Today again I am calling you to pray. You, dear children, are not able to understand how great the value of prayer is as long as you yourselves do not say: 'now is the time for prayer, now nothing else is important to me, now not one person is important to me but God.' Dear children, consecrate yourselves to prayer with a special love so that God will be able to render graces back to you. Thank you for having responded to my call."

October 9, 1986
"Dear children! You know that I desire to lead you on the way of holiness, but I do not want to compel you to be saints by force. I desire that each of you by your own little self-denials help yourself and me so I can lead you from day to day closer to holiness. Therefore, dear children, I do not desire to force you to observe the messages. But rather this long time that I am with you is a sign that I love you immeasurably and what I desire of each individual is to become holy. Thank you for having responded to my call."

October 16, 1986
"Dear children! Today again I want to show you how much I love you, but I am sorry that I am not able to help each one to understand my love. Therefore, dear children, I am calling you to prayer and complete surrender to God, because Satan wants to sift you through everyday affairs and in your life he wants to snatch the first place. Therefore, dear children, pray

without ceasing! Thank you for having responded to my call."

October 23, 1986
"Dear children! Today again I am calling you to pray. Especially, dear children, do I call you to pray for peace. Without your prayers, dear children, I cannot help you to fulfill the message which the Lord has given me to give to you. Therefore, dear children, pray, so that in prayer you realize what God is giving you. Thank you for having responded to my call."

October 30, 1986
"Dear children! Today again I desire to call you to take seriously and carry out the messages which I am giving you. Dear children, it is for your sake that I have stayed this long so I could help you to fulfill all the messages which I am giving you. Therefore, dear children, out of love for me carry out all the messages which I am giving you. Thank you for having responded to my call."

November 6, 1986
"Dear children! Today I wish to call you to pray daily for souls in purgatory. For every soul prayer and grace is necessary to reach God and the love of God. By doing this, dear children, you obtain new intercessors who will help you in life to realize that all the earthly things are not important for you, that only Heaven is that for which it is necessary to strive. Therefore, dear children, pray without ceasing that you may be able to help yourselves and the others to whom your prayers will bring joy. Thank you for having responded to my call."

November 13, 1986
"Dear children! Today again I am calling you to pray with your whole heart and day by day to change your life.

Especially, dear children, I am calling that by your prayers and sacrifices you begin to live in holiness, because I desire that each one of you who has been to this fountain of grace will come to Paradise with the special gift which you shall give me, and that is holiness. Therefore, dear children, pray and daily change your life in order to become fully holy. I shall always be close to you. Thank you for having responded to my call."

November 20, 1986
"Dear children! Today also I am calling you to live and follow with a special love all the messages which I am giving you. Dear children, God does not want you lukewarm and undecided, but that you totally surrender to Him. You know that I love you and that out of love I long for you. Therefore, dear children, you also decide for love so that you will long for and daily experience God's love. Dear children, decide for love so that love prevails in all of you, but not human love, rather God's love. Thank you for having responded to my call."

November 27, 1986
"Dear children! Again today I call you to consecrate your life to me with love, so I am able to guide you with love. I love you, dear children, with a special love and I desire to bring you all to Heaven unto God. I want you to realize that this life lasts briefly compared to the one in Heaven. Therefore, dear children, decide again today for God. Only that way will I be able to show how much you are dear to me and how much I desire all to be saved and to be with me in Heaven. Thank you for having responded to my call."

December 4, 1986
"Dear children! Today I call you to prepare your hearts for these days when the Lord particularly desires to purify you from all the sins of your past. You, dear children, are not

able by yourselves, therefore I am here to help you. You pray, dear children! Only that way shall you be able to recognize all the evil that is in you and surrender it to the Lord so the Lord may completely purify your hearts. Therefore, dear children, pray without ceasing and prepare your hearts in penance and fasting. Thank you for having responded to my call."

December 11, 1986
"Dear children! I am calling you to pray especially at this time in order to experience the joy of meeting with the new-born Jesus. Dear children, I desire that you experience these days just as I experience them. With joy I wish to guide you and show you the joy into which I desire to bring each one of you. Therefore, dear children, pray and surrender completely to me. Thank you for having responded to my call."

December 18, 1986
"Dear children! Once again I desire to call you to prayer. When you pray you are much more beautiful, like flowers, which after the snow, show all their beauty and all their colors become indescribable. So also you, dear children, after prayer show before God all so much more what is beautiful and are beloved by Him. Therefore, dear children, pray and open your inner self to the Lord so that He makes of you a harmonious and beautiful flower for Paradise. Thank you for having responded to my call."

December 25, 1986 (Christmas Day)
"Dear children! Today also I give thanks to the Lord for all that He is doing for me, especially for this gift that I am able to be with you also today. Dear children, these are the days in which the Father grants special graces to all who open their hearts. I bless you and I desire that you too, dear children, become alive to the graces and place everything at God's disposal so that He may be glorified through you. My

heart carefully follows your progress. Thank you for having responded to my call."

1987

January 1, 1987
"Dear children! Today I wish to call on all of you that in the New Year you live the messages which I am giving you. Dear children, you know that for your sake I have remained a long time so I might teach you how to make progress on the way of holiness. Therefore, dear children, pray without ceasing and live the messages which I am giving you for I am doing it with great love toward God and toward you. Thank you for having responded to my call."

January 8, 1987
"Dear children! I desire to thank you for every response to the messages. Especially, dear children, thank you for all the sacrifices and prayers which you have presented to me. Dear children, I desire to keep on giving you still further messages, only not every Thursday, dear children, but on each 25th in the month. The time has come when what my Lord desired has been fulfilled. Now I will give you less messages, but I am still with you. Therefore, dear children, I beseech you, listen to my messages and live them, so I can guide you. Dear children, thank you for having responded to my call."

January 25, 1987
"Dear children! Behold, also today I want to call you to start living a new life as of today. Dear children, I want you to comprehend that God has chosen each one of you, in order to use you in His great plan for the salvation of mankind. You are not able to comprehend how great your role is in God's

design. Therefore, dear children, pray so that in prayer you may be able to comprehend what God's plan is in your regard. I am with you in order that you may be able to bring it about in all its fullness. Thank you for having responded to my call."

February 25, 1987
"Dear children! Today I want to wrap you all in my mantle and lead you all along the way of conversion. Dear children, I beseech you, surrender to the Lord your entire past, all the evil that has accumulated in your hearts. I want each one of you to be happy, but in sin nobody can be happy. Therefore, dear children, pray, and in prayer you shall realize a new way of joy. Joy will manifest in your hearts and thus you shall be joyful witnesses of that which I and My Son want from each one of you. I am blessing you. Thank you for having responded to my call."

March 25, 1987
"Dear children! Today I am grateful to you for your presence in this place, where I am giving you special graces. I call each one of you to begin to live as of today that life which God wishes of you and to begin to perform good works of love and mercy. I do not want you, dear children, to live the message and be committing sin which is displeasing to me. Therefore, dear children, I want each of you to live a new life without destroying all that God produces in you and is giving you. I give you my special blessing and I am remaining with you on your way of conversion. Thank you for having responded to my call."

April 25, 1987
"Dear children! Today also I am calling you to prayer. You know, dear children, that God grants special graces in prayer. Therefore, seek and pray in order that you may be able to comprehend all that I am giving here. I call you, dear

children, to prayer with the heart. You know that without prayer you cannot comprehend all that God is planning through each one of you. Therefore, pray! I desire that through each one of you God's plan may be fulfilled, that all which God has planted in your heart may keep on growing. So pray that God's blessing may protect each one of you from all the evil that is threatening you. I bless you, dear children. Thank you for having responded to my call."

May 25, 1987
"Dear children! I am calling everyone of you to start living in God's love. Dear children, you are ready to commit sin, and to put yourselves in the hand of Satan without reflecting. I call on each one of you to consciously decide for God and against Satan. I am your Mother and, therefore, I want to lead you all to perfect holiness. I want each one of you to be happy here on earth and to be with me in Heaven. That is, dear children, the purpose of my coming here and it's my desire. Thank you for having responded to my call."

June 25, 1987
"Dear children! Today I thank you and I want to invite you all to God's peace. I want each one of you to experience in your heart that peace which God gives. I want to bless you all today. I am blessing you with God's blessing and I beseech you, dear children, to follow and to live my way. I love you, dear children, and so not even counting the number of times, I go on calling you and I thank you for all that you are doing for my intentions. I beg you, help me to present you to God and to save you. Thank you for having responded to my call."

July 25, 1987
"Dear children! I beseech you to take up the way of holiness beginning today. I love you and, therefore, I want you to be holy. I do not want Satan to block you on that way. Dear

children, pray and accept all that God is offering you on a way which is bitter. But at the same time, God will reveal every sweetness to whomever begins to go on that way, and He will gladly answer every call of God. Do not attribute importance to petty things. Long for Heaven. Thank you for having responded to my call."

August 25, 1987
"Dear children! Today also I am calling you all in order that each one of you decides to live my messages. God has permitted me also in this year, which the Church has dedicated to me, to be able to speak to you and to be able to spur you on to holiness. Dear children, seek from God the graces which He is giving you through me. I am ready to intercede with God for all that you seek so that your holiness may be complete. Therefore, dear children, do not forget to seek, because God has permitted me to obtain graces for you. Thank you for having responded to my call."

September 25, 1987
"Dear children! Today also I want to call you all to prayer. Let prayer be your life. Dear children, dedicate your time only to Jesus and He will give you everything that you are seeking. He will reveal Himself to you in fullness. Dear children, Satan is strong and is waiting to test each one of you. Pray, and that way he will neither be able to injure you nor block you on the way of holiness. Dear children, through prayer grow all the more toward God from day to day. Thank you for having responded to my call."

October 25, 1987
"My dear children! Today I want to call all of you to decide for Paradise. The way is difficult for those who have not decided for God. Dear children, decide and believe that God is offering Himself to you in His fullness. You are invited and you need to answer the call of the Father, Who is calling

you through me. Pray, because in prayer each one of you will be able to achieve complete love. I am blessing you and I desire to help you so that each one of you might be under my motherly mantle. Thank you for having responded to my call."

November 25, 1987
"Dear children! Today also I call each one of you to decide to surrender again everything completely to me. Only that way will I be able to present each of you to God. Dear children, you know that I love you immeasurably and that I desire each of you for myself, but God has given to all a freedom which I lovingly respect and humbly submit to. I desire, dear children, that you help so that everything God has planned in this parish shall be realized. If you do not pray, you shall not be able to recognize my love and the plans which God has for this parish and for each individual. Pray that Satan does not entice you with his pride and deceptive strength. I am with you and I want you to believe me, that I love you. Thank you for having responded to my call."

December 25, 1987
"Dear children! Rejoice with me! My heart is rejoicing because of Jesus and today I want to give Him to you. Dear children, I want each one of you to open your heart to Jesus and I will give Him to you with love. Dear children, I want Him to change you, to teach you and to protect you. Today I am praying in a special way for each one of you and I am presenting you to God so He will manifest Himself in you. I am calling you to sincere prayer with the heart so that every prayer of yours may be an encounter with God. In your work and in your everyday life, put God in the first place. I call you today with great seriousness to obey me and to do as I am calling you. Thank you for having responded to my call."

1988

January 25, 1988

"Dear children! Today again I am calling you to complete conversion, which is difficult for those who have not chosen God. God can give you everything that you seek from Him. But you seek God only when sicknesses, problems and difficulties come to you and you think that God is far from you and is not listening and does not hear your prayers. No, dear children, that is not the truth. When you are far from God, you cannot receive graces because you do not seek them with a firm faith. Day by day, I am praying for you, and I want to draw you ever more near to God, but I cannot if you don't want it. Therefore, dear children put your life in God's hands. I bless you all. Thank you for having responded to my call."

February 25, 1988

"Dear children! Today again I am calling you to prayer to complete surrender to God. You know that I love you and am coming here out of love so I could show you the path to peace and salvation for your souls. I want you to obey me and not permit Satan to seduce you. Dear children, Satan is very strong and, therefore, I ask you to dedicate your prayers to me so that those who are under his influence can be saved. Give witness by your life. Sacrifice your lives for the salvation of the world. I am with you, and I am grateful to you, but in heaven you shall receive the Father's reward which He has promised to you. Therefore, dear children, do not be afraid. If you pray, Satan cannot injure you even a little bit because you are God's children and He is watching over you. Pray and let the rosary always be in your hand as a sign to Satan that you belong to me. Thank you for having responded to my call."

March 25, 1988
"Dear children! Today also I am inviting you to a complete surrender to God. Dear children, you are not conscious of how God loves you with such a great love because He permits me to be with you so I can instruct you and help you to find the way of peace. This way, however, you cannot discover if you do not pray. Therefore, dear children, forsake everything and consecrate your time to God and God will bestow gifts upon you and bless you. Little children, don't forget that your life is fleeting like a spring flower which today is wondrously beautiful but tomorrow has vanished. Therefore, pray in such a way that your prayer, your surrender to God, may become like a road sign. That way, your witness will not only have value for yourselves but for all eternity. Thank you for having responded to my call."

April 25, 1988
"Dear children! God wants to make you holy. Therefore, through me He is inviting you to complete surrender. Let holy mass be your life. Understand that the church is God's palace, the place in which I gather you and want to show you the way to God. Come and pray. Neither look at others nor slander them, but rather, let your life be a testimony on the way of holiness. Churches deserve respect and are set apart as holy because God, who became man, dwells in them day and night. Therefore, little children, believe and pray that the Father increase your faith, and then ask for whatever you need. I am with you and I am rejoicing because of you conversion and I am protecting you with my motherly mantle. Thank you for having responded to my call."

May 25, 1988
"Dear children! I am inviting you to a complete surrender to God. Pray, little children, that Satan may not carry you about like the branches in the wind. Be strong in God. I desire that through you the whole world may get to know the God of

joy. By your life bear witness for God's joy. Do not be anxious nor worried. God himself will help you and show you the way. I desire that you love all men with my love. Only in that way can love reign over the world. Little children, you are mine. I love you and want you to surrender to me so that I can lead you to God. Never cease praying so that Satan cannot take advantage of you. Pray for the knowledge that you are mine. I bless you with blessings of joy. Thank you for having responded to my call."

June 25, 1988
"Dear children! I am calling you to that love which is loyal and pleasing to God. Little children, love bears everything bitter and difficult for the sake of Jesus who is love. Therefore, dear children, pray that God come to your aid, not however according to your desire, but according to His love. Surrender yourself to God so that He may hear you, console you and forgive everything inside you which is a hindrance on the way of love. In this way God can move your life, and you will grow in love. Dear children, glorify God with a hymn of love so that God's love may be able to grow in you day by day to its fullness. Thank you for having responded to my call."

July 25, 1988
"Dear children! Today I am calling you to a complete surrender to God. Everything you do and everything you possess give over to God so that He can take control in your life as the King of all that you possess. That way, through me, God can lead you into the depths of the spiritual life. Little children, do not be afraid, because I am with you even if you think there is no way out and that Satan is in control. I am bringing peace to you I am your mother, the Queen of Peace. I am blessing you with the blessings of joy so that for you God may be everything in your life. Thank you for having responded to my call."

August 25, 1988
"Dear children! Today I invite you all to rejoice in the life which God gives you. Little children, rejoice in God, the Creator, because He has created you so wonderfully. Pray that your life be joyful thanksgiving which flows out of your heart like a river of joy. Little children, give thanks unceasingly for all that you possess, for each little gift which God has given you, so that a joyful blessing always comes down from God upon your life. Thank you for having responded to my call."

September 25, 1988
"Dear children! Today I am inviting all of you, without exception, to the way of holiness in your life. God gave you the grace, the gift of holiness. Pray that you may, more and more, comprehend it, and in that way, you will be able, by your life, to bear witness for God. Dear children, I am blessing you and I intercede to God for you so that your way and your witness may be a complete one and a joy for God. Thank you for having responded to my call."

October 25, 1988
"Dear children! My invitation that you live the messages which I am giving you is a daily one, specially, little children, because I want to draw you closer to the Heart of Jesus. Therefore, little children, I am inviting you today to the prayer of consecration to Jesus, my dear Son, so that each of you may be His. And then I am inviting you to the consecration of my Immaculate Heart. I want you to consecrate yourselves as parents, as families and as parishioners so that all belong to God through my heart. Therefore, little children, pray that you comprehend the greatness of this message which I am giving you. I do not want anything for myself, rather all for the salvation of your soul. Satan is strong and therefore, you, little children, by

constant prayer, press tightly against my motherly heart. Thank you for having responded to my call."

November 25, 1988
"Dear children! I call you to prayer, to have an encounter with God in prayer. God gives Himself to you, but He wants you to answer in your own freedom to his invitation. That is why little children during the day, find yourself a special time when you could pray in peace and humility, and have this meeting with God the creator. I am with you and I intercede for you in front of God, so watch in vigil, so that every encounter in prayer be the joy of your contact with God. Thank you for having responded to my call."

December 25, 1988
"Dear children! I call you to peace. Live it in your heart and all around you, so that all will know peace, peace that does not come from you but from God. Little children, today is a great day. Rejoice with me. Glorify the Nativity of Jesus through the peace that I give you. It is for this peace that I have come as your Mother, Queen of Peace. Today I give you my special blessing. Bring it to all creation, so that all creation will know peace. Thank you for having responded to my call."

1989

January 25, 1989
"Dear children! Today I am calling you to the way of holiness. Pray that you may comprehend the beauty and the greatness of this way where God reveals himself to you in a special way. Pray that you may be open to everything that God does through you that in your life you may be enabled to give thanks to God and to rejoice over everything that He

does through each individual. I give you my blessing. Thank you for having responded to my call."

February 25, 1989
"Dear children! Today I invite you to prayer of the heart. Throughout this season of grace I wish each of you to be united with Jesus, but without unceasing prayer you cannot experience the beauty and greatness of the grace which God is offering you. Therefore, little children, at all times fill your heart with even the smallest prayers. I am with you and unceasingly keep watch over every heart which is given to me. Thank you for having responded to my call."

March 25, 1989
"Dear children! I am calling you to a complete surrender to God. I am calling you to great joy and peace which only God can give. I am with you and I intercede for you every day before God. I call you, little children, to listen to me and to live the messages that I am giving you. Already for years you are invited to holiness but you are still far away. I am blessing you. Thank you for having responded to my call."

April 25, 1989
"Dear children! I am calling you to a complete surrender to God. Let everything that you possess be in the hands of God. Only in that way shall you have joy in your heart. Little children, rejoice in everything that you have. Give thanks to God because everything is God's gift to you. That way in your life you shall be able to give thanks for everything and discover God in everything even in the smallest flower. Thank you for having responded to my call."

May 25, 1989
"Dear children! I invite you now to be open to God. See, children, how nature is opening herself and is giving life and fruits. In the same way I invite you to live with God and to

surrender completely to him. Children, I am with you and I want to introduce you continuously to the joy of life. I desire that everyone may discover the joy and love which can be found only in God and which only God can give. God doesn't want anything from you only your surrender. Therefore, children, decide seriously for God because everything else passes away. Only God doesn't pass away. Pray to be able to discover the greatness and joy of life which God gives you. Thank you for having responded to my call."

June 25, 1989
"Dear children! Today I am calling you to live the messages I have been giving you during the past eight years. This is the time of grace and I desire the grace of God be great for every single one of you. I am blessing you and I love you with a special love. Thank you for having responded to call."

July 25, 1989
"Dear children! Today I am calling you to renew your hearts. Open yourselves to God and surrender to him all your difficulties and crosses so, God may turn everything into joy. Little children, you cannot open yourselves to God if you do not pray. Therefore, from today, decide to consecrate a time in the day only for an encounter with God in silence. In that way you will be able, with God, to witness my presence here. Little children, I do not wish to force you. Rather freely give God your time, like children of God. Thank you for having responded to my call."

August 25, 1989
"Dear children! I call you to prayer. By means of prayer, little children, you obtain joy and peace. Through prayer you are richer in the mercy of God. Therefore, little children, let prayer be the life of each one of you. Especially I call you to pray so that all those who are far away from God may be

converted. Then our hearts shall be richer because God will rule in the hearts of all men. Therefore, little children, pray, pray, pray! Let prayers begin to rule in the whole world. Thank you for having responded to my call."

September 25, 1989
"Dear children! Today I invite you to give thanks to God for all the gifts you have discovered in the course of your life and even for the least gift that you have perceived. I give thanks with you and want all of you to experience the joy of these gifts. And I want God to be everything for each one of you. And then, little children, you can grow continuously on the way of holiness. Thank you for responding to my call."

October 25, 1989
"Dear children! Today also I am inviting you to prayer. I am always inviting you, but you are still far away. Therefore, from today, decide seriously to dedicate time to God. I am with you and I wish to teach you to pray with the heart. In prayer with the heart you shall encounter God. Therefore, little children, pray, pray, pray! Thank you for having responded to my call."

November 25, 1989
"Dear children! I am inviting you for years by these messages which I am giving you. Little children, by means of the messages I wish to make a very beautiful mosaic in your hearts, so I may be able to present each one of you to God like the original image. Therefore, little children, I desire that your decisions be free before God, because He has given you freedom. Therefore pray, so that, free from any influence of Satan, we may decide only for God. I am praying for you before God and I am seeking your surrender to God. Thank you for responding to my call."

December 25, 1989
"Dear children! Today I bless you in a special way with my motherly blessing and I am interceding for you before God that He gives you the gift of conversion of the heart. For years I am calling you and exhorting you to a deep spiritual life in simplicity, but you are so cold. Therefore, little children, I ask you to accept and live the messages with seriousness, so that your soul will not be sad when I will no longer be with you, and when I will no longer lead you like insecure children in their first steps. Therefore, little children, every day read the messages that I have given you and transform them into life. I love you and therefore I am calling you all to the way of salvation with God. Thank you for having responded to my call."

1990

January 25, 1990
"Dear children! Today I invite you to decide for God once again and to choose Him before everything and above everything, so that He may work miracles in your life and that day by day your life may become joy with Him. Therefore, little children, pray and do not permit Satan to work in your life through misunderstandings, the non-understanding and non-acceptance of one another. Pray that you may be able to comprehend the greatness and the beauty of the gift of life. Thank you for having responded to my call."

February 25, 1990
"Dear children! I invite you to surrender to God. In this season I specially want you to renounce all the things to which you are attached but which are hurting your spiritual life. Therefore, little children, decide completely for God,

and do not allow Satan to come into your life through those things that hurt both you and your spiritual life. Little children, God is offering Himself to you in fullness, and you can discover and recognize Him only in prayer. Therefore make a decision for prayer. Thank you for having responded to call."

March 25, 1990
"Dear children! I am with you even if you are not conscious of it. I want to protect you from everything that Satan offers you and through which he wants to destroy you. As I bore Jesus in my womb, so also, dear children, do I wish to bear you into holiness. God wants to save you and sends you messages through men, nature, and so many things which can only help you to understand that you must change the direction of your life. Therefore, little children, understand also the greatness of the gift which God is giving you through me, so that I may protect you with my mantle and lead you to the joy of life. Thank you for having responded to my call."

April 25, 1990
"Dear children! Today I invite you to accept with seriousness and to live the messages which I am giving you. I am with you and I desire, dear children, that each one of you be ever closer to my heart. Therefore, little children, pray and seek the will of God in your everyday life. I desire that each one of you discover the way of holiness and grow in it until eternity. I will pray for you and intercede for you before God that you understand the greatness of this gift which God is giving me that I can be with you. Thank you for having responded to my call."

May 25, 1990
"Dear children! I invite you to decide with seriousness to live this novena. Consecrate the time to prayer and to sacrifice. I

am with you and I desire to help you to grow in renunciation and mortification, that you may be able to understand the beauty of the life of people who go on giving themselves to me in special way. Dear children, God blesses you day after day and desires a change of your life. Therefore, pray that you may have the strength to change your life. Thank you for having responded to my call."

June 25, 1990
"Dear children! Today I desire to thank you for all your sacrifices and for all your prayers. I am blessing you with my special motherly blessing. I invite you all to decide for God, so that from day to day you will discover His will in prayer. I desire, dear children, to call all of you to a full conversion so that joy will be in your hearts. I am happy that you are here today in such great numbers. Thank you for having responded to my call."

July 25, 1990
"Dear children! Today I invite you to peace. I have come here as the Queen of Peace and I desire to enrich you with my motherly peace. Dear children, I love you and I desire to bring all of you to the peace which only God gives and which enriches every heart. I invite you to become carriers and witnesses of my peace to this unpeaceful world. Let peace reign in the whole world which is without peace and longs for peace. I bless you with my motherly blessing. Thank you for having responded to my call."

August 25, 1990
"Dear children! I desire to invite you to take with seriousness and put into practice the messages which I am giving you. You know, little children, that I am with you and I desire to lead you along the same path to heaven, which is beautiful for those who discover it in prayer. Therefore, little children, do not forget that those messages which I am giving you

have to be put into your everyday life in order that you might be able to say: "There, I have taken the messages and tried to live them." Dear children, I am protecting you before the heavenly Father by my own prayers. Thank you for having responded to my call."

September 25, 1990
"Dear children! I invite you to pray with the heart in order that your prayer may be a conversation with God. I desire each one of you to dedicate more time to God. Satan is strong and wants to destroy and deceive you in many ways. Therefore, dear children, pray every day that your life will be good for yourselves and for all those you meet. I am with you and I am protecting you even though Satan wishes to destroy my plans and to hinder the desires which the Heavenly Father wants to realize here. Thank you for having responded to my call."

October 25, 1990
"Dear children! Today I call you to pray in a special way that you offer up sacrifices and good deeds for peace in the world. Satan is strong and with all his strength, desires to destroy the peace which comes from God. Therefore, dear children, pray in a special way with me for peace. I am with you and I desire to help you with my prayers and I desire to guide you on the path of peace. I bless you with my motherly blessing. Do not forget to live the messages of peace. Thank you for having responded to my call."

November 25, 1990
"Dear children! Today I invite you to do works of mercy with love and out of love for me and for your and my brothers and sisters. Dear children, all that you do for others, do it with great joy and humility towards God. I am with you and day after day I offer your sacrifices and prayers to God

for the salvation of the world. Thank you for having responded to my call."

December 25, 1990
"Dear children! Today I invite you in a special way to pray for peace. Dear children, without peace you cannot experience the birth of the little Jesus neither today nor in your daily lives. Therefore, pray the Lord of Peace that He may protect you with His mantle and that He may help you to comprehend the greatness and the importance of peace in your heart. In this way you shall be able to spread peace from your heart throughout the whole world. I am with you and I intercede for you before God. Pray, because Satan wants to destroy my plans of peace. Be reconciled with one another and by means of your lives help peace reign in the whole earth. Thank you for having responded to my call."

1991

January 25, 1991
"Dear children! Today, like never before, I invite you to prayer. Let your prayer be a prayer for peace. Satan is strong and desires to destroy not only human life, but also nature and the planet on which you live. Therefore, dear children, pray that through prayer you can protect yourselves with God's blessing of peace. God has sent me among you so that I may help you. If you so wish, grasp for the rosary. Even the rosary alone can work miracles in the world and in your lives. I bless you and I remain with you for as long as it is God's will. Thank you for not betraying my presence here and I thank you because your response is serving the good and the peace."

February 25, 1991

"Dear children! Today, I invite you to decide for God, because distance from god is the fruit of the lack of peace in your hearts. God is only peace. Therefore, approach Him through your personal prayer and then live peace in your hearts and in this way peace will flow from your hearts like a river into the whole world. Do not talk about peace, but make peace. I am blessing each of you and each good decision of yours. Thank you for having responded to my call."

March 25, 1991

"Dear children! Again today I invite you to live the passion of Jesus in prayer, and in union with Him. Decide to give more time to God who gave you these days of grace. Therefore, dear children, pray and in a special way renew the love for Jesus for in your hearts. I am with you and I accompany you with my blessing any my prayers. Thank you for having responded to my call."

April 25, 1991

"Dear children! Today I invite you all so that your prayer be prayer with the heart. Let each of you find time for prayer so that in prayer you discover God. I do not desire you to talk about prayer, but to pray. Let your every day be filled with prayer of gratitude to God for life and for all that you have. I do not desire your life to pass by in words but that you glorify God with deeds. I am with you and I am grateful to God for every moment spent with you. Thank you for having responded to my call."

May 25,1991

"Dear Children! Today I invite all of you who have heard my message of peace to realize it with seriousness and with love in your life. There are many who think that they are doing a lot by talking about the messages, but do not live them. Dear children, I invite you to life and to change all the negative in you, so that it all turns into the positive and life. Dear children, I am with you and I desire to help each of you to live and by living, to witness the good news. I am here, dear children, to help you and to lead you to heaven, and in heaven is the joy through which you can already live heaven now. Thank you for having responded to my call!"

June 25,1991

"Dear children! Today on this great day which you have given to me, I desire to bless all of you and to say: these days while I am with you are days of grace. I desire to teach you and help you to walk the way of holiness. There are many people who do not desire to understand my messages and to accept with seriousness what I am saying. But you I therefore call and ask that by your lives and by your daily living you witness my presence. If you pray, God will help you to discover the true reason for my coming. Therefore, little children, pray and read the Sacred Scriptures so that through my coming you discover the message in Sacred Scripture for you. Thank you for having responded to my call."

July 25, 1991

"Dear Children! Today I invite you to pray for peace. At this time peace is being threatened in a special way, and I am seeking from you to renew fasting and prayer in your families. Dear children, I desire you to grasp the seriousness of the situation and that much of what will happen depends on your prayers and you are praying a little bit. Dear children, I am with you and I am inviting you to begin to pray and fast seriously as in the first days of my coming. Thank you for having responded to my call."

August 25, 1991
"Dear Children! Today also I invite you to prayer, now as never before when my plan has begun to be realized. Satan is strong and wants to sweep away plans of peace and joy and make you think that my Son is not strong in his decisions. Therefore, I call all of you, dear children to pray and fast still more firmly. I invite you to realize through the secrets I began in Fatima may be fulfilled. I call you, dear children, to grasp the importance of my coming and the seriousness of the situation. I want to save all souls and present them to God. Therefore, let us pray that everything I have begun be fully realized. Thank you for having responded to my call."

September 25, 1991
"Dear children! Today in a special way I invite you all to prayer and renunciation. For now as never before Satan wants to show the world his shameful face by which he wants to seduce as many people as possible onto the way of death and sin. Therefore, dear children, help my Immaculate Heart to triumph in the sinful world. I beseech all of you to offer prayers and sacrifices for my intentions so I can present them to God for what is most necessary. Forget your desires, dear children, and pray for what God desires, and not for what you desire. Thank you for having responded to my call."

October 25, 1991
"Dear children! Pray! Pray! Pray!"

November 25, 1991
"Dear Children! This time also I am inviting you to prayer. Pray that you might be able to comprehend what God desires to tell you through my presence and through the messages I am giving you. I desire to draw you ever closer to Jesus and to His wounded heart that you might be able to comprehend the immeasurable love which gave itself for each one of you.

Therefore, dear children, pray that from your heart would flow a fountain of love to every person both to the one who hates you and to the one who despises you. That way you will be able through Jesus' love to overcome all the misery in this world of sorrows, which is without hope for those who do not know Jesus. I am with you and I love you with the immeasurable love of Jesus. Thank you for all your sacrifices and prayers. Pray so I might be able to help you still more. Your prayers are necessary to me. Thank you for having responded to my call."

December 25, 1991
"Dear children! Today in a special way I bring the little Jesus to you, that He may bless you with His blessing of peace and love. Dear children, do not forget that this is a grace which many people neither understand nor accept. Therefore, you who have said that you are mine, and seek my help, give all of yourself. First of all, give your love and example in your families. You say that Christmas is a family feast. Therefore, dear children, put God in the first place in your families, so that He may give you peace and may protect you not only from war, but also in peace protect you from every satanic attack. When God is with you, you have everything. But when you do not want Him, then you are miserable and lost, and you do not know on whose side you are. Therefore, dear children, decide for God. Then you will get everything. Thank you for having responded to my call."

1992

January 25, 1992
"Dear Children! Today, I am inviting you to a renewal of prayer in your families so that way every family will become a joy to my son Jesus. Therefore, dear children, pray and

seek more time for Jesus and then you will be able to understand and accept everything, even the most difficult sicknesses and crosses. I am with you and I desire to take you into my heart and protect you, but you have not yet decided. Therefore, dear children, I am seeking for you to pray, so through prayer you would allow me to help you. Pray, my dear little children, so prayer becomes your daily bread. Thank you for having responded to my call."

February 25, 1992
"Dear children! Today I invite you to draw still closer to God through prayer. Only that way will I be able to help you and to protect you from every attack of Satan. I am with you and I intercede for you with God, that He protect you. But I need your prayers and your - "Yes." You get lost easily in material and human things, and forget that God is your greatest friend. Therefore, my dear little children, draw close to God so He may protect you and guard you from every evil. Thank you for having responded to my call!"

March 25, 1992
"Dear children! Today as never before I invite you to live my messages and to put them into practice in your life. I have come to you to help you and, therefore, I invite you to change your life because you have taken a path of misery, a path of ruin. When I told you: convert, pray, fast, be reconciled, you took these messages superficially. You started to live them and then you stopped, because it was difficult for you. No, dear children, when something is good, you have to persevere in the good and not think: God does not see me, He is not listening, He is not helping. And so you have gone away from God and from me because of your miserable interest. I wanted to create of you an oasis of peace, love and goodness. God wanted you, with your love and with His help, to do miracles and, thus, give an example. Therefore, here is what I say to you: Satan is playing with

you and with your souls and I cannot help you because you are far away from my heart. Therefore, pray, live my messages and then you will see the miracles of God's love in your everyday life. Thank you for having responded to my call."

April 25, 1992

"Dear children! Today also I invite you to prayer. Only by prayer and fasting can war be stopped. Therefore, my dear little children, pray and by your life give witness that you are mine and that you belong to me, because Satan wishes in these turbulent days to seduce as many souls as possible. Therefore, I invite you to decide for God and He will protect you and show you what you should do and which path to take. I invite all those who have said "yes" to me to renew their consecration to my Son Jesus and to His Heart and to me so we can take you more intensely as instruments of peace in this unpeaceful world. Medjugorje is a sign to all of you and a call to pray and live the days of grace that God is giving you. Therefore, dear children, accept the call to prayer with seriousness. I am with you and your suffering is also mine. Thank you for having responded to my call."

May 25, 1992

"Dear children! Today also I invite you to prayer, so that through prayer you come still nearer to God. I am with you and I desire to lead you on the path to salvation that Jesus gives you. From day to day, I am nearer to you although you are not aware of it and you do not want to admit that you are only linked to me in a small way with your few prayers. When trials and problems arise, you say, "O God! O Mother! Where are you?" As for me, I only wait for your "Yes" to present to Jesus for Him to fill you with His grace. That is why, once more, please accept my call and start to pray in a new way until prayer becomes joy to you. Then you will discover that God is all-powerful in your daily life. I am with you and I am waiting for you. Thank you for having responded to my call."

June 25, 1992
"Dear children! Today I am happy, even if in my heart there is still a little sadness for all those who have started on this path and then have left it. My presence here is to take you on a new path, the path to salvation. This is why I call you, day after day to conversion. But if you do not pray, you cannot say that you are on the way to being converted. I pray for you and I intercede to God for peace; first peace in your hearts and also peace around you, so that God may be your peace. Thank you for having responded to my call."

July 25, 1992
"Dear children! Today also I invite you to prayer, a prayer of joy so that in these sad days no one amongst you may feel sadness in prayer, but a joyful meeting with God His Creator. Pray, little children, to be able to come closer to me and to feel through prayer what it is I desire from you. I am with you and each day I bless you with my maternal blessing so that Our Lord may fill you abundantly with His grace for your daily life. Give thanks to God for the grace of my being able to be with you because I assure you it is a great grace. Thank you for having responded to my call."

August 25, 1992
"Dear children! Today I desire to tell you that I love you. I love you with my maternal love and I invite you to open yourselves completely to me so that, through each one of you, I can convert and save this world which is full of sin and bad things. That is why, my dear little children, you should open yourselves completely to me so that I may carry you always further toward the marvelous love of God the Creator who reveals Himself to you from day to day. I am

with you and I wish to reveal to you and show you the God who loves you. Thank you for having responded to my call."

September 25, 1992
"Dear children! Today again I would like to say to you that I am with you also in these troubled days during which Satan wishes to destroy all that my Son Jesus and I are building. He desires especially to destroy your souls. He wants to take you away as far as possible from the Christian life and from the commandments that the Church calls you to live. Satan wishes to destroy everything that is holy in you and around you. This is why, little children, pray, pray, pray to be able to grasp all that God is giving you through my coming. Thank you for having responded to my call."

October 25, 1992
"Dear children! I invite you to prayer now when Satan is strong and wishes to make as many souls as possible his own. Pray, dear children, and have more trust in me because I am here in order to help you and to guide you on a new path toward a new life. Therefore, dear little children, listen and live what I tell you because it is important for you when I shall not be with you any longer that you remember my words and all that I told you. I call you to begin to change your life from the beginning and that you decide for conversion not with words but with your life. Thank you for having responded to my call."

November 25, 1992
"Dear Children! Today, more than ever, I am calling you to pray. May your life become a continuous prayer. Without love you cannot pray. That is why I am calling you to love God, the Creator of your lives, above everything else. Then you will come to know God and will love Him in everything as He loves you. Dear children, it is a grace that I am with you. That is why you should accept and live my messages

for your own good. I love you and that is why I am with you, in order to teach you and to lead you to a new life of conversion and renunciation. Only in this way will you discover God and all that which now seems so far away from you. Therefore, my dear children, pray. Thank you for having responded to my call."

December 25, 1992
"Dear children! I desire to place all of you under my mantle and protect you from all satanic attacks. Today is a day of peace, but in the whole world there is a great lack of peace. That is why I call you all to build a new world of peace with me through prayer. This I cannot do without you, and this is why I call all of you with my motherly love and God will do the rest. So, open yourselves to God's plan and to His designs to be able to cooperate with Him for peace and for everything that is good. Do not forget that your life does not belong to you, but is a gift with which you must bring joy to others and lead them to eternal life. May the tenderness of the little Jesus always accompany you. Thank you for having responded to my call."

1993

January 25, 1993
"Dear children! Today I call you to accept and live my messages with seriousness. These days are the days when you need to decide for God, for peace and for the good. May every hatred and jealousy disappear from your life and your thoughts, and may there only dwell love for God and for your neighbor. Thus, and only thus shall you be able to discern the signs of the time. I am with you and I guide you into a new time, a time which God gives you as grace so that

you may get to know him more. Thank you for having responded to my call."

February 25, 1993
"Dear children! Today I bless you with my motherly blessing and I invite you all to conversion. I wish that each of you decide for a change of life and that each of you works more in the Church not through words and thoughts but through example, so that your life may be a joyful testimony for Jesus. You cannot say that you are converted, because your life must become a daily conversion. In order to understand what you have to do, little children, pray and God will give you what you completely have to do, and where you have to change. I am with you and place you all under my mantle. Thank you for having responded to my call."

March 25, 1993
"Dear children! Today like never I call you to pray for peace, for peace in your hearts, peace in your families and peace in the whole world, because Satan wants war, wants lack of peace, wants to destroy all which is good. Therefore, dear children, pray, pray, pray. Thank you for having responded to my call."

April 25, 1993
"Dear children! Today I invite you all to awaken your hearts to love. Go into nature and look how nature is awakening and it will be a help to you to open your hearts to the love of God, the Creator. I desire you to awaken love in your families so that where there is unrest and hatred, love will reign and when there is love in your hearts then there is also prayer. And, dear children, do not forget that I am with you and I am helping you with my prayer that God may give you the strength to love. I bless and love you with my motherly love. Thank you for having responded to my call."

May 25, 1993

"Dear children! Today I invite you to open yourselves to God by means of prayer so the Holy Spirit may begin to work miracles in you and through you. I am with you and I intercede before God for each one of you because, dear children, each one of you is important in my plan of salvation. I invite you to be carriers of good and peace. God can give you peace only if you convert and pray. Therefore, my dear little children, pray, pray, pray and do that which the Holy Spirit inspires you. Thank you for having responded to my call."

June 25, 1993

"Dear children! Today I also rejoice at your presence here. I bless you with my motherly blessing and intercede for each one of you before God. I call you anew to live my messages and to put them into life and practice. I am with you and bless all of you day by day. Dear children, these are special times and, therefore, I am with you to love and protect you; to protect your hearts from Satan and to bring you all closer to the heart of my Son, Jesus. Thank you for having responded to my call."

July 25, 1993

"Dear children! I thank you for your prayers and for the love you show toward me. I invite you to decide to pray for my intentions. Dear children, offer novenas, making sacrifices wherein you feel the most bound. I want your life to be bound to me. I am your Mother, little children, and I do not want Satan to deceive you for He wants to lead you the wrong way, but he cannot if you do not permit him. Therefore, little children, renew prayer in your hearts, and then you will understand my call and my live desire to help you. Thank you for having responded to my call."

August 25, 1993
"Dear children! I want you to understand that I am your Mother, that I want to help you and call you to prayer. Only by prayer can you understand and accept my messages and practice them in your life. Read Sacred Scripture, live it, and pray to understand the signs of the times. This is a special time, therefore, I am with you to draw you close to my heart and the heart of my Son, Jesus. Dear little children, I want you to be children of the light and not of the darkness. Therefore, live what I am telling you. Thank you for having responded to my call."

September 25, 1993
"Dear children! I am your Mother and I invite you to come closer to God through prayer because only He is your peace, your savior. Therefore, little children, do not seek comfort in material things, but rather seek God. I am praying for you and I intercede before God for each individual. I am looking for your prayers that you accept me and accept my messages as in the first days of the apparitions and only then when you open your hearts and pray will miracles happen. Thank you for having responded to my call."

October 25, 1993
"Dear children! These years I have been calling you to pray, to live what I am telling you, but you are living my messages a little. You talk, but do not live, that is why little children, this war is lasting so long. I invite you to open yourselves to God and in your hearts to live with God, living the good and giving witness to my messages. I love you and wish to protect you from every evil, but you do not desire it. Dear children, I cannot help you if you do not live God's commandments, if you do not live the mass, if you do not give up sin. I invite you to be apostles of love and goodness. In this world of unrest give witness to God and God's love,

and God will bless you and give you what you seek from Him. Thank you for having responded to my call."

November 25, 1993
"Dear children! I invite you in this time like never before to prepare for the coming of Jesus. Let little Jesus reign in your hearts and only then when Jesus is your friend will you be happy. It will not be difficult for you either to pray or offer sacrifices or to witness Jesus' greatness in your life because He will give you strength and joy in this time. I am close to you by my intercession and prayer and I love and bless all of you. Thank you for having responded to my call."

December 25, 1993
"Dear children! Today i rejoice with the little Jesus and I desire that Jesus' joy may enter into every heart. Little children, with the message I give you a blessing with my son Jesus, so that in every heart peace may reign. I love you, little children, and I invite all of your to come closer to me by means of prayer. You talk and talk but do not pray. Therefore, little children, decide for prayer. Only in this way will you be happy and God will give your what you seek from Him. Thank you for having responded to my call."

1994

January 25,1994
"Dear children! You are all my children. I love you. But, little children, you must not forget that without prayer you cannot be close to me. In these times Satan wants to create disorder in your hearts and in your families. Little children, do not give in. You should not allow him to lead you and your life. I love you and intercede before God for you. Little children, pray. Thank you for having responded to my call."

February 25, 1994

"Dear children! Today I thank you for your prayers. All of you have helped me so that this war may end as soon as possible. I am close to you and I pray for each one of you and I beg you: pray, pray, pray. Only through prayer can we defeat evil and protect all that Satan wants to destroy in your lives. I am your Mother and I love you all equally, and I intercede for you before God. Thank you for having responded to my call."

March 25, 1994

"Dear children! Today I rejoice with you and I invite you to open yourselves to me, and become an instrument in my hands for the salvation of the world. I desire, little children, that all of you who have felt the odor of holiness through these messages which I am giving you to carry, to carry it into this world, hungry for God and God's love. I thank you all for having responded in such a number and I bless you all with my motherly blessing. Thank you for having responded to my call."

April 25, 1994

"Dear children! Today I invite you to decide to pray according to my intention. Little children, I invite each one of you to help my plan to be realized through this parish. Now I invite you in a special way, little children, to decide to go along the way of holiness. Only this way will you be close to me. I love you and I desire to conduct you all with me to Paradise. But, if you do not pray and if you are not humble and obedient to the messages which I am giving you, I cannot help you. Thank you for having responded to my call."

May 25, 1994

"Dear children! I invite you all to have more trust in me and to live my messages more deeply. I am with you and I intercede before God for you but also I wait for your hearts to open up to my messages. Rejoice because God loves you and gives you the possibility to convert every day and to believe more in God the Creator. Thank you having responded to my call."

June 25, 1994

"Dear children! Today I rejoice in my heart in seeing you all present here. I bless you and I call you all to decide to live my messages which I give you here. I desire, little children, to guide you all to Jesus because He is your salvation. Therefore, little children, the more you pray the more you will be mine and of my Son, Jesus. I bless you all with my motherly blessing and I thank you for having responded to my call."

July 25, 1994

"Dear children! Today I invite you to decide to give time patiently for prayer. Little children, you cannot say you are mine and that you have experienced conversion through my messages if you are not ready to give time to God every day. I am close to you and I bless you all. Little children, do not forget that if you do not pray you are not close to me, nor are you close to the Holy Spirit who leads you along the path to holiness. Thank you for having responded to my call."

August 25, 1994

"Dear children! Today I am united with you in prayer in a special way, praying for the gift of the presence of my most beloved son in your home country. Pray, little children, for the health of my most beloved son, who suffers, and whom I have chosen for these times. I pray and intercede before my Son, Jesus, so that the dream that your fathers had may be fulfilled. Pray, little children, in a special way, because Satan is strong and wants to destroy hope in your heart. I bless you. Thank you for having responded to my call."

September 25, 1994
"Dear children! I rejoice with you and I invite you to prayer. Little children, pray for my intention. Your prayers are necessary to me, through which I desire to bring you closer to God. He is your salvation. God sends me to help you and to guide you towards paradise, which is your goal. Therefore, little children, pray, pray, pray. Thank you for having responded to my call."

October 25, 1994
"Dear children! I am with you and I rejoice today because the Most High has granted me to be with you and to teach you and to guide you on the path of perfection. Little children, I wish you to be a beautiful bouquet of flowers which I wish to present to God for the day of All Saints. I invite you to open yourselves and to live, taking the saints as an example. Mother Church has chosen them, that they may be an impulse for your daily life. Thank you for having responded to my call!"

November 25, 1994
"Dear children! Today I call you to prayer. I am with you and I love you all. I am your Mother and I wish that your hearts be similar to my heart. Little children, without prayer you cannot live and say that you are mine. Prayer is joy. Prayer is what the human heart desires. Therefore, get closer, little children, to my Immaculate Heart and you will discover God. Thank you for having responded to my call."

December 25, 1994
"Dear children! Today I rejoice with you and I am praying with you for peace: peace in your hearts, peace in your

families, peace in your desires, peace in the whole world. May the King of Peace bless you today and give your peace. I bless you and I carry each one of your in my heart. Thank you for having responded to my call."

1995

January 25, 1995
"Dear children! I invite you to open the door of your heart to Jesus as the flower opens itself to the sun. Jesus desires to fill your hearts with peace and joy. You cannot, little children, realize peace if your are not at peace with Jesus. Therefore, I invite you to confession so Jesus may be your truth and peace. So, little children, pray to have the strength to realize what I am telling you. I am with your and I love your. Thank you for having responded to my call."

February 25, 1995
"Dear children! Today I invite you to become missionaries of my messages, which I am giving here through this place that is dear to me. God has allowed me to stay this long with you and therefore, little children, I invite you to live with love the messages I give and to transmit them to the whole world, so that a river of love flows to people who are full of hatred and without peace. I invite you, little children, to become peace where there is no peace and light where there is darkness, so that each heart accepts the light and the way of salvation. Thank you for having responded to my call."

March 25, 1995
"Dear Children! Today I invite you to live the peace in your hearts and families. There is no peace, little children, where there is no prayer and there is no love, where there is no faith. Therefore, little children, I invite you all, to decide

again today for conversion. I am close to you and I invite you all, little children, into my embrace to help you, but you do not want and in this way, Satan is tempting you, and in the smallest thing, your faith disappears. This is why little children, pray and through prayer, you will have blessing and peace. Thank you for having responded to my call."

April 25, 1995
"Dear children! Today I call you to love. Little children, without love you can neither live with God nor with brother. Therefore, I call all of you to open your hearts to the love of God that is so great and open to each one of you. God, out of love for man, has sent me among you to show you the path of salvation, the path of love. If you do not first love God, then you will neither be able to love neighbor nor the one you hate. Therefore, little children, pray and through prayer you will discover love. Thank you for having responded to my call."

May 25, 1995
"Dear Children! I invite you, little children, to help me through your prayers so that as many hearts as possible come close to my Immaculate Heart. Satan is strong and with all his forces wants to bring closer the most people possible to himself and to sin. That is why he is on the prowl to snatch more every moment. I beg you, little children, pray and help me to help you. I am your mother and I love you and that is why I wish to help you. Thank you for having responded to my call."

June 25, 1995
"Dear Children! Today I am happy to see you in such great numbers, that you have responded and have come to live my messages. I invite you, little children, to be my joyful carriers of peace in this troubled world. Pray for peace so that as soon as possible a time of peace, which my heart

waits impatiently for, may reign. I am near to you, little children, and intercede for every one of you before the Most High. I bless you with my motherly blessing. Thank you for having responded to my call."

July 25, 1995
"Dear children! Today I invite you to prayer because only in prayer can you understand my coming here. The Holy Spirit will enlighten you to understand that you must convert. Little children, I wish to make of you a most beautiful bouquet prepared for eternity but you do not accept the way of conversion, the way of salvation that I am offering you through these apparitions. Little children, pray, convert your hearts and come closer to me. May good overcome evil. I love you and bless you. Thank you for having responded to my call."

August 25, 1995
"Dear children! Today I invite you to prayer. Let prayer be life for you. A family cannot say that it is in peace if it does not pray. Therefore, let your morning begin with morning prayer, and the evening end with thanksgiving. Little children, I am with you, and I love you and I bless you and I wish for every one of you to be in my embrace. You cannot be in my embrace if you are not ready to pray every day. Thank you for having responded to my call."

September 25, 1995
"Dear Children! Today I invite you to fall in love with the Most Holy Sacrament of the Altar. Adore Him, little children, in your Parishes and in this way you will be united with the entire world. Jesus will become your friend and you will not talk of Him like someone whom you barely know. Unity with Him will be a joy for you and you will become witnesses to the love of Jesus that He has for every creature.

Little children, when you adore Jesus you are also close to me. Thank you for having responded to my call."

October 25, 1995

"Dear Children! Today I invite you to go into nature because there you will meet God the Creator. Today I invite you, little children, to thank God for all that He gives you. In thanking Him you will discover the Most High and all the goods that surround you. Little children, God is great and His love for every creature is great. Therefore, pray to be able to understand the love and goodness of God. In the goodness and the love of God the Creator, I also am with you as a gift. Thank you for having responded to my call."

November 25, 1995

"Dear Children! Today I invite you that each of you begin again to love, in the first place, God who saved and redeemed each of you, and then brothers and sisters in your proximity. Without love, little children, you cannot grow in holiness and cannot do good deeds. Therefore, little children, pray without ceasing that God reveals His love to you. I have invited all of you to unite yourselves with me and to love. Today I am with you and invite you to discover love in your hearts and in the families. For God to live in your hearts, you must love. Thank you for having responded to my call."

December 25, 1995

"Dear Children! Today I also rejoice with you and I bring you little Jesus, so that He may bless you. I invite you, dear children, so that your life may be united with Him. Jesus is the King of Peace and only He can give you the peace that you seek. I am with you and I present you to Jesus in a special way, now in this new time in which one should decide for Him. This time is the time of grace. Thank you for having responded to my call."

1996

January 25, 1996
"Dear Children! Today I invite you to decide for peace. Pray that God give you the true peace. Live peace in your hearts and you will understand, dear children, that peace is the gift of God. Dear children, without love you cannot live peace. The fruit of peace is love and the fruit of love is forgiveness. I am with you and I invite all of you, little children, that before all else forgive in the family and then you will be able to forgive others. Thank you for having responded to my call."

February 25, 1996
"Dear children! Today I invite you to conversion. This is the most important message that I have given you here. Little children, I wish that each of you become a carrier of my messages. I invite you, little children, to live the messages that I have given you over these years. This time is a time of grace. Especially now, when the Church also is inviting you to prayer and conversion. I also, little children, invite you to live my messages that I have given you during the time since I appear here. Thank you for having responded to my call."

March 25, 1996
"Dear children! I invite you to decide again to love God above all else. In this time when due to the spirit of consumerism one forgets what it means to love and to cherish true values, I invite you again, little children, to put God in the first place in your life. Do not let Satan attract you through material things but, little children, decide for God who is freedom and love. Choose life and not death of the soul, little children, and in this time when you meditate upon the suffering and death of Jesus I invite you to decide for life which blossomed through the Resurrection, and that

your life may be renewed today through conversion that shall lead you to eternal life. Thank you for having responded to my call."

April 25, 1996
"Dear children! Today I invite you again to put prayer in the first place in your families. Little children, when God is in the first place, then you will, in all that you do, seek the will of God. In this way your daily conversion will become easier. Little children, seek with humility that which is not in order in your hearts, and you shall understand what you have to do. Conversion will become a daily duty that you will do with joy. Little children, I am with you, I bless you all and I invite you to become my witnesses by prayer and personal conversion. Thank you for having responded to my call."

May 25, 1996
"Dear children! Today I wish to thank you for all your prayers and sacrifices that you, during this month which is consecrated to me, have offered to me. Little children, I also wish that you all become active during this time that is through me connected to heaven in a special way. Pray in order to understand that you all, through your life and your example, ought to collaborate in the work of salvation. Little children, I wish that all people convert and see me and my son, Jesus, in you. I will intercede for you and help you to become the light. In helping the other, your soul will also find salvation. Thank you for having responded to my call."

June 25, 1996
"Dear children! Today I thank you for all the sacrifices you have offered me these days. Little children, I invite you to open yourselves to me and to decide for conversion. Your hearts, little children, are still not completely open to me and therefore, I invite you again to open to prayer so that in prayer the Holy Spirit will help you, that your hearts become

of flesh and not of stone. Little children, thank you for having responded to my call and for having decided to walk with me toward holiness."

July 25, 1996
"Dear children! Today I invite you to decide every day for God. Little children, you speak much about God, but you witness little with your life. Therefore, little children, decide for conversion, that your life may be true before God, so that in the truth of your life you witness the beauty God gave you. Little children, I invite you again to decide for prayer because through prayer, you will be able to live the conversion. Each one of you shall become in the simplicity, similar to a child which is open to the love of the Father. Thank you for having responded to my call."

August 25, 1996
"Dear children! Listen, because I wish to speak to you and to invite you to have more faith and trust in God, who loves you immeasurably. Little children, you do not know how to live in the grace of God, that is why I call you all anew, to carry the word of God in your heart and in thoughts. Little children, place the Sacred Scripture in a visible place in your family, and read and live it. Teach your children, because if you are not an example to them, children depart into godlessness. Reflect and pray and then God will be born in your heart and your heart will be joyous. Thank you for having for responded to my call."

September 25, 1996
"Dear children! Today I invite you to offer your crosses and suffering for my intentions. Little children, I am your mother and I wish to help you by seeking for you the grace from God. Little children, offer your sufferings as a gift to God so they become a most beautiful flower of joy. That is why, little children, pray that you may understand that suffering

can become joy and the cross the way of joy. Thank you for having for responded to my call."

October 25, 1996
"Dear children! Today I invite you to open yourselves to God the Creator, so that He changes you. Little children, you are dear to me. I love you all and I call you to be closer to me and that your love towards my Immaculate Heart be more fervent. I wish to renew you and lead you with my Heart to the Heart of Jesus, which still today suffers for you and calls you to conversion and renewal. Through you, I wish to renew the world. Comprehend, little children, that you are today the salt of the earth and the light of the world. Little children, I invite you and I love you and in a special way implore: Convert!" Thank you for having responded to my call."

November 25, 1996
"Dear children! Today, again, I invite you to pray, so that through prayer, fasting and small sacrifices you may prepare yourselves for the coming of Jesus. May this time, little children, be a time of grace for you. Use every moment and do good, for only in this way will you feel the birth of Jesus in your hearts. If with your life you give an example and become a sign of God's love, joy will prevail in the hearts of men. Thank you for having responded to my call."

December 25, 1996
"Dear children! Today I am with you in a special way, holding little Jesus in my lap and I invite you, little children, to open yourselves to His call. He calls you to joy. Little children, joyfully live the messages of the Gospel, which I am repeating in the time since I am with you. Little children, I am your Mother and I desire to reveal to you the God of love and the God of peace. I do not desire for your life to be in sadness but that it be realized in joy for eternity, according

to the Gospel. Only in this way will your life have meaning. Thank you for having responded to my call."

1997

January 25, 1997
"Dear children! I invite you to reflect about your future. You are creating a new world without God, only with your own strength and that is why you are unsatisfied and without joy in the heart. This time is my time and that is why, little children, I invite you again to pray. When you find unity with God, you will feel hunger for the word of God and your heart, little children, will overflow with joy. You will witness God's love wherever you are. I bless you and I repeat to you that I am with you to help you. Thank you for having responded to my call."

February 25, 1997
"Dear children! Today I invite you in a special way to open yourselves to God the Creator and to become active. I invite you, little children, to see at this time who needs your spiritual or material help. By your example, little children, you will be the extended hands of God, which humanity is seeking. Only in this way will you understand, that you are called to witness and to become joyful carriers of God's word and of His love. Thank you for having responded to my call."

March 25, 1997
"Dear children! Today, in a special way, I invite you to take the cross in the hands and to meditate on the wounds of Jesus. Ask of Jesus to heal your wounds, which you, dear children, during your life sustained because of your sins or the sins of your parents. Only in this way, dear children, you

will understand that the world is in need of healing of faith in God the Creator. By Jesus' passion and death on the cross, you will understand that only through prayer you, too, can become true apostles of faith; when, in simplicity and prayer, you live faith which is a gift. Thank you for having responded to my call."

April 25, 1997
"Dear children! Today I call you to have your life be connected with God the Creator, because only in this way will your life have meaning and you will comprehend that God is love. God sends me to you out of love, that I may help you to comprehend that without Him there is no future or joy and, above all, there is no eternal salvation. Little children, I call you to leave sin and to accept prayer at all times, that you may in prayer come to know the meaning of your life. God gives Himself to him who seeks Him. Thank you for having responded to my call."

May 25, 1997
"Dear children! Today I invite you to glorify God and for the Name of God to be holy in your hearts and in your life. Little children, when you are in the holiness of God, He is with you and gives you peace and joy which come from God only through prayer. That is why, little children, renew prayer in your families and your heart will glorify the holy Name of God and heaven will reign in your heart. I am close to you and I intercede for you before God. Thank you for having responded to my call."

June 25, 1997
"Dear children! Today I am with you in a special way and I bring you my motherly blessing of peace. I pray for you and I intercede for you before God, so that you may comprehend that each of you is a carrier of peace. You cannot have peace if your heart is not at peace with God. That is why, little

children, pray, pray, pray, because prayer is the foundation of your peace. Open your heart and give time to God so that He will be your friend. When true friendship with God is realized, no storm can destroy it. Thank you for having responded to my call."

July 25, 1997
"Dear children! Today I invite you to respond to my call to prayer. I desire, dear children, that during this time you find a corner for personal prayer. I desire to lead you towards prayer with the heart. Only in this way will you comprehend that your life is empty without prayer. You will discover the meaning of your life when you discover God in prayer. That is why, little children, open the door of your heart and you will comprehend that prayer is joy without which you cannot live. Thank you for having responded to my call."

August 25, 1997
"Dear children! God gives me this time as a gift to you, so that I may instruct and lead you on the path of salvation. Dear children, now you do not comprehend this grace, but soon a time will come when you will lament for these messages. That is why, little children, live all of the words which I have given you through this time of grace and renew prayer, until prayer becomes a joy for you. Especially, I call all those who have consecrated themselves to my Immaculate Heart to become an example to others. I call all priests and religious brothers and sisters to pray the rosary and to teach others to pray. The rosary, little children, is especially dear to me. Through the rosary open your heart to me and I am able to help you. Thank you for having responded to my call."

September 25, 1997
"Dear children! Today I call you to comprehend that without love you cannot comprehend that God needs to be in the first

place in your life. That is why, little children, I call you all to love, not with a human but with God's love. In this way, your life will be more beautiful and without an interest. You will comprehend that God gives Himself to you in the simplest way out of love. Little children, so that you may comprehend my words which I give you out of love, pray, pray, pray and you will be able to accept others with love and to forgive all who have done evil to you. Respond with prayer; prayer is a fruit of love towards God the Creator. Thank you for having responded to my call."

October 25, 1997
"Dear children! Also today I am with you and I call all of you to renew yourselves by living my messages. Little children, may prayer be life for you and may you be an example to others. Little children, I desire for you to become carriers of peace and of God's joy to today's world without peace. That is why, little children, pray, pray, pray! I am with you and I bless you with my motherly peace. Thank you for having responded to my call."

November 25, 1997
"Dear children! Today I invite you to comprehend your Christian vocation. Little children, I led and am leading you through this time of grace, that you may become conscious of your Christian vocation. Holy martyrs died witnessing: I am a Christian and love God over everything. Little children, today also I invite you to rejoice and be joyful Christians, responsible and conscious that God called you in a special way to be joyfully extended hands toward those who do not believe, and that through the example of your life, they may receive faith and love for God. Therefore, pray, pray, pray that your heart may open and be sensitive for the Word of God. Thank you for having responded to my call."

December 25, 1997

"Dear children! Also today I rejoice with you and I call you to the good. I desire that each of you reflect and carry peace in your heart and say: I want to put God in the first place in my life. In this way, little children, each of you will become holy. Little children, tell everyone, I want the good for you and he will respond with the good and, little children, good will come to dwell in the heart of each man. Little children, tonight I bring to you the good of my Son who gave His life to save you. That is why, little children, rejoice and extend your hands to Jesus who is only good. Thank you for having responded to my call."

1998

January 25, 1998

"Dear children! Today again I call all of you to prayer. Only with prayer, dear children, will your heart change, become better, and be more sensitive to the Word of God. Little children, do not permit Satan to pull you apart and to do with you what he wants. I call you to be responsible and determined and to consecrate each day to God in prayer. May Holy Mass, little children, not be a habit for you, but life. By living Holy Mass each day, you will feel the need for holiness and you will grow in holiness. I am close to you and intercede before God for each of you, so that He may give you strength to change your heart. Thank you for having responded to my call."

February 25, 1998

"Dear children! Also today I am with you and I, again, call all of you to come closer to me through your prayers. In a special way, I call you to renunciation in this time of grace. Little children, meditate on and live, through your little sacrifices, the passion and death of Jesus for each of you. Only if you come closer to Jesus will you comprehend the immeasurable love He has for each of you. Through prayer and your renunciation you will become more open to the gift of faith and love towards the Church and the people who are around you. I love you and bless you. Thank you for having responded to my call."

March 25, 1998
"Dear children! Also today I call you to fasting and renunciation. Little children, renounce that which hinders you from being closer to Jesus. In a special way I call you: Pray, because only through prayer will you be able to overcome your will and discover the will of God even in the smallest things. By your daily life, little children, you will become an example and witness that you live for Jesus or against Him and His will. Little children, I desire that you become apostles of love. By loving, little children, it will be recognized that you are mine. Thank you for having responded to my call."

April 25, 1998
"Dear children! Today I call you, through prayer, to open yourselves to God as a flower opens itself to the rays of the morning sun. Little children, do not be afraid. I am with you and I intercede before God for each of you so that your heart receives the gift of conversion. Only in this way, little children, will you comprehend the importance of grace in these times and God will become nearer to you. Thank you for having responded to my call."

May 25, 1998
"Dear children! Today I call you, through prayer and sacrifice, to prepare yourselves for the coming of the Holy Spirit. Little children, this is a time of grace and so, again, I call you to decide for God the Creator. Allow Him to

transform and change you. May your heart be prepared to listen to, and live, everything which the Holy Spirit has in His plan for each of you. Little children, allow the Holy Spirit to lead you on the way of truth and salvation towards eternal life. Thank you for having responded to my call."

June 25, 1998
"Dear children! Today I desire to thank you for living my messages. I bless you all with my motherly blessing and I bring you all before my Son Jesus. Thank you for having responded to my call."

July 25, 1998
"Dear children! Today, little children, I invite you, through prayer, to be with Jesus, so that through a personal experience of prayer you may be able to discover the beauty of God's creatures. You cannot speak or witness about prayer, if you do not pray. That is why, little children, in the silence of the heart, remain with Jesus, so that He may change and transform you with His love. This, little children, is a time of grace for you. Make good use of it for your personal conversion, because when you have God, you have everything.
Thank you for having responded to my call."

August 25, 1998
"Dear children! Today I invite you to come still closer to me through prayer. Little children, I am your mother, I love you and I desire that each of you be saved and thus be with me in Heaven. That is why, little children, pray, pray, pray until your life becomes prayer. Thank you for having responded to my call."

September 25, 1998
"Dear children! Today, I call you to become my witnesses by living the faith of your fathers. Little children, you seek signs

and messages and do not see that, with every morning sunrise, God calls you to convert and to return to the way of truth and salvation. You speak much, little children, but you work little on your conversion. That is why, convert and start to live my messages, not with your words but with your life. In this way, little children, you will have the strength to decide for the true conversion of the heart. Thank you for having responded to my call."

October 25, 1998

"Dear children! Today I call you to come closer to my Immaculate Heart. I call you to renew in your families the fervor of the first days when I called you to fasting, prayer and conversion. Little children, you accepted my messages with open hearts, although you did not know what prayer was. Today, I call you to open yourselves completely to me so that I may transform you and lead you to the heart of my son Jesus, so that He can fill you with His love. Only in this way, little children, will you find true peace - the peace that only God gives you. Thank you for having responded to my call."

November 25, 1998

"Dear children! Today I call you to prepare yourselves for the coming of Jesus. In a special way, prepare your hearts. May holy Confession be the first act of conversion for you and then, dear children, decide for holiness. May your conversion and decision for holiness begin today and not tomorrow. Little children, I call you all to the way of salvation and I desire to show you the way to Heaven. That is why, little children, be mine and decide with me for holiness. Little children, accept prayer with seriousness and pray, pray, pray. Thank you for having responded to my call."

December 25, 1998
"Dear children! In this Christmas joy I desire to bless you with my blessing. In a special way, little children, I give you the blessing of little Jesus. May He fill you with His peace. Today, little children, you do not have peace and yet you yearn for it. That is why, with my Son Jesus, on this day I call you to pray, pray, pray, because without prayer you do not have joy or peace or a future. Yearn for peace and seek it, for God is true peace. Thank you for having responded to my call."

1999

January 25, 1999
"Dear children! I again invite you to prayer. You have no excuse to work more because nature still lies in deep sleep. Open yourselves in prayer. Renew prayer in your families. Put Holy Scripture in a visible place in your families, read it, reflect on it and learn how God loves His people. His love shows itself also in present times because He sends me to call you upon the path of salvation. Thank you for having responded to my call."

February 25, 1999
"Dear children! Also today I am with you in a special way contemplating and living the passion of Jesus in my heart. Little children, open your hearts and give me everything that is in them: joys, sorrows and each, even the smallest, pain, that I may offer them to Jesus; so that with His immeasurable love, He may burn and transform your sorrows into the joy of His resurrection. That is why, I now call you in a special way, little children, for your hearts to open to prayer, so that through prayer you may become friends of Jesus. Thank you for having responded to my call."

March 25, 1999
"Dear children! I call you to prayer with the heart. In a special way, little children, I call you to pray for conversion of sinners, for those who pierce my heart and the heart of my Son Jesus with the sword of hatred and daily blasphemies. Let us pray, little children, for all those who do not desire to come to know the love of God, even though they are in the Church. Let us pray that they convert, so that the Church may resurrect in love. Only with love and prayer, little children, can you live this time which is given to you for conversion. Place God in the first place, then the risen Jesus will become your friend. Thank you for having responded to my call."

April 25, 1999
"Dear children! Also today I call you to prayer. Little children, be joyful carriers of peace and love in this peaceless world. By fasting and prayer, witness that you are mine and that you live my messages. Pray and seek! I am praying and interceding for you before God that you convert; that your life and behavior always be Christian. Thank you for having responded to my call."

May 25, 1999
"Dear children! Also today I call you to convert and to more firmly believe in God. Children, you seek peace and pray in different ways, but you have not yet given your hearts to God for Him to fill them with His love. So, I am with you to teach you and to bring you closer to the love of God. If you love God above all else, it will be easy for you to pray and to open your hearts to Him. Thank you for having responded to my call."

June 25, 1999
"Dear children! Today I thank you for living and witnessing my messages with your life. Little children, be strong and pray so that prayer may give you strength and joy. Only in this way will each of you be mine and I will lead you on the way of salvation. Little children, pray and with your life witness my presence here. May each day be a joyful witness for you of God's love. Thank you for having responded to my call."

July 25, 1999
"Dear children! Also today I rejoice with you and I call you all to prayer with the heart. I call all of you, little children, to give thanks to God here with me for the graces which He gives to you through me. I desire for you to comprehend that I want to realize here, not only a place of prayer but also a meeting of hearts. I desire for my, Jesus' and your heart to become one heart of love and peace. That is why, little children, pray and rejoice over everything that God does here, despite that Satan provokes quarrels and unrest. I am with you and I lead you all on the way of love. Thank you for having responded to my call."

August 25, 1999
"Dear children! Also today I call you to give glory to God the Creator in the colors of nature. He speaks to you also through the smallest flower about His beauty and the depth of love with which He has created you. Little children, may prayer flow from your hearts like fresh water from a spring. May the wheat fields speak to you about the mercy of God towards every creature. That is why, renew prayer of thanksgiving for everything He gives you. Thank you for having responded to my call."

September 25, 1999
"Dear children! Today again I call you to become carriers of my peace. In a special way, now when it is being said that God is far away, He has truly never been nearer to you. I call you to renew prayer in your families by reading the Sacred Scripture and to experience joy in meeting with God who infinitely loves His creatures. Thank you for having responded to my call."

October 25, 1999
"Dear children! Do not forget: this is a time of grace; that is why, pray, pray, pray! Thank you for having responded to my call."

November 25, 1999
"Dear children! Also today I call you to prayer. In this time of grace, may the cross be a sign-post of love and unity for you through which true peace comes. That is why, little children, pray especially at this time that little Jesus, the Creator of peace, may be born in your hearts. Only through prayer will you become my apostles of peace in this world without peace. That is why, pray until prayer becomes a joy for you. Thank you for having responded to my call."

December 25, 1999
"Dear children! This is the time of grace. Little children, today in a special way with little Jesus, whom I hold in my embrace, I am giving you the possibility to decide for peace. Through your 'yes' for peace and your decision for God, a new possibility for peace is opened. Only in this way, little children, this century will be for you a time of peace and well-being. Therefore, put little newborn Jesus in the first place in your life and He will lead you on the way of salvation. Thank you for having responded to my call."

2000

January 25, 2000
"Dear children! I call you, little children, to pray without ceasing. If you pray, you are closer to God and He will lead you on the way of peace and salvation. That is why I call you today to give peace to others. Only in God is there true peace. Open your hearts and become those who give a gift of peace and others will discover peace in you and through you and in this way you will witness God's peace and love which He gives you. Thank you for having responded to my call."

February 25, 2000
"Dear children! Wake up from the sleep of unbelief and sin, because this is a time of grace which God gives you. Use this time and seek the grace of healing of your heart from God, so that you may see God and man with the heart. Pray in a special way for those who have not come to know God's love, and witness with your life so that they also can come to know God and His immeasurable love. Thank you for having responded to my call."

March 25, 2000
"Dear children! Pray and make good use of this time, because this is a time of grace. I am with you and I intercede for each one of you before God, for your heart to open to God and to God's love. Little children, pray without ceasing, until prayer becomes a joy for you. Thank you for having responded to my call."

April 25, 2000
"Dear children! Also today I call you to conversion. You are concerned too much about material things and little about spiritual ones. Open your hearts and start again to work more on your personal conversion. Decide everyday to dedicate

time to God and to prayer until prayer becomes a joyful meeting with God for you. Only in this way will your life have meaning and with joy you will contemplate eternal life. Thank you for having responded to my call."

May 25, 2000
"Dear children! I rejoice with you and in this time of grace I call you to spiritual renewal. Pray, little children, that the Holy Spirit may come to dwell in you in fullness, so that you may be able to witness in joy to all those who are far from faith. Especially, little children, pray for the gifts of the Holy Spirit so that in the spirit of love, every day and in each situation, you may be closer to your fellow-man; and that in wisdom and love you may overcome every difficulty. I am with you and I intercede for each of you before Jesus. Thank you for having responded to my call."

June 25, 2000
"Dear children! Today I call you to prayer. The one who prays is not afraid of the future. Little children do not forget, I am with you and I love you all. Thank you for having responded to my call."

July 25, 2000
"Dear children! Do not forget that you are here on earth on the way to eternity and that your home is in Heaven. That is why, little children, be open to God's love and leave egoism and sin. May your joy be only in discovering God in daily prayer. That is why, make good use of this time and pray, pray, pray; and God is near to you in prayer and through prayer. Thank you for having responded to my call."

August 25, 2000
"Dear children! I desire to share my joy with you. In my Immaculate Heart I feel that there are many of those who have drawn closer to me and are, in a special way, carrying

the victory of my Immaculate Heart in their hearts by praying and converting. I desire to thank you and to inspire you to work even more for God and His kingdom with love and the power of the Holy Spirit. I am with you and I bless you with my motherly blessing. Thank you for having responded to my call."

September 25, 2000
"Dear children! Today I call you to open yourselves to prayer. May prayer become joy for you. Renew prayer in your families and form prayer groups. In this way, you will experience joy in prayer and togetherness. All those who pray and are members of prayer groups are open to God's will in their hearts and joyfully witness God's love. I am with you, I carry all of you in my heart and I bless you with my motherly blessing. Thank you for having responded to my call."

October 25, 2000
"Dear children! Today I desire to open my motherly heart to you and to call you all to pray for my intentions. I desire to renew prayer with you and to call you to fast which I desire to offer to my Son Jesus for the coming of a new time – a time of spring. In this Jubilee year many hearts have opened to me and the Church is being renewed in the Spirit. I rejoice with you and I thank God for this gift; and you, little children, I call to pray, pray, pray – until prayer becomes a joy for you. Thank you for having responded to my call."

November 25, 2000
"Dear children! Today when Heaven is near to you in a special way, I call you to prayer so that through prayer you place God in the first place. Little children, today I am near you and I bless each of you with my motherly blessing so that you have the strength and love for all the people you meet in your earthly life and that you can give God's love. I

rejoice with you and I desire to tell you that your brother Slavko has been born into Heaven and intercedes for you. Thank you for having responded to my call."

December 25, 2000

"Dear children! Today when God granted to me that I can be with you, with little Jesus in my arms, I rejoice with you and I give thanks to God for everything He has done in this Jubilee year. I thank God especially for all the vocations of those who said 'yes' to God completely. I bless you all with my blessing and the blessing of the newborn Jesus. I pray for all of you for joy to be born in your hearts so that in joy you too carry the joy I have today. In this Child I bring to you the Savior of the your hearts and the One who calls you to the holiness of life. Thank you for having responded to my call."

2001

January 25, 2001

"Dear children! Today I call you to renew prayer and fasting with even greater enthusiasm until prayer becomes a joy for you. Little children, the one who prays is not afraid of the future and the one who fasts is not afraid of evil. Once again, I repeat to you: only through prayer and fasting also wars can be stopped – wars of your unbelief and fear for the future. I am with you and am teaching you little children: your peace and hope are in God. That is why draw closer to God and put Him in the first place in your life. Thank you for having responded to my call."

February 25, 2001

"Dear children! This is a time of grace. That is why pray, pray, pray until you comprehend God's love for each of you. Thank you for having responded to my call."

March 25, 2001
"Dear children! Also today I call you to open yourselves to prayer. Little children, you live in a time in which God gives great graces but you do not know how to make good use of them. You are concerned about everything else, but the least for the soul and spiritual life. Awaken from the tired sleep of your soul and say yes to God with all your strength. Decide for conversion and holiness. I am with you, little children, and I call you to perfection of your soul and of everything you do. Thank you for having responded to my call."

April 25, 2001
"Dear children! Also today, I call you to prayer. Little children, prayer works miracles. When you are tired and sick and you do not know the meaning of your life, take the Rosary and pray; pray until prayer becomes for you a joyful meeting with your Savior. I am with you, little children, and I intercede and pray for you. Thank you for having responded to my call."

May 25, 2001
"Dear children! At this time of grace, I call you to prayer. Little children, you work much but without God's blessing. Bless and seek the wisdom of the Holy Spirit to lead you at this time so that you may comprehend and live in the grace of this time. Convert, little children, and kneel in the silence of your hearts. Put God in the center of your being so that, in that way, you can witness in joy the beauty that God continually gives in your life. Thank you for having responded to my call."

June 25, 2001
"Dear children! I am with you and I bless you all with my motherly blessing. Especially today when God gives you abundant graces, pray and seek God through me. God gives

you great graces, that is why, little children make good use of this time of grace and come closer to my heart so that I can lead you to my Son Jesus. Thank you for having responded to my call."

July 25, 2001
"Dear children! In this time of grace, I call you to come even closer to God through your personal prayer. Make good use of the time of rest and give your soul and your eyes rest in God. Find peace in nature and you will discover God the Creator Whom you will be able to give thanks to for all creatures; then you will find joy in your heart. Thank you for having responded to my call."

August 25, 2001
"Dear children! Today I call all of you to decide for holiness. May for you, little children, always in your thoughts and in each situation holiness be in the first place, in work and in speech. In this way, you will also put it into practice; little by little, step by step, prayer and a decision for holiness will enter into your family. Be real with yourselves and do not bind yourselves to material things but to God. And do not forget, little chlidren, that your life is as passing as a flower. Thank you for having responded to my call."

September 25, 2001
"Dear children! Also today I call you to prayer, especially today when Satan wants war and hatred. I call you anew, little children: pray and fast that God may give you peace. Witness peace to every heart and be carriers of peace in this world without peace. I am with you and intercede before God for each of you. And you do not be afraid because the one who prays is not afraid of evil and has no hatred in the heart. Thank you for having responded to my call."

October 25, 2001
"Dear children! Also today I call you to pray from your whole heart and to love each other. Little children, you are chosen to witness peace and joy. If there is no peace, pray and you will receive it. Through you and your prayer, little children, peace will begin to flow through the world. That is why, little children, pray, pray, pray, because prayer works miracles in human hearts and in the world. I am with you and I thank God for each of you who has accepted and lives prayer with seriousness. Thank you for having responded to my call."

November 25, 2001
"Dear children! In this time of grace, I call you anew to prayer. Little children, pray and prepare your hearts for the coming of the King of Peace, that with His blessing He may give peace to the whole world. Peacelessness has begun to reign in hearts and hatred reigns in the world. That is why, you who live my messages be the light and extended hands to this faithless world that all may come to know the God of Love. Do not forget, little children, I am with you and bless you all. Thank you for having responded to my call."

December 25, 2001
"Dear children! I call you today and encourage you to prayer for peace. Especially today I call you, carrying the newborn Jesus in my arms for you, to unite with Him through prayer and to become a sign to this peaceless world. Encourage each other, little children, to prayer and love. May your faith be an encouragement to others to believe and to love more. I bless you all and call you to be closer to my heart and to the heart of little Jesus. Thank you for having responded to my call."

2002

January 25, 2002
"Dear children! At this time while you are still looking back to the past year I call you, little children, to look deeply into your heart and to decide to be closer to God and to prayer. Little children, you are still attached to earthly things and little to spiritual life. May my call today also be an encouragement to you to decide for God and for daily conversion. You cannot be converted, little children, if you do not abandon sins and do not decide for love towards God and neighbor. Thank you for having responded to my call."

February 25, 2002
"Dear children! In this time of grace, I call you to become friends of Jesus. Pray for peace in your hearts and work for your personal conversion. Little children, only in this way will you be able to become witnesses of peace and of the love of Jesus in the world. Open yourselves to prayer so that prayer becomes a need for you. Be converted, little children, and work so that as many souls as possible may come to know Jesus and His love. I am close to you and I bless you all. Thank you for having responded to my call."

March 25, 2002
"Dear children! Today I call you to unite with Jesus in prayer. Open your heart to Him and give Him everything that is in it: joys, sorrows and illnesses. May this be a time of grace for you. Pray, little children, and may every moment belong to Jesus. I am with you and I intercede for you. Thank you for having responded to my call."

April 25, 2002
"Dear children! Rejoice with me in this time of spring when all nature is awakening and your hearts long for change. Open yourselves, little children, and pray. Do not forget that I am with you and I desire to take you all to my Son that He may give you the gift of sincere love towards God and everything that is from Him. Open yourselves to prayer and seek a conversion of your hearts from God; everything else He sees and provides. Thank you for having responded to my call."

May 25, 2002
"Dear children! Today I call you to put prayer in the first place in your life. Pray and may prayer, little children, be a joy for you. I am with you and intercede for all of you, and you, little children, be joyful carriers of my messages. May your life with me be joy. Thank you for having responded to my call."

June 25, 2002
"Dear children! Today I pray for you and with you that the Holy Spirit may help you and increase your faith, so that you may accept even more the messages that I am giving you here in this holy place. Little children, comprehend that this is a time of grace for each of you; and with me, little children, you are secure. I desire to lead you all on the way of holiness. Live my messages and put into life every word that I am giving you. May they be precious to you because they come from heaven. Thank you for having responded to my call."

July 25, 2002
"Dear children! Today I rejoice with your patron saint and call you to be open to God's will, so that in you and through you, faith may grow in the people you meet in your everyday life. Little children, pray until prayer becomes joy for you.

Ask your holy protectors to help you grow in love towards God. Thank you for having responded to my call."

August 25, 2002
"Dear children! Also today I am with you in prayer so that God gives you an even stronger faith. Little children, your faith is small and you are not even aware how much, despite this, you are not ready to seek the gift of faith from God. That is why I am with you, little children, to help you comprehend my messages and put them into life. Pray, pray, pray and only in faith and through prayer your soul will find peace and the world will find joy to be with God. Thank you for having responded to my call."

September 25, 2002
"Dear children! Also in this peaceless time, I call you to prayer. Little children, pray for peace so that in the world every person would feel love towards peace. Only when the soul finds peace in God, it feels content and love will begin to flow in the world. And in a special way, little children, you are called to live and witness peace – peace in your hearts and families – and, through you, peace will also begin to flow in the world. Thank you for having responded to my call."

October 25, 2002
"Dear children! Also today I call you to prayer. Little children, believe that by simple prayer miracles can be worked. Through your prayer you open your heart to God and He works miracles in your life. By looking at the fruits, your heart fills with joy and gratitude to God for everything He does in your life and, through you, also to others. Pray and believe little children, God gives you graces and you do not see them. Pray and you will see them. May your day be filled with prayer and thanksgiving for everything that God gives you. Thank you for having responded to my call."

November 25, 2002
"Dear children! I call you also today to conversion. Open your heart to God, little children, through Holy Confession and prepare your soul so that little Jesus can be born anew in your heart. Permit Him to transform you and lead you on the way of peace and joy. Little children, decide for prayer. Especially now, in this time of grace, may your heart yearn for prayer. I am close to you and intercede before God for all of you. Thank you for having responded to my call."

December 25, 2002
"Dear children! This is a time of great graces, but also a time of great trials for all those who desire to follow the way of peace. Because of that, little children, again I call you to pray, pray, pray, not with words but with the heart. Live my messages and be converted. Be conscious of this gift that God has permitted me to be with you, especially today when in my arms I have little Jesus - the King of Peace. I desire to give you peace, and that you carry it in your hearts and give it to others until God's peace begins to rule the world. Thank you for having responded to my call."

2003

January 25, 2003
"Dear children! With this message I call you anew to pray for peace. Particularly now when peace is in crisis, you be those who pray and bear witness to peace. Little children, be peace in this peaceless world. Thank you for having responded to my call."

February 25, 2003

"Dear children! Also today I call you to pray and fast for peace. As I have already said and now repeat to you, little children, only with prayer and fasting can wars also be stopped. Peace is a precious gift from God. Seek, pray and you will receive it. Speak about peace and carry peace in your hearts. Nurture it like a flower which is in need of water, tenderness and light. Be those who carry peace to others. I am with you and intercede for all of you. Thank you for having responded to my call."

March 25, 2003

"Dear children! Also today I call you to pray for peace. Pray with the heart, little children, and do not lose hope because God loves His creatures. He desires to save you, one by one, through my coming here. I call you to the way of holiness. Pray, and in prayer you are open to God's will; in this way, in everything you do, you realize God's plan in you and through you. Thank you for having responded to my call."

April 25, 2003

"Dear children! I call you also today to open yourselves to prayer. In the foregone time of Lent you have realized how small you are and how small your faith is. Little children, decide also today for God, that in you and through you He may change the hearts of people, and also your hearts. Be joyful carriers of the risen Jesus in this peaceless world, which yearns for God and for everything that is from God. I am with you, little children, and I love you with a special love. Thank you for having responded to my call."

May 25, 2003
"Dear children! Also today I call you to prayer. Renew your personal prayer, and in a special way pray to the Holy Spirit to help you pray with the heart. I intercede for all of you, little children, and call all of you to conversion. If you convert, all those around you will also be renewed and prayer will be a joy for them. Thank you for having responded to my call."

June 25, 2003
"Dear children! Also today, I call you with great joy to live my messages. I am with you and I thank you for putting into life what I am saying to you. I call you to renew my messages even more, with new enthusiasm and joy. May prayer be your daily practice. Thank you for having responded to my call."

July 25, 2003
"Dear children! Also today I call you to prayer. Little children, pray until prayer becomes a joy for you. Only in this way each of you will discover peace in the heart and your soul will be content. You will feel the need to witness to others the love that you feel in your heart and life. I am with you and intercede before God for all of you. Thank you for having responded to my call."

August 25, 2003
"Dear children! Also today I call you to give thanks to God in your heart for all the graces which He gives you, also through the signs and colors that are in nature. God wants to draw you closer to Himself and moves you to give Him glory and thanks. Therefore, little children, I call you anew to pray, pray, pray and do not forget that I am with you. I intercede

before God for each of you until your joy in Him is complete. Thank you for having responded to my call."

September 25, 2003

"Dear children! Also today I call you to come closer to my heart. Only in this way, will you comprehend the gift of my presence here among you. I desire, little children, to lead you to the heart of my Son Jesus; but you resist and do not desire to open your hearts to prayer. Again, little children, I call you not to be deaf but to comprehend my call, which is salvation for you. Thank you for having responded to my call."

October 25, 2003

"Dear children! I call you anew to consecrate yourselves to my heart and the heart of my Son Jesus. I desire, little children, to lead you all on the way of conversion and holiness. Only in this way, through you, we can lead all the more souls on the way of salvation. Do not delay, little children, but say with all your heart: "I want to help Jesus and Mary that all the more brothers and sisters may come to know the way of holiness." In this way, you will feel the contentment of being friends of Jesus. Thank you for having responded to my call."

1 Peter 2:24

He himself bore our sins in his body upon the cross, so that, free from sin, we might live for righteousness. By his wounds you have been healed.

Luke 9:23

Then he said to all, "If anyone wishes to come after me, he must deny himself and take up his cross daily and follow me.

Luke 14:27

Whoever does not carry his own cross and come after me cannot be my disciple.

John 19:25

Standing by the cross of Jesus were his mother and his mother's sister, Mary the wife of Clopas, and Mary of Magdala.

Appendix Four

Resources

NEW AMERICAN BIBLE – I particularly like this Bible because it contains the Dogmatic Constitution On Divine Revelation from Vatican II, maps, photographs, cross references, commentary notes, explanatory paragraphs to each book and other information useful to thorough Bible study.

CATECHISM OF THE CATHOLIC CHURCH, SECOND EDITION – ISBN 1-57455-110-8

ON THE MOST HOLY ROSARY – Apostolic Letter of Pope John Paul II, printed in the United States by Pauline Books and Media, 50 Saint Pauls Avenue, Boston, MA 02130-3491.

MEDJUGORJE OFFICIAL SHRINE WEBSITE – www.medjugorje.hr

PEACE – Three hour mini-retreat prepared by Jeffrey Maria D. Arnold. Includes PowerPoint® presentation. Telephone toll free 866 585-1555 or 949 463-1730 or email to jmdarnold@hotmail.com

MORNING STAR MINISTRY – for a copy of the video of Our Lady in apparition on Cross Mountain or to join a tour group to Medjugorje or obtain general travel information, contact Paul and Grace Millard at PH/FAX 909 845-9227 or email to msmpng@juno.com

THE MEDJUGORJE WEB – popular informative website; order books from official Franciscan gift store in Medjugorje; join tour group to Medjugorje. www.medjugorje.org

SISTER EMMANUEL AND DENIS NOLAN – another good website www.childrenofmedjugorje.com

CNEWA – a papal agency for humanitarian and pastoral support. 1011 First Avenue, New York, New York, 10022-4195, 800-442-6392, www.cnewa.org

BOOKS

PEACE – MEDJUGORJE MIRACLE AND MESSAGE
ISBN 0-9745156-0-4 LCCN 2003112618 For additional copies of this book order direct from the publisher or from Amazon.com. Check your local book store as well.

MEDJUGORJE – ISBN 9958-775-14-X. Official Shrine Information Book. Many color photographs. Very informative. Order from The Medjugorje Web

MEDUGORJE TODAY – ISBN 3-924902-03-8. Beautiful information and pictorial coffee-table book. Difficult to obtain. Probably have to go to Medjugorje to get it.

IN THE SCHOOL OF LOVE – Father Slavko Barbaric. Order from The Medjugorje Web.

THE VISIONS OF THE CHILDREN – Janice T. Connell. ISBN 0-312-18204-X. Published by St. Martin's Press, New York, NY. Includes interviews of the visionaries and locutionists.

THE APPARITIONS OF OUR LADY AT MEDJUGORJE – Svetozar Kraljevic, O.F.M. ISBN 981221083. Historical account of events at Medjugorje from 1981 to 1983. Order through The Medjugorje Web.

THEOTÓKOS - WOMAN, MOTHER, DISCIPLE – John Paul II. ISBN 0-8198-7401-9 A Catechesis on Mary, Mother of God, by the Holy Father.